Attending to the Wounds on Christ's Body

Attending to the Wounds on Christ's Body

Teresa's Scriptural Vision

ELIZABETH NEWMAN

CASCADE *Books* • Eugene, Oregon

ATTENDING TO THE WOUNDS ON CHRIST'S BODY
Teresa's Scriptural Vision

Cascade Books
An Imprint of Wipf and Stock Publishers
199 W. 8th Ave., Suite 3
Eugene, OR 97401

www.wipfandstock.com

ISBN 13: 978-1-4982-1345-5

Cataloguing-in-Publication data:

Newman, Elizabeth.

Attending to the wounds on Christ's body : Teresa's scriptural vision / Elizabeth Newman.

x + 220 pp. ; 23 cm. Includes bibliographical references and indexes.

ISBN 13: 978-1-4982-1345-5

1. Teresa, of Avila, Saint, 1515–1582. 2. Bible—Criticism, interpretation, etc.—Spain—History—16th century. 3. Christian union. I. Title.

BX4700 T4 N40 2012

Manufactured in the U.S.A.

To my parents,
Harold and Ernestine Newman

Contents

Acknowledgments

I AM GRATEFUL TO have had the opportunity to teach for twelve years at Saint Mary's College, Notre Dame, and for ten years at the Baptist Theological Seminary at Richmond. This "cross-pollination," while at times disorienting, has nonetheless been a wonderful gift. Being a Baptist Christian in a mostly Catholic context formed me in ways I still cannot fully name. I am appreciative especially to my Saint Mary's colleagues Joseph Incandela and Kevin McDonnell for both their friendship and astute theological insights.

It was while reading Teresa's *Interior Castle* with BTSR students that the idea for this book came to me one day as I was walking to the library. I wish to thank all my theology students as BTSR for their commitment, their passion, their inquisitiveness, and their willingness to enter worlds other than their own. My teaching assistants, Emily Riley and Matthew Williams, have been especially helpful.

I am particularly thankful to BTSR for allowing me the opportunity to take a yearlong sabbatical to work on this book. I also wish to express my deep appreciation to the Association of Theological Schools and to the Henry Luce III Foundation for their generous support for this project in appointing me a 2009 Luce Fellow in Theology. Their funding enabled my family and me to spend time with the Community of Sant'Egidio in Rome, during which we received the gracious hospitality of Claudio Betti. It also enabled us to visit such amazing places as the catacombs, the Church of Saint Clemente, the town of Assisi, and many other wonderful Italian places (and to enjoy the Italian food).

I also wish to acknowledge and thank both M. Therese Lysaught and Murray Jardine for their early enthusiastic support of this project. Therese especially helped me see more clearly the kinds of ecumenical connections that I was hoping to make.

Keith J. Egan has been supportive of my project and generous with his time and extensive knowledge of the Carmelite tradition. Our friendship goes back to 1990 when Keith, as chair of Saint Mary's Department of Religion, took the risk of hiring me, fresh out of graduate school. I am deeply grateful to his support over the years, support that has helped sustain my own passion for Christian unity.

Finally, I am blessed with a wonderful family. I especially thank my husband for his support. I also thank my wonderful children: my daughter, Jessica, and my son, Jacob, who recently accused me of writing about the "theoretical theories" of God. I hope this book is not *that* abstract, but rather is a concrete theory—or way of seeing—about how we might yet look more fully upon one another as brothers and sisters in Christ.

I dedicate this book to my parents, Harold and Ernestine Newman, whose love and support over the years have been immeasurable.

Introduction

L IKE MANY FOLKS, I grew up in a hymn-singing church. At Snyder Me-morial Baptist Church in Fayetteville, North Carolina, we often sang "I Love to Tell the Story," with its familiar refrain, "'Twill be my theme in glory, to tell the old, old story of Jesus and his love." The hymn describes the story of Jesus as "old" but also ever new, inviting us to a continual per-formance of the gospel. How do we come to terms, though, with the fact that Christians have told this story differently from one another, often in ways that divide rather than unite? Some divisions have indeed secured the truth and vitality of the story: maintaining the divinity of Jesus, for example, over against the Arians' version about Jesus as less than divine. If Jesus is not fully divine, Athanasius and others concluded, then the Son is not the One through whom God saves and recreates the world. In this instance, storytellers rightly discerned the difference between telling the "story differently and telling a different story."[1]

In the wake of the Reformation, however, Christians have accepted as normal telling different stories about Christ, the church, and the world. The result has been that Christians often tell their stories in opposition to one another. Some Baptists, for example, describe a key plot line by say-ing, "We are not a creedal people." On this point, they tell a different story than Catholics and some other Protestants because of the belief that creeds stifle freedom.[2] Some Catholics, on the other hand, describe Catholicism

1. Barry Harvey describes the Christian drama as "an ongoing drama performed by a people who live in a wide variety of times and places." Harvey adds, however, that we must attend "with all the critical tools at our disposal to the 'crucial difference . . . between telling a story differently and telling a different story'" (*Another City*, 19). Harvey is quoting Nicholas Lash, *Theology on the Way to Emmaus*.

2. For one example, Baptist historian and theologian Walter Shurden writes, "Sadly, tragically, Baptist denominations have a tendency to lose their way. They get waylaid with a dangerous case of historical amnesia. . . . They get dangerous because they move from a Christ-centered to a creed-centered faith. They get dangerous because they move from freedom for the individual to fear of the individual" ("Coalition for Baptist Principles"). While this is an emphasis amongst some modern Baptists, others have

as a richly complex church in contrast to the simple Protestant churches down the street.[3] To tell the story in this way is to contrast rich complexity with an often-benighted simplicity.

A deeper Christian conviction, however, calls the church to tell a shared story, one that enables Christians to look upon others—Protestant, Catholics, and Orthodox—as brothers and sisters in Christ. This calling is far more than learning to get along. It rests on the astounding conviction that God has created and continues to create *a people* (Israel and the church) to be Christ's body for the world, a light to enlighten all nations.[4] This is not to deny that some might be better at telling and living the Christian story than others.[5] One of the ways of living God's truth, however, is the humility to receive as well as give, seeing in even the im-

---

no objection to reciting the ancient creeds as hard-won summaries of the gospel, a view held by some earlier Baptists as well. See, for example, the work of contemporary Baptist theologians Stephen Harmon (*Toward Baptist Catholicity*) and Paul Fiddes (*Tracks and Traces*). Fiddes notes that "a model covenant service recently published by the Baptist Union of Great Britain includes the Creed of Nicaea-Constantinople in its resources," and it urges Baptist readers to note that the creed is a "better vehicle than modern statements of faith for the making of covenant, because it sets out a story of salvation, not a set a principles." Fiddes adds that this Creed is "the great missionary story of the Triune God, beginning with the making of heaven and earth and ending with a new creation; it tells of the part played in the drama of creation and redemption by Father, Son and Spirit in the unity of the divine koinonia; it enables those who say the creed to be drawn anew into God's story, and so into God's own fellowship of life" (Fiddes, *Tracks and Traces*, 217).

3. In *The Catholic Faith: An Introduction*, Larry Cunningham contrasts Catholic practice to that of the Baptists he knew growing up: "As a kid growing up in the deep south, I rather envied the simple church style of my overwhelmingly Baptist neighbors. They had a church, a preacher, a Bible, a few doctrines, two ordinances and a straightforward service: sing, pray, listen to the Bible readings and the preacher's sermon, and *go home*" (7; my emphasis). The difficulty for me with Cunningham's otherwise helpful introduction is that he feels the need to tell the Catholic story in a way that simplifies and thus distorts Baptist practice.

4. In saying this, I do not intend to suggest that Israel or Jews today are to be the body of Christ. They are, however, the original covenantal people that God called and continues to call into being, a people who carry the promise and covenant fulfilled in Messiah Jesus.

5. It is also the case that differences in storytelling can be complementary. The Second Vatican Council's "Degree on Ecumenism: *Unitatis Redintegratio*," states, for example, "In the study of revealed truth East and West have used different methods and approaches in understanding and confessing divine things. It is hardly surprising, then, if sometimes one tradition has come nearer to a full appreciation of some aspects of a mystery of revelation than the other, or has expressed them better. In such cases, these various theological formulations are often to be considered complementary rather than conflicting" (§17).

poverished Christian brother, sister, congregation, or denomination the light and presence of Christ. What Augustine says about himself applies to churches as well: "for I have been healed by the same doctor who has granted him the grace not to fall ill, or at least to fall ill less seriously." Therefore, Augustine prays, "Let such a person love you just as much, or even more, on seeing that the same physician who rescued me from sinful diseases of such gravity has kept him immune."[6] Applied more broadly to the church, Augustine is describing how one Physician heals and preserves us all. Those "stronger" churches are sustained and healed by the same Savior who watches over the weak.

One of the ways that God heals the church is by providing saints from across time and place. God never leaves a congregation without at least one saint.[7] The same concept applies to the church universal: God provides saints across time and space as gifts for the whole church. It is my conviction that these saints are potential sources of unity and of shared storytelling. As Geoffrey Wainwright states, ". . . a significant step towards ecclesial unity would be taken by the increased formal and mutual recognition of saints."[8] Such a statement rests upon the conviction that, as Pope John Paul II states in his encyclical *Ut Unum Sint* ("May they be one"), our common heritage is "first and foremost this reality of holiness."[9] Such holiness is not about being better or more pure than others. In its scriptural sense, holiness has to do first of all with God setting a people or person aside for his purposes.

That holiness refers to a people means that the language of "saints" can describe all members of the church; the church, like Israel, is set aside to be God's people for the sake of the world. Paul uses the language of "saints" to refer to all Christians in the early churches at Ephesus, Philippi, Colossae, and so forth. The disciples at Corinth, for example, are

---

6. Augustine, *Confessions*, 72.

7. I am indebted to Stanley Hauerwas for this point.

8. Wainwright, *Embracing Purpose*, 184. Wainwright acknowledges that recognition of the saints would necessarily involve questions about "canonization," and this would become part of the dialogue about "the condition of the faithful departed in general."

9. John Paul II, *Ut Unum Sint*, §84. John Paul II adds, "When we speak of a common heritage, we must acknowledge as part of it not only the institutions, rites, means of salvation and the traditions which all the communities have preserved and by which they have been shaped, but first and foremost this reality of holiness." This reality of holiness refers to the saints that are not confined by particular ecclesial boundaries. As he notes, "This universal presence of the Saints is in fact a proof of the transcendent power of the Spirit."

"sanctified in Christ Jesus, called to be saints together with all those who in every place call on the name of our Lord Jesus Christ . . ." (1 Cor 1:2, RSV). In the Apostles' Creed, Christians confess belief in "the communion of saints." "Communion" indicates a *present* reality that is possible because the saints are not dead but alive in Christ. In this sense, "saints" refer to those often unnamed but faithful Christians who have kept the faith alive across generations.

"Saint" is also a term the church has used to describe those whom God has called in extraordinary ways—Saint Francis, for example. In my Baptist context, well-known saints include Lottie Moon (a missionary to China), Clarence Jordan (founder of Koinonia Farm), and Fannie Lou Hamer (African-American prophet for civil rights). Our saints represent our respective stories and histories, and might be unknown across ecclesial division. Even so, the great saints can be ecumenical luminaries, providing a way to move forward in our call to unity. It is my conviction that Teresa of Ávila (1515–1582) stands out as a sixteenth-century luminary in this grand ecumenical parade.

If it is true that the saints are alive in Christ and that there is thus a shared communion, then it follows that the saints can continue to teach, preach, and prophesy in the present. It is therefore legitimate to ask of a particular saint, "How does she speak to the church today?" Just as the gospel enters into particular cultures and contexts in different tongues and ways, so also do saints expand the gospel so that it can be heard anew in different times. Luther's "justification by faith," for example, was heard one way in the heated Reformation debates, but in quite another way during recent Roman Catholic-Lutheran efforts at reconciliation.[10] Shifts and changes in context indicate that saints can continue to illumine the gospel in rich and creative ways. More fully stated, if it is true that holiness and sainthood are ultimately gifts from God, then God can continue to extend this gift across generations in the life of the church.

In this light, then, I examine how Teresa continues to be a gift to the church—the whole church—today. I particularly look at how Teresa's embodiment and understanding of the Word builds up a way of being church together. As I discuss especially in chapter 1, many today assume Teresa's mysticism or spirituality is about the individual subject. At its best, this interpretation fosters personal holiness. At its worse, it makes the church irrelevant to "spirituality" and personal growth. By contrast, I argue that the dwellings that Teresa narrates are not simply about the individual soul

10. Lutheran World Federation and the Catholic Church, "Joint Declaration."

but are rather about God's gift of unity to the church. I do not wish to deny that in other times and places Teresa could have been heard in a different key. If and when "church" seems an extrinsic reality disconnected from ordinary lives, then Teresa might well be read as advocating a personal spirituality, where "personal" is here understood as friendship with Christ and others. It is my conviction, however, that in our late modern time a subjective emphasis has often distorted Teresa's wisdom. Instead of revitalizing the church, it has made the church a mere stage prop for an individual's spiritual quest. Even more worrisome, a focus on "spirituality" divorced from church (or, more broadly, religion) makes it possible to accept division in the church as normal. Thus, late modernity has easily come to assume that church divides, while spirituality unites.[11]

In what follows, I explore how Teresa *illumines* God's Word in a way that aims for unity in the body of Christ. More particularly, I argue that Teresa perceives and narrates how key providential patterns, grounded in Scripture, give form to the church in ways that extend Christ's body in the world. This analysis is not primarily an exercise in Teresian scholarship, much less late medieval Catholicism. Others have written on these topics in helpful and insightful ways. My focus is rather on how Teresa as a doctor and saint of the Catholic Church offers healing for the whole body of Christ. In my view, Teresa is not only a Roman Catholic saint, though Spanish Catholicism no doubt deeply shaped her. Nor is Teresa bound by sixteenth-century customs and worldviews, though she is naturally a product of her time in many ways. As a luminary in the communion of saints, Teresa is a gift to the church universal.

On a personal note, as I have already indicated, I am a Baptist, the granddaughter of a Baptist minister who served small churches in Louisa County, Virginia, for some forty years. Both of us attended Southern Baptist Theological Seminary in Louisville, my grandfather in the 1920s and I some sixty years later. My parents faithfully raised me in the ecclesial life of the Baptist church: Sunday school, church training, G.A.'s (Girls' Auxiliary), Bible studies, prayer meetings, youth council, youth choir, dinner on the grounds, retreats, mission trips, and hundreds of folks who loved, encouraged, and prayed for me. So the reader might legitimately wonder how it is I am writing about a Catholic saint from the sixteenth century, a medieval figure who gave much of her life to reforming Carmelite monasteries. If this were purely an academic enterprise, one could safely assume, "She's a professor and this is an area of specialty, for those who

11. Such a conviction drives the common sentiment, "I'm spiritual but not religious."

are interested in this type of thing." Such academic categorizing, however, does not provide an adequate frame of reference. The reason I am writing about Teresa is that, while I am Baptist, I identify myself as a Baptist within the church universal. Some refer to this as Baptist Catholicity.[12] What exactly this means is not fully clear, but at minimum it names the attempt to see oneself as a member of not only a particular congregation or denomination but also as living within and as part of the one, holy, catholic, and apostolic church. This means that I share a passion for the unity of the church, which I hope colors my understanding of our various ecclesial worlds. Baptist philosopher Douglas V. Henry states well a conviction I share: "Though we carry on as divided and denominated Christians, our scattered, tattered ecclesial communities depend upon a legacy of Christian unity that antedates our brokenness and that still defines the better part of the faith we profess."[13] In a similar way, I would add that we carry on even though divided because we participate proleptically, through the gift of the Spirit, in the Son's unity with the Father, a unity already given to the church.

How this connection between Baptist, Catholic, and the church universal happened in my own life is hard fully to say. I had a wonderful campus minister in college, Dr. Betty Talbert, who introduced me to some of the lives and writings of saints such as Francis of Assisi. Dr. Ralph Wood introduced me to such powerful Catholic writers as Flannery O'Connor and Walker Percy. I also spent a semester in Spain my junior year in college, immersed in a kind of Catholic culture (albeit a dying one in the sense that the young people had mostly stopped going to church). When in seminary, I had the opportunity to live and study for a month at Saint Meinrad's, a Benedictine abbey and seminary in the beautiful hills of southern Indiana. Certainly, my studies at Duke with Geoffrey Wainwright, Stanley Hauerwas, and William H. Poteat opened ways of thinking about the church more catholic than I had previously imagined. Most significantly, however, I taught for twelve years at Saint Mary's College, Notre Dame, Indiana. While many faculty were following the typical path of modern academia (which meant they believed that the Catholic faith belonged in campus ministry rather than the classroom), I still, nonetheless, partially "absorbed" what I will presumptuously call a kind of "Catholic" way of thinking. Perhaps better stated, I became aware—sometimes painfully so— that to be Baptist was to be Catholic in a sense. That is, I saw

12. See especially Harmon, *Toward Baptist Catholicity*; and Harvey, *Can These Bones Live?*

13. Henry, "End(s) of Baptist Dissert," 13.

that Christian divisions cannot be kept in tight compartments, especially when the academic convictions of late modernity seek to banish all such convictions to a private space, separate from economics, politics and other academic disciplines and areas of life.

This juxtaposition of "Catholic" and "Baptist" will no doubt be jarring to some. Are not Baptists and Catholics at the opposite end of the church continuum? Is this not like trying to combine water and oil? My own conviction is that while the church is broken and divided in all sorts of ways, it is nonetheless one. This oneness has nothing to do with our ability to patch things up. It is rather a statement about the nature and grace of God. In Christ, through the gift of the Spirit, we are one body. The body is, of course, broken by our own sin, hardheartedness, and blindness; it is thus covered over, like the ivy that used to wrap around objects in my grandmother's backyard, making it difficult to see or even know what was there. Yet, the oneness of the church is "there" because Christ is present, giving his body the unity he shares with the Father in the Spirit.

All this is to say that I think the phrase "Catholic Baptist" is not as odd as the belief that the church should remain forever divided. This is not to say that we should ignore our differences and celebrate a vapid pluralism. Genuine reconciliation requires prayerful attention, charity, and hope. It calls for seeking together the mind of Christ. It calls as well for paying attention to things we cannot, for now, fix. It can also mean feeling, at times, placeless. I have by no means resolved within myself "Catholic" or "Baptist" or "Protestant" identities. These currents run together in my life, as they do also in the church. I turn to Teresa as someone who can help navigate the waters, not only for me but also for a church divided by the rivers of time.

I write, then, with and about Teresa as a friend, albeit an odd one. How might we see in her person a glimpse of who God is calling all of us to be, divided though we are? How might Protestants see in Teresa's understanding of the Word something of their own sense of the gospel, reflected from a different, illuminating angle? How might Catholics see Teresa as a reformer, as *protesting* that which diminishes Christ's body? Such looking again at saints like Teresa does not mean that Baptists (or other Protestants) should become Catholic or vice versa. It does mean attending to one another with an awareness that God might yet transform us in ways that we cannot at this point fully imagine.

An initial word about my approach to Teresa is necessary. In what follows, I argue that Teresa ought to be read as a scriptural commentator. This is part of a larger claim about theology: that theology itself is a way of interpreting Scripture and, more fully, a way of participating in knowing God.[14] In our day, as others have observed, the disciplines of biblical interpretation and theology have for too long been divorced, to the detriment of both. In my view, Teresa is a theologian *because* she is a scriptural commentator and vice versa.

It is no doubt true that Teresa could not have foreseen the varied ways that she would be received by the church; least of all could she have imagined becoming the first woman doctor of the church. Yet, what Matthew Levering says about Scripture is surely true of saints like Teresa as well: "God the Teacher may teach more through the human teachers' words than the human teachers know . . ."[15] This book is an account of how God the Teacher may continue to teach through Teresa's words, words that are themselves deeply immersed in Scripture and scriptural figures. Michael Hanby makes the provocative claim about Augustine that "the best literal reading of Augustine would be a figurative reading of Augustine."[16] As I interpret it, Hanby means by this that the more illuminative readings of Augustine will not be strictly literal ones, as if Augustine is only writing for his time and place. Rather, these readings will participate providentially and thus simultaneously in the same Triune communion that so deeply marks Augustine's life. I think the same is true for Teresa: the best literal reading of her is a figurative one. This means, to refer to the example mentioned above, that the journey that Teresa narrates in the mansions is not simply that of her own soul, much less that of the modern individual. Rather, to read Teresa figuratively is to "read" ourselves as participating in the same communion that Teresa charts. This means that the journey of the "soul" through the castle is ultimately the journey of the church universal since it is the church that participates through grace in the communion between the Father, Son, and Holy Spirit. In what follows, I seek to make sense of this claim, aiming, as I believe Teresa also did, to attend to the wounds of disunity on the body of Christ.

14. Robert Jenson states, "Theology is thinking what to say to be saying the Gospel" (*Systematic Theology*, 38). For an illuminative account of theology, participation, and knowing God, see Hollon, "Knowledge of God."

15. Levering, *Participatory Biblical Exegesis*, 70.

16. Hanby, *Augustine and Modernity*, 5. The statement that precedes this one is significant: "By Augustine's own lights, the best literal reading of Augustine's theology would be a new Augustinian theology."

1

How to Read Teresa after Modernity

The good Jesus is too good company for us to forsake Him . . .[1]

YEARS AGO, AS A college student, I had the opportunity to visit the birthplace of Teresa in Ávila, Spain. The town was charming, with a medieval castle that must have resembled the ones that Teresa also saw, and that no doubt shaped her imagination when she penned her classic, *Interior Castle*. A friar from Teresa's same Carmelite order served as our patient guide. As a Discalced Carmelite, he was wearing sandals, a sign of the reforms that Teresa herself had initiated four hundred years earlier. My most vivid memory of the place, however, was Teresa's mummified heart encased in an ornate glass container. A faint line could be traced across the heart, where, I was told, the Holy Spirit had pierced her. Teresa writes about this divine "arrow" in *Interior Castle*, as well as in her autobiography, *The Book of Her Life*. Such a mark on Teresa's heart could well be understood as a sign of Teresa's own reception of the Holy Spirit as ultimately a gift to the church.

The modern person, however, might have difficulty not only with this "heart-arrow," but also with the descriptions that Teresa gives of various unusual visions and locutions. Is she a kind of female Don Quixote, chasing giants that are really windmills and generally imagining things that are not there? Like most well-known saints, Teresa has been the subject of various interpretations: not only that of a benighted nun, but also

1. Teresa, *Interior Castle*, 175.

9

an advocate of a modern "spirituality," and, more recently, one who speaks the postmodern absence of God.

My own conviction is that these various readings miss the wisdom that Teresa has to offer. Teresa rather ought to be read as an interpreter and performer of Scripture. Further, I argue that her interpretation can offer healing for wounds of division in the body of Christ. Such a reading might sound odd. Teresa's various writings can seem highly autobiographical, not particularly focused on Scripture, the liturgy, the church, or any other theological topic. Furthermore, Teresa was a reforming nun who advocated for a cloistered way of life, hardly conducive it would seem to overcoming division in the church. Teresa herself even appears to have little knowledge of the ways the church in the sixteenth century was beginning to tear apart.

Even so, it is my conviction that modern assumptions about religion and spirituality have domesticated Teresa. To see Teresa as writing simply about the "soul" or "spiritual experience" rather than Scripture, theology, or the church says more about the modern reader than it does about Teresa. In order to understand why this is so, I examine these domesticated readings of Teresa more clearly before turning to Teresa as a performer of God's Word.

MODERN READINGS

Teresa and Modern *Eros*

Those who know little else about Teresa of Ávila have often seen Giovanni Lorenzo Bernini's famous sculpture, *The Ecstasy of Saint Teresa* (ca. 1647–1652), located in the Santa Maria de la Vittoria Church in Rome. The sculpture, at least to most modern viewers, appears to be deeply erotic; an assumption confirmed when they read the words from Teresa's autobiography on which the sculpture is based:

> I saw in his hands a large golden dart and at the end of the iron tip there appeared to be a little fire. It seemed to me this angel plunged the dart several times into my heart and that it reached deep within me. When he drew it out, I thought he was carrying off with him the deepest part of me; and he left me all on fire with great love of God. The pain was so great that it made me moan, and the sweetness this greatest pain caused me was so

superabundant that there is no desire capable of taking it away; nor is the soul content with less than God.[2]

Modern viewers understandably question this so-called ecstasy. Is this really about God? Is this not obviously about Teresa's own unfulfilled sexuality, as one might expect from a celibate nun? Indeed, this is how some popular works, such as Dan Brown's *Angels and Demons*, describe it.[3]

This reading, however, while understandable from a purely modern view, casts Teresa into a kind of Freudian narrative in which "religion" serves as a mask for something else (psychological-erotic projection, for example). Christianity is explained on some other more factual or "scientific" grounds. From this perspective, the disciples' joy in the resurrection easily becomes a projected desire not to be abandoned by a father figure, similar in explanatory power to Teresa's joy representing her repressed need for a lover/spouse.

While this understanding of Teresa reads her through a modern psychological lens to the exclusion of a theological one, it nonetheless raises an important question about the place of desire and *eros* not only in Teresa's work but in the Christian life more generally: How does Teresa understand *eros* vis-à-vis other loves, such as *philia* and *agape*? I return to this question in chapter 3, while examining the figure of divine marriage in Teresa's life and work.

Teresa and Modern Interiority

In contrast to this first reading of Teresa as unenlightened and premodern, other interpreters embrace Teresa as a "mystic for *our* time." From their perspective, *Interior Castle* narrates the inward journey of a soul making its way to God, free from religious dogma. Teresa's interior castle, according to one interpreter, shows people how "to find life's answers deep within their own souls."[4] Author Barbara Mujica states that Teresa's "spirituality is an interior spirituality that does not hang on ritual but rather teaches people to find God within." In this "time of sectarianism," Mujica adds, "Teresa is a person who reaches across cultures and religions. She speaks

2. Teresa, *Book of Her Life*, 200.

3. Brown, *Angels and Demons*. In the novel, Papal authorities banish the Bernini statue to an "obscure chapel" because it is apparently "too risqué and sexual" (337).

4. Shlumpf, "Mystic for Our Times." For a similar understanding of Teresa, see Mirabai Starr in her recent translation of *Interior Castle*, as well as Caroline Myss in *Entering the Castle: An Inner Path to God and Your Soul*.

to everyone."[5] The reason that Teresa speaks to everyone is because she is not confined by the church, which, for these authors, is either invisible in Teresa's work or appears over against Teresa (as an inquisitorial force, for example).[6] In contrast to the previous understanding of a naïve Teresa, this view portrays her instead as an *enlightened* mystic. In the famous words of Immanuel Kant, she is not bound "by self-incurred tutelage."[7]

Such an interpretation of Teresa reflects a pervasive understanding of the religious journey of the soul as a journey within. Since it is primarily interior, religious dogma and creeds easily obstruct the immediate experience between the individual soul and God. The church too can appear as an intrusion between the soul and God. This way of interpreting Teresa as mystic can easily turn her crystal castle into a "hall of mirrors, a peculiar sort of labyrinth where it is possible to become so entrapped in the corridors of our own interiority that, though we believe we are seeking God, we are actually reflecting only on ourselves."[8]

While this reading of Teresa is also misguided, it does raise important questions about how Christians ought to think about "interiority" vis-à-vis doctrine and the church. What if these are in conflict? Such a question is irresolvable if one accepts the modern dichotomy between the "interior" self and the "exterior" community, or between personal experience and public, ecclesial ritual. Yet, as I intend to show, Teresa's performance of Scripture disallows this kind of stark dualism. For Teresa, rather, church is the condition of the possibility for spirituality because all Christian experiences of God are structured by ecclesial practices, which are themselves grounded in God's Word.[9]

5. Cited in Shlumpf, "Mystic for Our Times"; my emphasis. Mujica is author of the novel *Sister Teresa* and of *Teresa de Avila, Lettered Woman*.

6. This is not to deny that the Inquisition directly impacted Teresa. The ecclesiastical tribunal, under direct control of the Spanish monarchy at the time, examined three of Teresa's books. In 1485 the Inquisition accused Teresa's paternal grandfather, Juan Sanchez, of being a *judaizante*, a Christian convert who secretly practiced Jewish customs. He was found guilty and sentenced to walk with his children in penitential processions to Toledo's churches on seven consecutive Fridays. Soon after this humiliation, he moved his family to Ávila, and by 1493 he was successfully running a "rich shop of woolens and silks." For an account of this, see especially Bilinkoff, *Avila of Teresa*.

7 This well-known phrase is from Kant's classic definition of "enlightenment": "Enlightenment is man's release from his self-incurred tutelage" (*Foundations for the Metaphysics of Morals*, 85).

8. Grief, "Teresa of Ávila," 231.

9. My thanks to Jacob Goodson for assistance in making this point. This is another

Teresa and Modern/Postmodern Absence

A third misreading of Teresa is one shaped by the modern epistemological claim that one can only know "God-images," but not God. Immanuel Kant most famously represents this epistemological position. Kant found it necessary "to deny *knowledge* of *God, freedom* and *immortality* in order to find a place for *faith*."[10] Kant could make such a statement because he believed that beyond the confines of reason existed a realm of the unfathomable and mysterious. One could have no direct knowledge of objects in this supersensible realm. While this realm was without meaning from the standpoint of knowledge, it nonetheless had existential and moral significance. For my purposes, the Kantian dichotomy between knowledge and faith is significant. Such a quintessential modern move underwrites the subjectivity of faith (a conviction that shaped the previous misreading of Teresa) and the objectivity of knowledge/reason.

This kind of dichotomy, theologian Michel de Certeau states, has made possible a modern world that is "no longer perceived as spoken by God."[11] It is rather a world in which "discourses which script social bodies have ceased to be religious and theological."[12] Thus, the world of modernity "is characterized precisely by the fact of having been inaugurated, not without them [i.e. Christians] nor even essentially against them, but in terms of revolutions of which religion was no longer the principle."[13] In such a world, Christian institutions and discourses have moved from the center to the periphery.

In *The Mystic Fable*, de Certeau turns his analytical skills to mystic discourse, arguing that such speech has suffered a loss. According to de Certeau, early modern mysticism—where he locates Teresa—exemplifies this loss, following the breakup of the medieval Christian society. In this opaque world, the mystic takes up the following orientation: "since the Speaking Word must exist even though it may become inaudible, he (the mystic) temporarily substitutes his speaking *I* for the inaccessible divine *I*."[14]

---

way of saying that "spirituality" and "religious experiences" are not generic phenomena, but formed by larger stories and practices. One can no more have a purely private spiritual experience than one can have a private language. For a philosophical argument against the possibility of a private language, see Wittgenstein's *Philosophical Investigations*.

10. Kant, *Critique of Pure Reason*, 6; my emphasis. See also Jaspers, *Kant*, 85–87.

11. Certeau, *Mystic Fable*, 188.

12. Bauerschmidt, "Abrahamic Voyage," 14.

13. Certeau, *Mystic Fable*, 188.

14. Ibid.

De Certeau is thus claiming that as the space of a speaking God disappears in early modernity (which he locates in the sixteenth century), the mystic reimagines the voice of God as the voice of the self.

In Teresa's case, de Certeau refers to her writings as a "*fiction* [a 'mystic fable'] *of the soul.*" The "*I* who speaks in the place of (and instead of) the Other also requires a *space* of expression corresponding to what the world was in relation to the speech of God."[15] This space of expression for Teresa becomes the castle. De Certeau compares the seven mansions of Teresa's interior castle to the production of songs: different melodies and musical strings through which Teresa conducts a concert. The concert, however, ends on a solitary note. Filled with "outbursts" (dreams and madness) and returns (through men of letters or *letrados* and through order), "the amorous will go off alone singing its 'dreams' (chapter 41)."[16] De Certeau thus concludes that the "mystic" represents both ambiguity and loss. Teresa "can equally affirm that the castle is the book or the soul, that she is the author or that God is [*no es mío*], and that she is speaking of the writing, the soul, or prayer."[17]

In de Certeau's interpretation, the *absence* of God so defines modernity that God can no longer be heard. The modern landscape is barren. Mystics like Teresa are left to their own devices to *invent* the soul and its journey. De Certeau thus describes the "increasingly alien landscape of modernity, in which we all dwell, and in which the believer can find no home."[18]

It is hard not to see some truth in de Certeau's analysis, especially in his description of a deep homelessness and emptiness that characterizes much of modernity, a homelessness that propels one toward a yearning beyond a purely this-worldly orientation. Whereas the previous reading of Teresa celebrates the modern invention of a timeless spirituality, de Certeau sees this as symptomatic of a deep loss that leaves an individual to

15. Ibid.; italics in original.

16. Ibid., 192.

17. Ibid., 200.

18. Bauerschmidt, "Abrahamic Voyage," 2. De Certeau desires to make "space" for ruptures and absences that could not be fully accounted for in the institutional church. While this position allows for fluidity and dynamism, it also fails to account theologically for the church as institution, a position that can make Jesus seem oddly disconnected from time and place. De Certeau portrays Jesus Christ, the "Other," "as present but also absent; his coming and death founded Christianity, but the signifying event is not the crucifixion but the empty tomb; 'the 'follow me' [of Jesus] comes from a voice which has been effaced, forever irrecoverable'" ("The Question of Michel de Certeau").

his or her own devices. The inability to hear the Divine Word as *a people* is, for de Certeau, a fact to be mourned. Thus, one of his key convictions is that the individual, the mystic, can only inhabit the ruins of a "tattered Christendom."[19] His analysis rightly indicates that an adequate response to modern fragmentation must be more than purely "spiritual" in the modern sense.

De Certeau's conviction that modernity has made it difficult to perceive the world as spoken by God is confirmed, more recently, by Charles Taylor. In an oft-quoted passage from *A Secular Age*, Taylor writes, "Why was it virtually impossible not to believe in God in, say, 1500 in our Western society, while in 2000 many of us find this not only easy, but even inescapable?"[20] While de Certeau's rich description of modernity as suffering a growing deafness to God's Word is profound, his narration of Teresa as a modern figure is more problematic. This is not to deny that loss and absence figure in her writings. For example, there are times, Teresa writes, when "the soul thinks God has abandoned it because of what it is; it almost doubts His mercy."[21] Even so, Teresa continues, the person should continue receiving Communion and practicing private prayer. Teresa's turn to the practices of the church is not only typical but signals how her way is one of hearing the Word in the context of receiving this Word with the church. Thus, Teresa's way, while at times lonely and dark, is enfolded not into a story of postmodern absence but into God's story of communion through Christ. It is from this perspective that one can see how "the story of Teresa's life evolve[s] into a story of God's mercy,"[22] a mercy made known with and in the body called church. Teresa, then, does not offer a "mystic fable," but rather a scriptural and ecclesial journey that itself *is* a social reconfiguration. I return to this point in more depth in the following chapters as I show how Teresa's "dwellings" reconfigure politics, how her "divine marriage" imagines an alternative economy, and how her "pilgrimage" moves toward visible unity as Christ's body.

---

19. Certeau, *Mystic Fable*, 25. "Within the tattered Christendom they experienced a fundamental defection, that of the institutions of meaning. They lived the decomposition of a cosmos and were exiled from it. . . . They sought a firm footing, but in the end the Scripture appeared as 'corrupt' as the Churches" (ibid.).

20. Taylor, *Secular Age*, 25.

21. Teresa, *Collected Works*, 2:189.

22. Kavanaugh and Rodriguez in Teresa, *Collected Works*, 3:3.

TERESA AND THE WORD

For now, however, let us look more closely at Teresa and the Word. What do I mean by calling Teresa an interpreter and "performer" of Scripture?[23] At the outset, we can note that Teresa does not interpret Scripture according to contemporary expectations. She does not systematically offer a verse-by-verse commentary on particular books.[24] In fact, it is more typical for Teresa to quote Scripture sporadically and sometimes with a poor memory of where exactly a particular verse can be found. Like the majority of Christians in her day (as well as generations of Christians before her), Teresa would not have had personal access to the whole Bible. Further, she was not literate, meaning in this context that she did not read or speak Latin. Sections of the Bible translated into Spanish, however, would have been available to her in anthologies.

How, then, can we account for Teresa's interpretation and performance of Scripture? In a way that we might find difficult to imagine, Teresa inhabited a *liturgical* world. This world was marked by such practices as praying the daily office, making confession and having a confessor, frequent celebration of feast and fast days, and celebrating the sacrament of Mass as the culmination of all time. As Eamon Duffy describes this world, "Within the liturgy, birth, copulation, and death, journeying and homecoming, guilt and forgiveness, the blessing of homely things and the call to pass beyond them were all located, tested and sanctioned. In the liturgy and in the sacramental celebrations which were its central moments, medieval people found the key to the meaning and purpose of their lives."[25] To describe the breadth of liturgy in this way is to register that participants were inevitably hearers of Scripture in community. The Word would have been integral to all liturgical gatherings. Teresa would not have had the capacity, therefore, to imagine what some today refer to as "*Scriptura nuda*," the individual interpreting the text alone. She would have rather been formed to understand that "not only is Scripture within

23. The phrase "performing the Scripture" comes from Lash, *Theology on the Way to Emmaus*. Lash states, "the fundamental form of the *Christian* interpretation of scripture is the life, activity and organisation of the Christian community, construed as performance of the biblical text." He continues that "if, in the liturgy of the Word, the story is told, it is told not so that it may merely be relished or remembered, but that it may be performed, in the following of Christ" (45–46).

24. Teresa does write, though, *Meditations on the Song of Songs*.

25. Duffy, *Stripping of the Altars*, 11.

the church, but we, the church, are within Scripture—that is, our common life is located *inside* the story Scripture tells."[26]

In our modern context, some might find this dependence upon ecclesial reading and hearing problematic. What about the need to have a place to stand over against the church? Is this performance of Scripture simply one of strict conformity? These are important questions and ones to which, as I show more fully, Teresa's own life provides a response. Teresa herself was far from regarding the church as without blemish or hardship. Her own writings were at various points examined by the ecclesiastical tribunal.[27] Oddly, though, Teresa was not perturbed by the idea that she might have to appear before the Inquisition. "I knew quite well," she once wrote, "that in matters of faith no one would ever find me transgressing even the smallest ceremony of the church, and that for the church or for any truth of Holy Scripture I would undertake to die a thousand deaths."[28] Such strong confidence in the church, during either her time or ours, might well seem alien to modern readers. For Teresa, however, this confidence did not conflict with her conviction that the church, and thus the liturgical/scriptural world in which she lived, needed to be reformed. She noted repeatedly how she had to suffer from the ignorance and stupidity of many of her male superiors and confessors. She recounted trials of living in community with her sisters. Teresa herself, of course, led a reformation of her monastic order, establishing seventeen foundations of Discalced Carmelites. She was thus well aware of the sins and weaknesses of the church. Even so, eyewitnesses report that on her deathbed Teresa said many times over, "Finally, Lord, I am a daughter of the church." For Teresa, the ecclesial Word, even if received in distorted or incomplete ways, was what enabled one to live faithfully before God. Teresa was able to reform and renew the church not in spite of but because of her liturgical and scriptural formation.

Significantly, when Teresa's spiritual confessor, Fr. Jerome Gracián, told her to write *Interior Castle*, he requested that she "put down the *doctrine* in a general way without naming the one to whom the things you

---

26. Jenson, "Scripture's Authority in the Church," 30. Timothy George makes the following helpful distinction between *sola* and *nuda scriptura*: "*Sola Scriptura* does not mean *nuda scriptura* nor *scriptura solitaria*! It means instead that the Word of God, as it is communicated to us in the Scriptures, remains the final judge (norma normans) of all the teaching in the church" ("Evangelical Reflection," 206).

27. See note 5 above.

28. Cited by Boulay, *Teresa of Avila*, 80, as well as Egan, "Teresa of Jesus," 87.

mentioned happened." [29] Her confessor's statement indicates that he intended *Interior Castle* to be something other than simply Teresa's personal experience or reflections. Yet, just as *Interior Castle* seems to fall far short of being anything like a biblical commentary by modern standards, so also does it appear not to measure up to modern standards of "doctrine." For example, there are no divisions into various doctrinal topics, no organized system of analysis, and little reference to other works. What this indicates, however, is not that Teresa is not offering commentary or doctrine, but rather that she is offering it in a way that goes against modern expectations that divide biblical exegesis, theology, and spirituality into separate disciplines—divisions that have often wreaked havoc in contemporary Christian life. [30]

Words as Deeds

To see Teresa as a "performer of Scripture" is to see that she shares an understanding of words as deeds. [31] Words do things. Today, more often than not, many associate words-as-deeds with magic and superstition, as in the stories of Harry Potter. Teresa's late medieval culture would not have found this kind of magic alien. Teresa's capacity to see words as deeds, however, derives from Scripture. For example, the story of Jacob stealing Esau's birthright and blessing (the older son's due) shows how words, once spoken, are deeds that cannot be undone. Even though Esau weeps and cries out to his father, "have you only one blessing?" (Gen 27:38), Isaac cannot undo his words. A spoken blessing, "like an arrow shot toward its goal, was believed to release a power which could not be retracted." [32] The Hebrew word *dabhar*, as is well known, can mean either "word" or "deed." Most fully, God's *dabhar* "makes a world appear." [33] As the psalmist

29. Cited by Kavanaugh and Rodriguez in Teresa, *Collected Works*, 2:263; my emphasis.

30. That Teresa's work itself is often located under "spirituality" underwrites these kinds of modern divisions. Once one imagines spirituality as separate from Scripture or theology, then it easily becomes an experiential phenomena separate from the church. The notorious cliché, "I'm spiritual, but not religious . . ." (discussed in the second misreading above) reflects this split.

31. This comes in part because Teresa lived closer to an oral culture than we do today. The contrast between orality and literacy, and how it forms our ways of being, is a fascinating one. See especially Ong, *Orality and Literacy*.

32. NRSV note 35 on Gen 27:34.

33. For a theological and philosophical analysis of *dabhar*, see especially Poteat, *Polanyian Meditations*, 104–32.

writes, "By the word (deed) of the Lord were the heavens made, and all their host by the breath of his mouth" (Ps 33:6, RSV). In John's Gospel, "In the beginning was the Word" can also mean, "In the beginning was the deed" (John 1:1).

In *Interior Castle*, Teresa relies upon this understanding of words as deeds. At one point, she quotes Jesus' words to his disciples, "Peace be with you" (John 20:19), and his words to the "glorious Magdalen," "Go in peace" (Luke 7:50). She notes that these are more than "mere words." Rather, she says, "the words of the Lord are like *acts* wrought in us . . ."[34] They are deeds that produce an effect. Thus, Teresa can write,

> When Jesus Christ was praying for His Apostles (I do not know where this occurs), He asked that they might become one with the Father and with Him, even as Jesus Christ our Lord is in the Father and the Father is in Him. I do not know what greater love there can be than this. And we shall *none of us* fail to be included here, for His Majesty went on to say: "Not for them alone do I pray, but also for all who believe in Me" . . .[35]

Teresa's point here is that by virtue of Jesus' words/deeds she and her sisters are like the Apostles. More fully, even, she and her sisters are with the apostles through communion with Christ. This is not imaginary, esoteric, or wishful thinking. It is rather a reality made possible by Jesus' words, "that they may be one."

The distance between Christ's words of unity and the reality of the church—both in Teresa's time and in our own—might well leave one with the impression that these words are *mere* words. Christ's prayer for unity seems not to have made a world appear since division runs rampant. How exactly are the words of Scripture deeds? Teresa, in my view, understands God's words/deeds as gifts of love. Inasmuch as God's words are gifts, they call for our reception in order to be more fully manifest in the world. Such reception involves our identification and participation. Thus, Teresa is describing *how* her sisters and readers can more fully receive God's ever-faithful words/deeds. The words of Jesus cannot fail, Teresa writes, though "we ourselves fail by not preparing ourselves and departing from all that can shut out this light, we do not see ourselves in this mirror [Christ] into

---

34. Teresa, *Interior Castle*, 218; my emphasis. In a similar vein, Teresa writes, "And if the soul suffers dryness, agitation and worry, these are taken away as though by a stroke of the hand since it seems the Lord wants it to understand that He is powerful and that His words are works" (*Book of Her Life*, 162).

35. Teresa, *Interior Castle*, 133; my emphasis.

which we are gazing and in which our image is engraved."[36] For Teresa, *receptivity* is key to performing Scripture. Teresa's use of the metaphor of a mirror through which we *receive* our vision echoes 2 Corinthians 3:18: "And all of us, with unveiled faces, seeing the glory of the Lord as though reflected in a mirror, are being transformed into the same image from one degree of glory to another; for this comes from the Lord, the Spirit." It is not human deeds and speech that are efficacious, but rather the Word of God and human participation in it.

This deep-seated conviction that the Word of God cannot fail makes it possible for Teresa to use certain scriptural images, structures, or figures to order reality; they are the outworking of God's word/deed. To respond and participate in God's words/deeds is to allow our lives to become patterned in particular visible and unifying ways. The question remains, however, as to *how* to receive Christ and Scripture most fully.

For now, though, it is important to see that those who interpret Teresa as charting a journey of the soul *within* fail fully to grasp the nature of God's words as deeds as this plays itself out in Teresa's life and work. For interpreters of Teresa such as Heidi Shlumpf or Caroline Myss, mentioned earlier, the divine word is already within the soul and the challenge is to discover this internal phenomena. Wholeness lies in journeying toward this interior "light." On their view, Teresa is describing the soul at the center of which resides an inner spark (Christ). Is she not after all describing an *interior* journey?

In partial response to this question, it is significant that the original title of Teresa's classic, *Las Moradas*, does not mean "interior castle," as the standard English translation suggests, but "the dwellings" or "the abodes." This difference is significant especially in our context, where "interior" typically means private and highly subjective, whereas "dwellings" still maintains the connotation of exterior space. As I discuss more fully in chapter 2, the journey through Teresa's *moradas* or dwellings is not a matter of going inside oneself there to discover an interior light or self, but of becoming a visible part of God's saving deeds in history.

To illumine this difference, Bernd Wannenwetsch's description of two contrasting understandings of "word" is helpful. The Greek *logos*, he states, refers to the uncovering of already existing things. The Hebrew *dabhar*, on the other hand, is "an act of power that does what it says in the very power of its being spoken . . ."[37] The existence of an interior word means that the

---

36. Ibid., 219.

37. Wannenwetsch, "Inwardness and Commodification," 36. Wannenwetsch describes the inwardness of the word (typically expressed today through meaning or

spiritual journey is one in which an already existent meaning or essence needs to be discovered. This is the view that Myss and others mentioned earlier attribute to Teresa. Wannenwetsch describes this understanding of "inwardness" (a return from one's fallen state in the corruptible world back to a divine source) as more Platonic than Christian. By contrast, an understanding of word as deed, and of God's words as deeds that shape the course of history and our very lives, indicates that our journey is dependent upon God's mighty acts in time.

Teresa, the Word, and Augustine

It is against this background of the Word-as-deed that we can see a key way in which the work of Augustine influenced Teresa. In her autobiography, Teresa discusses how reading Augustine transformed her: "As I began to read the *Confessions*, it seemed to me I saw myself in them. When I came to the passage where he speaks about his conversion and read how he heard that voice in the garden, it only seemed to me, according to what I felt in my heart, that it was I the Lord called."[38] In this famous scene to which Teresa refers, Augustine hears a child singing, "Pick it up and read, pick it up and read," and hears in these words God's own word telling him to open the Scriptures. He then picks up his "book of the Apostle's letters" and reads Romans 13:13–14, part of which states, "put on the Lord Jesus Christ, and make no provision for the flesh or the gratification of your desires" (RSV). Realizing that the grace of Christ will transform his disordered life, Augustine writes, "the light of certainty flooded my heart and all dark shades of doubt fled away."[39]

When Teresa reads Augustine's account, she too undergoes a transformation. She writes, "I remained for a long time totally dissolved in tears and feeling within myself utter distress and weariness." [40] While reading God's Word as mediated through Augustine, Teresa like Augustine is "pierced" by the Word of God. As Augustine has stated, "You pierced my

---

sincerity) as a deformation of the Word of God. It deforms the Word by locating it already within us; it expresses "itself in concrete 'spiritual needs' which can be attended to by the [church] . . ." Wannenwetsch observes that the main assumption here, "borrowed from Greek philosophies of language, was that of a sort of common 'logos' . . . in which all share and which makes divinizing possible in the first place" (35).

38. Teresa, *Book of Her Life*, 51.

39. Augustine, *Confessions*, 207.

40. Teresa, *Book of Her Life*, 51.

heart with *your word*, and I fell in love with you."[41] Like Augustine, too, Teresa's senses are more fully opened to God's gifts and desires, so that she can later exclaim not only about the Word but also about the Eucharist, "Your delight is to be with the children of the earth."[42] It is against the backdrop of God's Word "piercing" Teresa that we ought to interpret her description of the Holy Spirit "wounding" her (in contrast to the Freudian *eros* misreading discussed above).

The Word that both Augustine and Teresa *hear* is not an existential inner word (always already present). But how do we know, one might ask? How is this word not simply their own projected inner voice, as some of the readings of Teresa that I discussed earlier imply? It is significant that the Word that Teresa reads comes to her mediated through particular people and communities: for example, Saint Paul, Antony (who inspired Augustine and who, Augustine recalls, had been instructed by a Gospel text), Augustine, and the Augustinian nuns of Our Lady of Grace (the convent where Teresa had stayed as a layperson). The passing on of the Word, so understood, occurs in the context of the church universal as it comes to be embodied in the lives of people in concrete ways. This Word is not already inside Augustine or Teresa. Augustine does say that he was without, trying to find order in his life, while God was *within*: "Lo, you were within, but I outside, seeking there for you . . ."[43] And Teresa, as I will discuss more fully, develops a key image of "His Majesty," Christ, as already *inside* the soul. These passages, however, need to be read in light of God's dwelling with humanity through Christ—not as an inner light that circumvents God's new creation, the church, and ourselves as members of it.

Teresa and the Four Senses of Scripture

I now turn more directly to how Teresa interprets Scripture. As practitioners of "scriptural reasoning" have recently emphasized, to use Scripture wisely is, ironically, to avoid simply *using* Scripture but rather to be nurtured and healed by Scripture.[44] Such an understanding of Scripture as

41. Augustine, *Confessions*, 241; my emphasis.

42. Teresa is citing Prov 8:31. The context that Teresa is focusing on at this point is particularly the sacrament of the Mass: "How You desire, Lord, thus to be with us and to be present in the Sacrament" (*Book of Her Life*, 86). This emphasis is significant because it displays how *both* the Word and the Sacrament form and transform Teresa.

43. Augustine, *Confessions*, 262.

44. In describing the practice of scriptural reasoning, Goodson writes, "The goal is

nourishment and medicine is commensurate with a wide-ranging tradition of reading Scripture in "four senses." [45] It is this way of reading that would have formed Teresa.

The "four senses" of Scripture goes back to John Cassian in the fifth century and developed out of Scripture's own way of reading Scripture. Briefly described, the four senses are as follows. The first sense, which is primary, is the "literal." Today this word often refers to "inerrantist" readings of Scripture, such that, for example, Genesis 1–2 is read through the lens of modern science. In the usage referred to here, however, the literal sense can be said to refer to the "Scriptures [bearing] witness to the mighty acts of God."[46] Others describe this use of literal sense as "the meanings that Christians conventionally ascribe to a passage in their ongoing struggles to live and worship faithfully before the Triune God."[47] While the literal sense remains primary, it gives rise to three other senses: the moral, the figurative, and the eschatological. The moral sense teaches persons what to do, and so aims to nurture the virtue of love. The figurative sense refers to the church and seeks to nurture the virtue of faith by teaching hearers what to believe. The eschatological sense, by reading in light of how the future impinges on the present, nurtures the virtue of hope. Seeing or hearing multiple senses does not mean that "a text can mean anything a later audience wants it to mean." According to David Steinmetz, "the language of the Bible opens up a field of possible meanings," not any and

---

not to use Scripture but to be healed by Scripture" ("Baptist Theology of Mary?" 13). Scriptural reasoning is the practice whereby Christians, Jews, and Muslims read scriptures together not in spite of but out of their unique commitments. Along similar lines, Henri de Lubac writes about Origen that he was "less intent on explaining Scripture than on illuminating everything by it" (*Scripture in the Tradition*, 46).

45. A well-known distich in the Latin Middle Ages (cited by Nicholas around 1330) sums up the four senses as follows: "The letter teaches what happened. Allegory teaches what you shall believe. The moral sense, what you shall do. Anagogy, where you shall aim." Cited by de Lubac, who gives the most systematic account of these four senses in *Medieval Exegesis* (quote in 1:4). For another account of "pre-critical" exegesis, see especially Steinmetz, "Superiority of Pre-Critical Exegesis." As I will discuss, this way of reading Scripture does not deny the usefulness of historical-critical methods. Its self-understanding, however, is to read Scripture with and for the church, rather than for some other purpose.

46. Wainwright, *Embracing Purpose*, 93.

47. Fowl, "Theological and Ideological Strategies," 171. Fowl notes that in the Christian theological tradition the "literal sense" does not correspond exactly with modern notions of "literal."

all meanings. [48] At the same time, the senses are inseparable; "they inter-penetrate each other." [49]

For our purposes, it is important to note that this fourfold pattern became a way of training the church and her members to see themselves and their own time and place in biblical terms. Within this tradition of reading, Scripture is more than a report of past events. Rather, as Balthasar summarizes, this fourfold pattern reflects how "God's word becomes incarnate in Christ and prepares for this incarnation in Israel through the living word addressed to Abraham and to the people in the Mosaic instructions and in the prophets." For this reason, Balthasar continues, "the theory of the senses of Scripture is not a curiosity of the history of theology but an instrument for seeking out the most profound articulations of salvation history." [50] An understanding of God's Word as living and speaking in time, culminating in the Word that is Christ, provides the basis for multiple senses of reading Scripture. Teresa, for her part, does not so much specifically identify these senses as rely upon them implicitly in her life and work.

This understanding of different senses of Scripture, along with the conviction that words are deeds, makes possible an expectation of scriptural abundance easily obscured by modern readings. In *Medieval Exegesis*, de Lubac describes this approach to Scripture as "undecipherable in its fullness and in the multiplicity of its meanings." [51] The fecundity of Scripture, he adds, is "a table arranged by Wisdom, laden with food, where the unfathomable divinity of the Savior is itself offered as nourishment to all." [52] The ancient fathers, in fact, compared Scripture received in this way "to a robe that was worn by the royal bride, woven of gold with a thousand colors." [53] God's Word is fruitful in spectacular ways. More recently, de Lubac observes, John Henry Newman describes this scriptural excess as follows:

48. Steinmetz, "Superiority of Pre-Critical Exegesis," 31. Steinmetz also notes how the four senses have been related to Christian virtues. The four senses can go by different names: the "tropological" (moral), the "allegorical" or "typological" (figurative), and the "anagogical" (eschatological).

49. Balthasar, *Theology of Henri de Lubac*, 80.

50. Ibid., 75 and 76.

51. De Lubac, *Medieval Exegesis*, 77.

52. Ibid., 77.

53. Ibid., 79.

[Scripture] cannot, as it were, be mapped, or its contents cata-
logued; but after all our diligence, to the end of our lives and to
the end of the Church, it must be an unexplored and unsubdued
land, with heights and valleys, forests and streams, on the right
and left of our path and close about us, full of concealed wonders and choice treasures.[54]

This superabundance is ultimately made possible by the Holy Spirit
who animates Scripture: "Scripture is 'fertilized by a miracle of the Holy
Spirit.'"[55]

At this point, I want to direct the reader's attention to how Teresa's
"spirituality" is of a piece with her scriptural performance. That is, she
imagines "spirituality" (though this term is not one that Teresa herself
would have used) within the context of Scripture's abundance. While I
display this conviction more fully in the following chapters, it is important
to register at this point how Teresa both writes and embodies this scriptural excess. "Let us not cease to believe," she states, "that even in this life
God gives the hundredfold."[56] Such a statement, typical of Teresa's counsel,
shows how she writes and thinks out of a superabundance made possible
through God's Word.

In contrast to these multiple senses, modern strategies for reading
Scripture have tended to read it monolithically. David Steinmetz observes
about the historical-critical method that "the primitive meaning of the
text is its only valid meaning, and the historical-critical method is the
only key which can unlock it."[57] Certainly, viewing Scripture "purely as
historians" can provide helpful resources or tools for understanding aspects of Scripture. It is interesting to consider, however, that neither the
historical-critical method nor, for that matter, the modern literal method
of reading Scripture aim to produce lives of abundance that manifest the
fruits of Christian virtue. The historical-critical method, in its claim to be
scientific and more objective, lacks the necessary *telos* since, for it, reading
Scripture is not about producing certain kinds of lives but about achieving
particular sorts of knowledge. There is no necessary identification on the

54. As quoted in ibid., 80.

55. Ibid., 82.

56. Teresa, *Book of Her Life*, 147. Teresa is echoing Mark 10:29–30: "Jesus said,
'Truly I tell you, there is no one who has left house or brothers or sisters or mother or
father or children or fields, for my sake and for the sake of the good news, who will
not receive a hundredfold now in this age—houses, brothers and sisters, mothers and
children, and fields with persecutions—and in the age to come eternal life.'"

57. Steinmetz, "Superiority of Pre-Critical Exegesis," 6.

part of the reader with the stories or events.[58] Similarly, a modern literal reading of the text, which involves the individual before the written word, ignores how the church makes possible the lives of Christians. By contrast, the *telos* of reading Scripture according to multiple senses is something radically different. As Augustine famously states, "whoever, then, thinks that he understands the Holy Scriptures, or any part of them, but puts such an interpretation upon them as does not tend to build up this twofold love of God and our neighbor, does not yet understand them."[59]

Like Augustine, Teresa understands Scripture within the context of liturgical transformation. Teresa, too, emphasizes the virtue of love as a key sign of faithfulness to God's Word. The language of "interior" or "interiority" that Teresa occasionally uses does not refer to a private sphere but to the necessity of *conversion*.[60] To interiorize God's Word is to become transformed. Teresa's "use" of Scripture can be compared to depictions of Saint John eating the book and being commanded to prophesy (Rev 10:9–11) as well as Ezekiel eating the scroll (Ezek 3:1–3). When eaten, the Word can be bitter or sweet as honey. Teresa's journey through the many dwellings ought to be read as a treatise for learning how to digest and thus internalize God's Word. Teresa herself, as indicated earlier, has feasted upon God's Word through the "exterior" habits of liturgy, prayer, the ordering of time, reading, and many other practices that sustain life together in Christ. When Teresa or her sisters hear the Spirit speaking, Teresa's counsel is always to discern the Spirit in the context of God's Word to a people.[61] It is this kind of interior reception of God's Word in the context of God's people that enables Teresa to use Scripture to attend to the wounds on the body of Christ, a point to which I return in subsequent chapters.

58. This is not to deny that the method is beneficial, or that the one using the method may well become a saint, but the method or practice itself does not call for the virtues that constitute a life of holiness. For a discussion of how the historical-critical and modern literal approaches to the Bible share similar assumptions, see Stanley Hauerwas, *Unleashing the Scripture*.

59. Augustine, *On Christian Doctrine*, 533.

60. To cite de Lubac, "The spiritual meaning of a mystery is the meaning we discover—or, rather, into which we penetrate—by living that mystery. Still more fundamentally, the entire process of spiritual understanding is, in its principle, identical to the process of conversion" (*Medieval Exegesis*, 13).

61. Thus Teresa writes, ". . . a locution bears the credentials of being from God if it is in conformity with Sacred Scripture" (*Book of Her Life*, 166–67).

TERESA, A MYSTIC

Earlier I noted that some contemporary authors have embraced Teresa as a "mystic for our time." They mean by this that Teresa's interior journey is one not bound by ritual, culture, or religion. From their perspective, a mystic is someone who embodies universal truths, someone who is enlightened, at peace, self-fulfilled, and so forth. Teresa's quest, so understood, is a universal journey of the soul within. She is ahead of her own time, in this sense, and is thus a "mystic for our time."

We can notice, at this point, however, that such a "mystic" does not so much cut across cultures as exemplify dominant convictions of late modern Western culture, chief of which is the idea that the journey to true selfhood lies within. As John Kenney notes, this contemporary use of "mysticism" can be traced to the early modern period.

> . . . it was the employment of the term "mysticism" by Romantics in the nineteenth century that first led to its wider popularity. This was part of the larger conceptual shift in the meaning of religion in Western culture, a change in emphasis from social and cultural aspects of spiritual life to personal experience. As collective rituals and institutions came to be seen by many as suspect, the experiences of the private self became more significant.[62]

So understood, "mysticism" refers to personal experience separate from wider religious and social phenomena. From this perspective, mysticism differs from dogma, and cannot be controlled or contained by the church. As one contemporary center for Christian mysticism states, "As Christian mystics, we find truth in our experiences, not dogma . . . deep mystical Christian teachings lead souls into direct relationship with God."[63] "Spiri-

---

62. Kenney, *Mysticism of Saint Augustine*, 1. Kenney adds, "It has become characteristic of modern thought that religion is understood primarily as a matter of personal experience, and only secondarily as a civic, social or institutional phenomenon." In a similar vein, Frederick Bauerschmidt observes about Max Weber's influential understanding of mysticism, "Thus while mysticism is rendered as the private ideal of individual peace, politics is the public reality of social violence" ("Politics of the Little Way," 78).

63. Centers of Light Online, "What Is Christian Mysticism?," online at http://online.centersoflight.org/what-is-christian-mysticism/. This understanding of mysticism is similar to Pope Benedict XVI's description of religious subjectivism: religion resides in "the subjective sphere and can therefore have no objective dogmatic contents that are binding on all; in this view, dogma in general seems to contradict man's reason" (Ratzinger, *Salt of the Earth*, 163).

tual communities," to the extent that they are relevant, serve as sources of support for one's individual journey. To read Teresa through this modern "mystical" lens is to assume that her life and writings have little to do with politics, economics, and ecclesial ways of life.

Many today, however, are drawn to mystics and mysticism because these seem to represent—in a world burdened with hard facts and sobering economic and political realities—a holy dimension beyond human control. I do not wish to deny that there is something compelling to this alternative sense of Divine reality breaking into where one is in a private and individual way. In late modernity, persons rightly yearn for something that will relieve them from the suffocating reality of living in a world absent the Divine.

At the same time, however, a mysticism relegated to the individual realm is a mysticism that easily leaves the so-called real world of politics, economics, and daily life as is. It is either escapist or underwrites the status quo, like the chaplain on a warship, attending to the spirituality of those on board while the ship heads off to make war on their political enemies. But mysticism, Christian or otherwise, cannot be isolated to a realm. It is rather always embedded in a particular politics, economics, and vision of society. Mysticism is not a generically "interior" reality, but is inevitably formed by institutions, practices, and traditions that sustain it and make it possible.

As we will see with Teresa, there is a sense in which the Christian mystic becomes *less* inward than others, living more externally and visibly in communion with Christ and his body. Archbishop Rowan Williams writes, "if the 'mystical' ultimately means the reception of a particular *pattern* of divine action (creative love, self-emptying incarnation), its test will be the presence or absence of something like that pattern in a human life seen as a whole, not the presence or absence of this or that phenomenon in the consciousness."[64] Christian mysticism is not a psychology or phenomenology of inner mystical states (though psychological transformation may well occur) but the embodiment of a Divine pattern in a whole way of life.

This embodiment is not first about humans behaving in a certain way, though it involves this. It is rather the reception of a divine pattern as displayed most fully in the Word of God. This Word comes in ordinary, liturgical ways (preaching, confession and forgiveness, baptism, Eucharist) or it may well come, as Teresa so vividly describes, in more unusual ways

---

64. Williams, *Teresa of Avila*, 187.

(dreams, visions, and so forth). But the reception of God's Word both creates and illumines ongoing patterns of God's deeds in time, revealed most fully in Christ. From this perspective, the mystic is one who participates in God's mysteries and illumines providential patterns in particularly vivid ways.

This understanding of "mystical" reflects an earlier usage. The word "mystical" is related to "mystery," to which both the Latin *mysterium* and *sacramentum* correspond.[65] Denys the Areopagite identifies "mystical theology" as that which illumines how "*Christian liturgy* displays the 'mysteries' of God's action in relation to the created order—the mystery of God going out from the depths of the divine nature to create and then to become incarnate in our nature, God binding creation together in communion and drawing creation back to its divine source."[66] So understood, "mystical" refers to the mystery of participating in a Divine communion. "Mystical" in this context is also related to the sacraments. As de Lubac has famously argued, early on in the church, "mystical" referred to the Eucharist; thus he writes, "the Eucharist corresponds to the Church as cause to effect, as means to end, as sign to reality."[67] The Eucharist is a "mystical" body because it realizes the mystery of God becoming flesh in those who partake of it. Both in the liturgy and exegesis, de Lubac notes, the words "mystery" and "mystical" always refers to "two fundamental senses": sign and secret, "which are still the two senses attached respectively to our two words sacrament and mystery."[68] Seen in this context, a "mystic" is a sign, a visible sign of Divine mysteries revealed in the life, death, and resurrection of Jesus.

A participation in the mysteries of God's actions may well involve a certain speechlessness. This is not because mystical experience transcends language by transcending the body, as is sometimes thought. Such an assumption reproduces a gnostic orientation by disconnecting knowledge from the body. Christian speechlessness rather reflects a silence before the excess of Divine Mystery, such as is recorded in the Psalms: "Great things are they that you have done, O Lord my God! . . . Oh, that I could make them known and tell them! But they are more than I can count" (Ps 40:5–6).[69] The Divine mystery is not fully speakable because God's Word

65. De Lubac, *Corpus Mysticum*, 45.

66. Williams, *Teresa of Avila*, 184.

67. Ibid., 13.

68. Ibid., 47.

69. The translation I have cited is from *The Psalter, or, Psalms of David, from the Book of Common Prayer* (1979).

abundantly exceeds human grasp. Teresa herself often acknowledges this reality. She writes, for example, "I am undoing myself, sisters, to give to you an understanding of this working of love, and I don't know how."[70] Teresa knows well the difficulty of writing about the mystery of divine patterns at work in the world. Yet she would surely agree with contemporary theologian Eugene Rogers when he writes,

> That empowerment of human beings to share in the divine celebration (of the Trinity) is mystagogical; that is, it leads human beings into a mystery. Theologically speaking, a mystery is not that which human beings do not understand, although they don't; it is that which overwhelms their understanding on account of its goodness. . . . To be led into a mystery is to be led into ever more wonderful goodness."[71]

Though the mystery that is God cannot be fully spoken or described because of its exceeding goodness, humans are nonetheless empowered through grace to speak of this Divine excess revealed as Trinity.

In this light, it is significant that Teresa thought it crucial to urge her sisters to pray to the *human* Christ. She did so because she wanted to avoid the dangers of the *alumbrados* (the "illuminated"), a group that focused on a purely inward spirituality. In contrast to the *alumbrados*, who believed the humanity of Christ was a hindrance to prayer and worship, Teresa stressed "seeing" the human Christ as much as possible. An emphasis on the humanity of Christ (and so implicitly on the *Theotokos* and Israel) shows that Teresa sees her identity and that of her sisters in relation to the flesh of Jesus, Jewish flesh, the flesh of Israel, and the flesh into which the church (and all impure blood) was grafted. Identity, for Teresa, is not drawn from a spiritual retreat within, nor does it conform to the dominant politics of her day, which was obsessed with "pure blood."[72] It is rather configured by the humanity and divinity of Christ. As Teresa puts it, "The good Jesus is too good company for us to forsake Him and His most

70. Teresa de Jesús, *Moradas*, 105; my translation. The original reads: "*Deshaciéndome estoy, hermanas, por daros a entender esta operación de amor, y no sé cómo.*"

71. Rogers, *After the Spirit*, 176. In a similar vein, Mark McIntosh states: "it is true that in classical Christianity mysticism speaks of the inexpressibility of God, but we ought not to assume this means that *God* is somehow *less* expressive than human beings, indeed the mystics regularly assert that the ineffability of God is the result of God's 'ever-greater' reality: God's existence speaks more than we know how to say and in that sense we are reduced to silence" (*Mystical Theology*, 113).

72. I discuss in chapter 2 how the concept of "pure blood" impacted the politics of Teresa's day.

sacred Mother."[73] Teresa rightly sees a denial of Christ's humanity is at the same time a distortion of his divinity. Only because Christ fully shares our humanity is it possible for humans to participate in the Son's communion with the Father. This communion, Teresa rightly sees, is a "company," a visible sign of God's friendship with the world. Such an understanding allows space to see how Teresa, as a Christian mystic, draws her sisters and readers not to a mysterious spiritual realm but into a company who shares together the mysteries of the Word made flesh, embodied in particular ways of life.

We are now in a better position to understand Fr. Gracián's words to Teresa, cited earlier: "put down the *doctrine* in a general way without naming the one to whom the things you mentioned happened."[74] Teresa's "doctrine" in her various writings can appear to be high autobiographical, and thus not really doctrine at all. How do we reconcile these very different genres, biography and doctrine? Is *Interior Castle*, for example, a veiled autobiography or is it, as Fr. Gracián hoped, doctrine? To respond to these questions, it is important to see that doctrine and experience are not at opposite ends of a continuum. Teresa's biography ought to be understood as an *exemplification* of Christian doctrine. Rightly understood, Christian doctrines are not interpretations of Christian mystical experiences, but rather mystical experiences are exemplifications of Christian doctrine.[75] But what does this mean? To discuss experience and doctrine in this way might sound like the question of whether the chicken or the egg came first. For my purposes, however, it is crucial to see that the experiences Teresa has and writes about are not unique or isolated phenomena, but are rather doctrinally shaped. It is not as if she has certain "experiences" and then tries to make them fit with the Christian story.[76] Nor does she learn Christian doctrine in some wooden way detached from a way of life. Rather, as the following chapters explore more fully, the ways that God

73. Teresa, *Interior Castle*, 175.

74. Cited by Kavanaugh and Rodriguez in Teresa, *Collected Works*, 2:263; my emphasis.

75. This is a gloss on a quote cited by Williams from Robert Gimello: "Rather than speak of Buddhist doctrines as interpretations of Buddhist mystical experiences, one might better speak of Buddhist mystical experiences as deliberately contrived exemplifications of Buddhist doctrine" (*Teresa of Ávila*, 194).

76. It might well be, of course, that discovering a divine pattern in our lives takes time, if not a lifetime and more. That is why individuals do not name themselves saints. It is the time taking task of the wider body of Christ to discover divine patterns in a particular life.

works in Teresa's life, the church, and the world reflect patterns of God's dealings with a people across time. Doctrines are those teachings that seek to name, describe, and explore the implications of these patterns for the life of the church and the world.

To modern ears, the use of "pattern" might sound predictable and stagnant. But the divine patterns have the capacity to be exemplified in countless ways. "Exemplify" even seems too domesticated to describe the movement of the Spirit since, according to Scripture, the Spirit makes everything new: "So if anyone is in Christ, there is a new creation: everything old has passed away; see, everything has become new" (2 Cor 5:7). How can we reconcile an emphasis on a pattern with Paul's description of a seeming explosion of newness? The pattern of God's ongoing work in creation is never static, but is rather what makes possible fresh and unique responses to the Spirit. Indeed, Teresa's own life embodies one such unique response. That is, the Word so *forms* the lives of saints and mystics that they become living signs of an ultimately unfathomable Divine reality. Turning away from this pattern leads to stasis, and ultimately non-being.

Talk of an unfathomable reality seems to contradict any grasp of a divine pattern. If a reality is unfathomable, how can one detect a pattern? Yet here I emphasize, as did Karl Barth, that God is incomprehensible not in God's remoteness but in God's nearness in Jesus Christ.[77] What is incomprehensible is the fact that God fully revealed himself as One among us. From this perspective, de Lubac writes about Scripture, "it [is] not a matter merely of a text being explicated, but of mysteries being explored . . ."[78] It is the particularity of the Word—both the Word that is the Son and the Word of Scripture—that opens up and makes possible a discovery of divine patterns that will always be ultimately deep mysteries.

In light of this expansive pattern, then, the Christian mystic is not one who has private or incommunicable experiences. Granted, certain truths *may* be hard to speak for a number of reasons, and therefore silence could be a faithful response. An example might be related to a context in which persons would be unable to hear echoes of a divine pattern, such as one suspicious of scientifically unverifiable claims. Or, the context might be the flipside to this scientific one: endless fascination with one's personal "spirituality" or attraction to New Age mysticism.[79] Speaking of a divine

77. Paraphrased by Hauerwas, *With the Grain*, 199.

78. De Lubac, *Medieval Exegesis*, 34. De Lubac is discussing a twelfth-century understanding of Scripture.

79. A scientific/"spiritual" dichotomy repeats a rationalism/romanticism duality

pattern in these or other dominant contexts calls for both discernment and hope.

A Christian mystic, however, like a saint,[80] cannot help but point to how the pattern of God's Word powerfully shapes our lives, pointing inevitably to a mysterious abundance. It is in this sense that we can properly speak of "interiorization," in that the mystic or saint is one who has interiorized the gospel in a unique way so that is has become more fully "exteriorized": she has allowed it to sink into the depths of her own life. In so doing, she illumines God's Word for the church and, ultimately, the world. A Christian mystic or saint, then, is like a two-way mirror. Scripture enables others to see the mystic more fully, even as the mystic becomes a kind of window for the Word, making real and expanding the patterns of Scripture in creative and penetrating ways. And this, I argue, is how we ought to see Teresa. Without mystics or saints like Teresa, Scripture could easily become a dead letter. But without Scripture, as integrated into prayer, confession, baptism, and other ecclesial practices, their lives would make no sense.

TERESA AS A DOCTOR OF THE CHURCH

It was exactly the desire to make fuller sense of Teresa's life and work that, after long years of debate, she was given the title *doctor ecclesiae* ("doctor of the church") in 1970, the first woman in the Catholic Church to be so designated. [81] From early on, *doctor ecclesiae* has referred to theologians who interpret and illumine Scripture for the whole church.[82] The title "has its roots in the Latin Bible's widespread use of the Latin word *doctor* for teacher."[83] *Doctrina* in Latin means the act of teaching. To be a "doctor of

---

inherited from the Enlightenment, a duality reflected more broadly in the opposition between objective "facts" and subjective "values."

80. Not all mystics are officially saints. As noted in the introduction, "saints" can refer both to those specifically designated so by the church as well as to all Christians. Ultimately, all saints (Christians) are called to display the divine pattern of Scripture. In fact, I would emphasize that they do display this pattern, as did Israel, even in their disobedience and apathy.

81. For fuller account of the Teresa's reception as *doctor ecclesiae*, see Egan, "Significance for Theology."

82. McGinn states that a *doctor ecclesiae* "speak[s] 'in the midst of the church' and therefore *to* the whole church" (*Doctors of the Church*, 1).

83. Egan, "Significance for Theology," 154. 1 Cor 12:28 states, "God has appointed in the church first apostles, second prophets, third teachers [*doctors*] . . ."

the church" is not simply to be "learned," however. As it developed in the West, to be declared *doctor ecclesiae* required eminent teaching along with outstanding sanctity and an affirmation by the church. Eminent teaching refers to those "tested authorities in understanding the scripture and church's tradition," and to "very lucid expositors of *sacred scripture*."[84]

Teresa is best read "after modernity" as one who seeks faithfully to interpret and perform Scripture. De Lubac, in fact, notes that there is a tradition of associating the fathers and doctors of the church with the four senses of spiritual exegesis, discussed earlier. Sixtus of Siena, for example, describes how different fathers of the church excelled in each of the senses. "Under the guidance of Jerome you will learn history derived from the Greek and Latin sources. Origen and Ambrose will lay open allegories and anagogy. Chrysostom and Gregory will set forth the senses that are apt to form morals. Aurelius sheds light on doubtful areas and places that are submerged in deep darkness."[85] While Teresa cannot be so neatly characterized, she is at her best, in my view, when she uses certain figures to understand her own time and place in scriptural terms: when she transports "the historical events of the past into the present and future."[86] In so doing, she enables the reader to see the future in the past and the present and so to interpret Scripture in terms of the divine economy.[87]

On this reading, *Interior Castle* is not an individual journey but rather encompasses a broader scriptural reality. To journey through Teresa's castle, then, is not to go alone or even with a community. It is rather to become part of what God is doing in the world: creating a people and *reforming* bodies so that the body of Christ becomes visible. This reforming takes place, as Teresa narrates it, through scriptural figures. As Ephraim Radner states about these figures, "the outworking of the scriptural figures—prophecies, forms, images, events—of Christ contain, in some way, the truth of his teaching. It did not matter that people did not always get the truth . . . the history of the Church will, inevitably, share the same form as the life of Jesus."[88] Such a passage reflects Teresa's own sensibility

84. The Third Council of Valence (855) describes the "doctors" Cyprian, Hilary, Jerome, Ambrose, and Augustine as "very lucid expositors of *sacred scripture*" (Egan, "Significance for Theology," 155).

85. Cited by de Lubac, *Medieval Exegesis*, 3–4.

86. Martens, citing Bienert, in "Revisiting the Allegory/Typology Distinction," 290.

87. Ibid. As J. J. O'Keefe notes, this way of reading Scripture was referred to by the fathers as "spiritual." Two figures are brought into association for the purpose of illuminating the "perceived fit" of the whole. See 294 n. 42.

88. Radner, *Hope among the Fragments*, 126. Radner further states that "a figure

of the outworking of God's Word. In the following chapters, I consider more fully how key scriptural figures, when digested, can heal wounds of division in the body of Christ.

---

is a form what God actually makes historical experience fit, like some providential mold."

2

The Politics of Teresa's Dwellings

The earth is the Lord's and the fullness thereof, the world and those who dwell therein ... (Ps 24:1, RSV)

"POLITICAL" IS NOT A word that, at first glance, would seem to fit Teresa. She was not, for example, a Catherine of Siena (fourteenth century) who worked to establish peace among the Italian city-states. At most, those who know Teresa's biography might point to the political savvy she employed, at times in the face of opposition, to establish her Carmelite foundations throughout Spain.[1] But this hardly makes her, much less her writings, political.

What was political in Teresa's day was the Spanish monarchy, one of the most visible political forces in all of Europe. Spain not only conquered other lands but also cast out a great number of Jews and Muslims who refused to convert. Such abuse at the hands of a Catholic state/monarchy seems clearly to suggest that religion and politics *ought* to remain in separate compartments. Religion and politics ought not to mix. In response to the abuse of "religious" power, such politics appears to makes sense. The difficulty with this line of thought, however, is that it limits politics to statecraft. This understanding imagines the empire or the nation-state as the primary, if not only, political body. It thus underwrites the idea that the space in which religion enters the political arena is through voting, running for office, lobbying, supporting a particular candidate, and so forth.

---

1. For an account of this, see Bilinkoff, *Avila of Saint Teresa*, particularly ch. 5, "Saint Teresa of Jesus and Carmelite Reform."

On this view, the bureaucratic structures of the nation-state, the propagation of national allegiance, the necessity of military force, and so forth all seem entirely natural.[2] Yet, Christians have the resources and freedom to imagine a different kind of politics. As Scott Moore rightly observes, "Christians have resources for a notion of politics which is much broader and more inclusive than that available to statecraft. Once we realize that, we can turn our gaze away from government as the place where the most important political work gets done."[3] It is from this perspective that I explore how Teresa's "dwellings" are already a politics, one that beckons those who hear and see toward a political unity that is an alternative to the unity of any empire or nation.

AN ECCLESIAL WAY OF BEING

Susan K. Wood, in writing about baptism, states, "the church is not simply the place of our baptism. We are baptized not simply *in* the church, but *into* the church. . . . This is much more than church membership or a matter of confessional identity; it is an ecclesial way of being in the world."[4] The key phrase in terms of politics and dwelling is that Christians are baptized into *an ecclesial way of being in the world*. Those who are baptized belong to a "we" that encompasses the church universal across time and geography. Thus, for example, Paul can write, "For if *we* have been united with him [Christ] in a death like his, *we* will certainly be united with him in a resurrection like his" (Rom 6:5; my emphasis). This ecclesial "we" signals a unity beyond family, class, nation, or race that is itself a political reality.

I use "political" here to refer to the church as a visible body gathered and ordered for a purpose, living in a time that differs from that of other

---

2. By contrast, Michael J. Baxter argues that, from the perspective of the Catholic radicalist tradition, this view of politics is unnatural: "Political theory in the Catholic radicalist tradition sees the nation-state—with its bureaucratic structures, defense of borders through military force, systems of surveillance, propagation of nationalist allegiance, and so on—as profoundly unnatural." Such a claim that the state is "natural" is a classic example of "ideology, whereby a particular political and economic arrangement that benefits certain classes is given the status of natural, universal, eternal" ("Notes on Catholic Americanism," 64).

3. Moore, *Academic*, 3. For a fuller analysis and criticism of politics as statecraft, see Moore, *Limits of Liberal Democracy*. Moore argues for an understanding of politics that is not restricted to modern statecraft or the enforcement of rights.

4. Wood, "I Acknowledge One Baptism," 199.

politics or nations.[5] Rightly understood, the church is not determined by the time of the nation-state, a time that will inevitably come to an end. Nations or empires come and go, and in so doing show how they depend upon a perception of time as linear, as passing away and giving rise to something else. A sense of the past (George Washington or Abraham Lincoln) may exist, as well might a sense of the future (the USA as an advocate of freedom for the world), but, even so, the past is gone and the future always remains not yet. The politics embedded in the Christian story, however, is not limited to the present but draws the church always into a past, present, and future in a way that makes us present to one another and God across time. Christians can "remember the future" not because God has planned everything out for us to see, but because the future is already in our midst. "The kingdom of God is upon us." In the politics of God's kingdom, time is "reshuffled" such that present, past, and future coexist, making possible a different kind of being together, a different politics.

Teresa imagines and inhabits this kind of time. Neither does she describe a timeless journey into the depths of the soul (a view criticized in the previous chapter) nor is time strictly chronological for her. She is at pains to emphasize that journeying through the multiple dwellings of the castle is not strictly sequential.[6] Rather, to dwell with Christ is to live in providential time in which the past and future are present as God's gift, enabling God's people to participate in *shared time*. From this perspective, for example, Moses' dwelling before the burning bush is not simply a past event, a mere memory kept alive in the minds of Jews and fellow Christians. Moses rather reveals a divine pattern that points to how God is present in all time, a pattern ultimately consummated in Christ yet still unfolding in our present.[7] Teresa herself is a kind of Moses figure, lead-

5. For descriptions of the church itself as a politics, see Yoder, *Politics of Jesus*, and Hauerwas, *In Good Company*, *Church as Polis*, and *Better Hope*.

6. Particularly important for Teresa is the room of humility, which she locates in the "first mansions." Teresa relates humility to self-knowledge since humility is the virtue that enables one to see oneself truthfully before God. Teresa emphasizes how important this dwelling is no matter where one is: "How necessary [self-knowledge] is (and be sure you understand me here) even to those whom the Lord keeps in the same mansion in which He Himself is!" (*Interior Castle*, 13).

7. For an example, Christian art has been able to place Mary in the burning bush with Moses standing before it. By placing Mary in the burning bush in this story of Moses and Israel, Mary becomes identified as one who leads God's people away from idolatry, by giving birth to the Word (just as Moses is the one through whom Israel receives the commandments). This Moses-Mary typology exemplifies how scriptural time bends back upon itself even as the future is made known in the present.

ing her sisters and the church more broadly through the time of dry land to that of the fresh waters of God's ever-present healing grace.[8] To dwell "ecclesially" in any particular place, then, is to share in this kind of divine pattern, a pattern that gives rise to a different way of living politically.[9]

Yet, one could respond, time in the church seems fragmented. Some churches live in Reformation time, others in Pentecostal time, and others in Orthodox time in a way that easily belies any shared dwelling together in time. A couple of questions might arise at this point. Which church or *ekklesia* am I talking about? The Baptist World Alliance recently responded to the question, "Are Baptist churches autonomous?" (a particularly Baptist kind of question since emphasis is often given to the "autonomy of the local church") as follows: "We affirm that for Baptists, the local church is wholly church but not the whole church."[10] Such a statement indicates that even as Baptists at the local level worship and hear Scripture together, they cannot understand themselves as strictly "autonomous" or separate from the church universal, which includes the church across time. In a related sense, Catholics and Orthodox affirm that the whole body of Christ is present whenever a particular congregation gathers. The church universal is of course broken; sin and division weaken, in sometimes appalling ways, the life of the church. Unity and wholeness are seldom apparent. Even so, as Brian Daley, SJ, notes about contemporary ecumenical efforts, though unity "is hindered or clouded by our sinfulness and 'slowness of heart' (Luke 24:25)," it nonetheless "already exists among us as God's gift." To live ecclesially (or, as Daley states, "ecumenically") is to allow this unity "to become more fully evident in the way Christians look upon each other,

8. In chapter 3 I discuss more fully how Teresa's pilgrimage through the multiple dwellings repeats, albeit in a different key, the exodus and journey toward the promised land.

9. Teresa does occasionally describe the "secrets" that pass between the soul and God. For example, ". . . *y en el centro y mitad de todas éstas tiene la más principal, que es adonde pasan las cosas de mucho secreto entre Dios y el alma*" ("and in the center and midst of all these [dwellings] is the main one, where very secret things pass between God and the soul"; my translation) (*Moradas*, 12). Such a passage can appear to underwrite a purely private, apolitical time between the soul and God. What Teresa is describing, however, is not the secret *gnosis* (knowledge) of either ancient or modern gnosticism. These "secret" graces should rather be understood as God drawing creatures, and indeed all of creation, to the fullness of time in Christ, thus enhancing the politics of ecclesial unity. For Teresa, the graces are thus not "secret" in the sense of purely private, but in the sense of mysterious, where mystery points to the communion of the Triune God. I return to a fuller discussion of this point in chapter 3, under the section, "Love in the Western World."

10. Baptist World Alliance, "Are Baptist Churches Autonomous?"

articulate their faith, carry out their worship, and act in the world."[11] Such a description provides an entrance into how Christians are to live politically in time.[12]

As I will show, Teresa's dwellings describe an ecclesial way of being in time, and thus the creation of a people living a politics different from the dominant politics of her day as well as ours. That Teresa imagines this creation of a people primarily in terms of reformed Carmelite monastic communities could seem as if her dwellings have little to do with our time today. Late medieval monasticism can easily seem like a relic from a bygone past. I am not advocating an idealized replication of sixteenth-century Carmelite monasticism, *descalzado* (shoeless) at that. To live by God's providential patterns is to be open to what some have called a "non-identical repetition." That is, to move through Teresa's seven dwellings is to repeat a scriptural pattern, not woodenly but creatively, in response to the Spirit's creative work.

POLITICS, MODERNITY, AND HOMOGENEOUS TIME

To see more fully how politics depends upon particular conceptions of time, I turn to political philosopher Michael Gillespie, who states that to think of oneself as modern is "to define one's being in terms of time." Gillespie observes that, whereas ancient people understood themselves in relation to a seminal event (an exodus from bondage or a major victory), to be modern is to be "new" in the sense of being in time in a novel, unprecedented way. Time becomes homogeneous in the sense that it is the same everywhere and for everyone. No particular time is more determinative than any other. "To understand oneself as new," Gillespie writes, "is also to understand oneself as *self-originating* . . . not merely as determined by tradition or governed by fate or providence. To be modern is to be self-liberating and self-making, and thus not merely to be *in* a history or tradition but to *make* history."[13] Thus, Gillespie can conclude,

11. Daley, "Rebuilding," 74.

12. As indicated in the previous chapter, Teresa was as much aware of the sinfulness of the church as she was of her own sins. This realization, however, did not negate providential time or the church as the body (dwelling) of Christ. Rather, the sinfulness and wounds in the church and the world drew Teresa to *see* Christ himself suffering visibly in space and time. Such awareness enabled her to participate in God's healing work in the world, making possible a different politics, one that sees others (no matter what religion *or* nationality) in the light of Christ who dwells with humanity in time.

13. Gillespie, *Theological Origins*, 2.

"modernity is above all convinced that it owes nothing to the past, that it has made itself, and that what matters is what is happening right now. Indeed, this is the meaning of the freedom, power, and progress that we all prize."[14] According to Gillespie, time—far from being a static concept— was transformed in modernity such that one perceived one's identity in a new way. The individual is now able to imagine that she is self-creating. To the extent that this is true, time then becomes homogeneous: the space in which the modern person understands that no time, outside of personal self-creation, is more determinative that any other.

Charles Taylor likewise describes a new kind of "time-conscious-ness" in modernity. According to Taylor, earlier time was understood in light of archetypes or an "ontic logos." For example, "the sacrifice of Isaac was seen as a 'type' of the sacrifice of Christ . . . two events are linked through something outside history, where their symbolic affinity reflects some deeper identity in regard to Divine Providence. Something other than *causal* relations in time connects them . . . there is a sense in which they are *simultaneous*."[15] In ways similar to Gillespie, Taylor notes that one consequence of the modern objectification of the world has been the development of time as homogeneous and empty, the time of phys-ics wherein events are related across time by "efficient causal relations," and "synchronically by mutual conditioning." From this perspective, it is the discipline of history that records "real time," in contrast to the earlier times of myth, symbol, or story. The modern mode of narration is now told "against traditional models, archetypes, or prefigurations" and instead "fits the experience of the disengaged particular self."[16] The self stands over against earlier time, no longer the subject of archetypes or prefigurations.

What would it mean, exactly, to be subject to archetypes and prefigu-rations? Taylor's point, as well as Gillespie's, is that the modern person has a difficult time imagining a response to this question. In late modernity, we do not tend to see *patterns* in time related to a transcendent entity or entities. Or if we do, we see this in movies where, for example, the vampires alive now were the same ones present during the Civil War (*Twilight*). But when we emerge from the darkened theater in the broad light of day, we know this is only fiction. "Real" time is homogeneous and chronological.

A crucial point to observe is that this shift in time—from archetypal, prefigured, and simultaneous to self-originating and causal—shapes our

14. Ibid., 293.

15. Taylor, *Sources*, 288; my emphasis.

16. Ibid., 289. See also Taylor, *Secular Age*, 54–59.

understanding of politics. Benedict Anderson, for example, in his well-known *Imagined Communities*, argues that a change in understanding time made possible the imagined community called a "nation."[17] While Anderson includes other factors in his analysis of nationalism (the fall of Latin, for example, and the rise of print) he observes that changes in the apprehension of time "made it possible to 'think' the nation."[18] This claim of a shift in understanding time as making it possible to "think the nation" might seem puzzling. Anderson elaborates,

> It is difficult today to recreate in the imagination a condition of life in which the nation was felt to be something utterly new. But so it was in that epoch. The Declaration of Independence of 1776 makes absolutely no reference to Christopher Columbus, Roanoke, or the Pilgrim Fathers, nor are the grounds put forward to justify independence in any way "historical," in the sense of highlighting the antiquity of the American people."[19]

Instead, the creation of the nation signals a break with the past. Memories of independence develop which emphasize identity as rupture. As Anderson states, "Because there is no Originator, the nation's biography can not be written evangelically, 'down time,' through a long procreative chain of begettings. The only alternative is to fashion it 'up time' . . . [a] fashioning . . . marked by deaths," an "inversion of conventional genealogy . . ."[20] What comes to mind here is the contrast between the begetting genealogies of Christ in the Gospels and the genealogies of war and death that constitute national memories. The key point is that the newness of the nation—through rupture and death—parallels the sense of time that makes possible the self-creating individual. The individual, like the nation, is always free to leave the past behind. Indeed, the individual must do so to become free. This trajectory is consistent with a Kantian plea not to follow tradition but instead to "use the mind without the guidance of another."[21] According to Anderson, it is the novelty of time that makes both the nation and the individual possible.

Furthermore, Anderson states that homogeneous time makes it possible for separate "individuals," though self-creating, to imagine themselves as connected temporally. An American has no idea what his other fellow

17. Anderson, *Imagined Communities*, 6.

18. Ibid., 22.

19. Ibid., 193.

20. Ibid., 205.

21. Kant, "What Is Enlightenment?" 85.

Americans are up to at one time, "but he has complete confidence in their steady, anonymous, simultaneous activity."[22] This remarkable confidence in a "community of anonymity" is "the hallmark of modern nations."[23] This kind of simultaneous time rests not on any sense of transcendence in relation to humanity, but rather in the simple observation that people are minimally connected by anonymous activities in empty time.

But, one might ask, are not Americans as well as other nations bound together by a common story? Do not Americans, for example, share common ideals and values? The answer to this is yes. Anderson would point out, however, that the independence Americans value—focused on life, liberty, and the pursuit of happiness—is first and foremost the individual's freedom to create his or her own happiness. The individual is free to create his or her own story; she is not "bound" by the past.[24] As Ernest Renan, in his classic essay "What Is a Nation?" states, "Forgetting, I would even go so far as to say historical error, is a crucial factor in the creation of a nation, which is why progress in historical studies often constitutes a danger for [the principle of] nationality." Renan adds that "historical enquiry brings to light deeds of violence which took place at the origin of all political formations, even of those whose consequences have been altogether beneficial. Unity is always effected by means of brutality."[25] Rupture, forgetfulness, and death, according to both Renan and Anderson, are byproducts of novel time. National "self-origination" rests upon a kind of forgetfulness, a break with the past. Such an observation exemplifies Gillespie's understanding of modernity as being in time in a novel way.

To call the nation an "imagined community," as Anderson does, provides some leverage for us to think about politics, time, and the church. The church, like the nation, is a kind of "imagined community," one that

22. Anderson, *Imagined Communities*, 26.

23. Ibid., 36. Elaborating on Anderson, William Cavanaugh notes, "The production of the nation-state depends especially on people imagining themselves as contemporaries not with the apostles and the saints, but with all the other presently living French (or Chileans or English)," even though, he adds, "one has no idea who they are or what they are up to" (*Torture and Eucharist*, 223).

24. Alasdair MacIntyre, in "Culture of Choices," observes that in our current context "choice" is not taken to be revelatory of character, but of identity. In contrast to character, identity is entirely self-generated: "I am what my choices have made me." The individual has no alternative other than that of now choosing what is to become good or bad for her. To criticize one's choices is to take a negative view of the individual making the choices, and more often than not, the response is a retreat into solidarity with those with whom one agrees.

25. Renan, "What Is a Nation?" 45.

imagines living in the same time as the communion of all saints. If a change in the nature of time made the nation possible, as Anderson argues, then it is also the case that a change in the nature of time makes the church possible. That is, as Teresa's use of seven dwellings suggests, the imagined community called "church" lives in a time not its own; it lives on God's time. This could sound presumptuous, but to live in God's time is to see all time in reference to God, which is to live in time providentially.

By contrast, Taylor lifts up John Locke (1632–1704) as one who relies upon homogeneous political time. According to Taylor, Locke creates a "punctual self." Taylor observes that Locke's self comes to exist in time disengaged, in a sense, from a past or future, and must therefore generate his own identity. "Disengagement," Taylor writes, "demands that we stop simply living in the body or within our traditions or habits and, by making them objects for us, subject them to radical scrutiny and remaking."[26]

The idea of a punctual self, a self that is able to disengage storied time, dovetails with Locke's thoughts on the mind as a *tabula rasa*. As Locke understood it, *tabula rasa* means that the individual is born with a "blank" mind, and subsequently has the freedom to "author" his own soul. Each individual is thus free to define the content of his character, though his identity as a member of the human species cannot be changed. Locke's doctrine of natural rights derives from this presumption of a free, self-authored mind combined with an unchangeable human nature.

In this light, it is interesting to note that when Locke approaches Christianity he considers it possible to start over again with primitive history. According to Eric Voegelin, Locke's method leads him to make "a *tabula rasa* of Western history."[27] Locke's punctual self thus underwrites homogeneous, novel time where the individual gets to interpret the text or the beliefs de novo. In his attempt to restore reason and Christian authority, A. J. Conyers states that Locke "decides that Christianity is identical with what he personally thinks and can understand."[28] While the Bible is central for Locke, states Conyers, it is also for him oddly timeless. Any punctual self can read the Bible as if for the first time; no prior figures, types, or "ontic logoi" need constrain him. He is, in a sense, *dwelling* alone in time. Teresa's dwellings, by contrast, are dependent upon an abundance of scriptural figures from across time, a point I discuss more fully below.

26. Taylor, *Sources*, 175.
27. Cited by Conyers, *Long Truce*, 133.
28. Ibid., 136.

To summarize, Anderson, Gillespie, and Taylor help us see how the creation of the modern individual and the creation of the modern state go hand in hand in that both are sustained and shaped by a concept of time as new, homogenous, and causal. The idea of not being bound by the past is part of the American story. Like the early European discoverers such as Christopher Columbus or the brave souls that ventured west, the American "spirit" depends upon the idea that the individual can start over again and create a new life. In this sense, Americans are self-originating, not bound by tradition, fate, or providence.[29]

There is much more that can be said about time, politics, and the nation. As we have seen, homogeneous time enables one to imagine the nation as new, free, and independent. By contrast, the politics of the church, unlike that of the nation-state, does not depend upon self-origination. It rather depends upon an "imagined community" that re-creates a people in light of a past, present, and future that is simultaneous. This simultaneity can be seen, for example, in the church as a figure or type of Israel, following her same pattern and thus depending upon Israel for her identity. Or, to take another example, the repetition of eucharistic practice relies upon the presence of Christ in the past, present, and future; the resurrected Christ is the historical Jesus, now present eschatologically drawing partakers into the fullness of communion with God. In what follows, I consider more fully how this figural, simultaneous time is a politics, and one that Teresa both embodies and describes. To see how this is so, I wish first to turn to the well-known Jewish theologian Abraham Heschel.

A PALACE IN TIME

Heschel reflects a sense of simultaneous time when he describes the Jewish Sabbath as a "palace in time." As Heschel states, Judaism is a *religion of time* "aiming at the *sanctification of time*."[30] To the contemporary reader, this might not seem quite accurate. Surely Judaism is above all a religion of *place*. Abraham left Ur of Chaldees to venture to the promised land; Moses led the Hebrew people towards freedom and salvation by leading them from the place of captivity to the place of promise. It might seem

29. There is a difference in being free from the past because one can supposedly leave it behind, and being freed from the past through the gift of forgiveness. In the former, time is ever new because the past is forgotten. In the latter, however, one does not forget the past but sees it rather in light of Christ's redeeming love.

30. Heschel, *Sabbath*, 8.

as if Judaism is more about land than time. Yet, as Heschel states, to keep the Sabbath is to refer all time to God and, by doing so, to sanctify time and place. Heschel's claim reflects the Jewish saying, "More than Jews have kept the Sabbath, the Sabbath has kept the Jews."[31] No matter where an individual Jew may be or what he or she may subjectively feel at a given moment, the Sabbath "keeps" the Jews by placing them in this "palace," enabling them to refer all time to God. The Sabbath is thus a palace in time; it continually keeps the time of God's covenant.

Such time can be seen as political in that even during the darkest atrocities of the Holocaust some Jews still kept the Sabbath. The time of National Socialism was grounded in total novelty; the Nazis wanted to recreate the German people, if not the human race. Keeping the Sabbath was a profoundly political act, resisting Nazism and at the same time ordering Jewish life to its true end. It might sound ridiculous, even morally repugnant, to refer to Sabbath in the concentration camps as also being a "palace in time." But the stories of Jewish faithfulness that emerge from this time of exile and overwhelming suffering indicate that in this battle over time the Nazis were unable fully to eradicate Jewish memory/time and so also Jewish politics—their ways of being a people. Even in the midst of an unspeakably evil and tragic politics, Sabbath keeping kept a politics at odds with that of a malevolent state.

Heschel's analysis of the Sabbath as a "palace in time" sheds light on how Teresa's dwellings also are a "castle in time." In our day, diamond castles are more reminiscent of Disney creations than anything else: a "magical kingdom" filled with travel to new lands, rides that appear to defy gravity, and hundreds of attractions aimed to entertain and enchant. It seems as if this kind of time is anything but homogeneous. In fact, vacation/Disney time breaks up the monotony of work, school, and so forth. Yet this kind of enchantment is itself completely dependent upon the politics and economics of the nation-state. If the politics of the nation-state relies upon time as homogeneous self-creation, then so too does the economics that sustains the nation-state. Nicholas Boyle aptly describes this market timelessness as follows: "In the unsleeping fluorescent glow of round-the-clock commerce, consumption is as instantaneous as the signature on the contract of sale, the electronic transfer of funds from account to account, the emptying of the supermarket shelf."[32] Time is defined by the homoge-

31. Attributed to Ahad Ha'am.

32. Boyle, *Who Are We Now?*, 154. Boyle adds that what the market *conceals* is telling: "behind the market scenes lies a world of people who have 'been there' a long

neity and the self-invention of buying and selling rather than by history, tradition, or even personal relations. Dwelling in the Disney World castle does not, therefore, escape homogeneous time as much as reinforce time as self-origination. We can re-create ourselves, if we have enough money.

At this point I fear that I am sounding like a killjoy. Children and many adults love the enchantment of Disney World: the stories, the lively characters, the imaginary travel to distant lands of dinosaurs and so forth. The attraction of Disney is that it does offer a kind of reprieve from homogeneous empty time. Time comes alive, if only for a week. While such vacations can do doubt be magical, the reality is that they have to end so that other vacationers can arrive. Workers, of course, remain on the scene carefully concealing anything that disrupts the imaginary world (such as trash). The magic time is thus not an alternative to homogeneous time, but rather an instance of it. That is, a place like Disney exemplifies time as novelty and self-creation. True, there are stories that shape such time, i.e., Star Wars, Mickey Mouse, Cinderella, and so forth. But these are constantly being created and recreated for the sake of the market. Ultimately, this kind of novelty and self-creation serves the dominant political and economic realities that so easily determine our lives.

Such a way of being "enchanted" is very different from learning to dwell within a divine pattern of the sort that Teresa is describing. To go on pilgrimage through "divine dwellings" is to retrace the steps of another and thus to acknowledge particular persons, places and times as holy, as set apart. Such a journey relies upon time as simultaneous: Divine providence brings two separate times into relation with each other. James McClendon describes this scriptural vision of time with the phrase "this is that." McClendon takes this phrase from the King James Version of Acts, in which Peter, on the day of Pentecost, says, "But *this is that* which was spoken by the prophet Joel; And it shall come to pass in the last days, saith God, I will pour out of my Spirit upon all flesh: and your sons and your daughters shall prophesy, and your young men shall see visions, and your old men shall dream dreams" (2:16–17, KJV; my emphasis). McClendon focuses on how the phrase "this is that" summarizes how providence enables us to see our time now as sharing in God's earlier time. As McClendon puts it, a past event discloses "the meaning and significance of the present"[33]

---

or a short time . . . who have seen changes, who have expectations and worries. . . . It is they who feel the consequences of the consumer choices out on the exchange-floor."

33. Myers, "Interview with James McClendon," 3. For a fuller account, see McClendon, *Ethics.*

precisely because it reveals a pattern of how God acts in time. Particular events and figures link the time of the past with the time of the present, displaying how God's future breaks into our time now in a recognizable pattern.

This type of simultaneous pattern is powerfully displayed in the Basilica of Saint Francis of Assisi, where scenes from his life are paired with the life of Christ, showing in vivid colors how Francis providentially embodies the life of Christ, present through the power of the Spirit in all time. Like other saints, Saint Francis can enable us now to see our dwelling in time as providentially patterned. Just as the life of Saint Francis participates in the present life of Christ, so also Teresa's dwellings describe a pattern of Christ with us in time. Such providential patterns make possible a sense of contemporaneity with the apostles and saints.

From a certain perspective, this claim seems bizarre. The saints are dead; we are alive. Only in some imaginary world could one think otherwise. But such a response rests upon the conviction that worldly, chronological time is the only *real* time that there is. If Christ is raised from the dead, however, he is not limited by merely sequential time. Rather all time is gathered up in him.

Gerhard Lohfink also observes that time in ancient Israel was not simply sequential. Ancient Israel, unlike modern Westerners, did not look to the future but rather imagined the future as behind it.

> [Israel] had the future at its back. The Hebrew word for future is "behind" (*'ahar*). The past, on the other hand, is "before" (*qedem*). The Israelites would not have said "Auschwitz is behind us," but "it is before us, it lies before our eyes." So even when Israel was moving into the future it did not look forward, but back to what had already happened, and it moved, still turned backward, another step into the future.[34]

This process, Lohfink notes, could be compared with rowing a boat: "always seated with back to the direction of travel and orienting oneself on points that have long been left behind." This is not simply a quirk of ancient Israel, but is rather how God leads people: "God leads God's people in the same way, by unfolding the past to them."[35] So understood, the past is not simply over and done with; it is still alive, a place where God is still present, a means through which God continues to draw a people into communion.

34. Lohfink, *Does God Need the Church?*, 105.
35. Ibid.

Whereas a "community of anonymity" relies upon homogenous, empty time (individuals inhabiting the same time in their own "self-originating" ways), simultaneous time gives rise to a particular kind of communion. This is a community that identifies with Abraham, Moses, Sarah, Peter, Mary and so forth because they dwell in the same providential time. The ancient creeds refer to this community as the "communion of saints," who dwell together in the time of Christ, who himself heals all time. It might seem odd to speak of the healing of time since time is an inanimate object. But if salvation includes the healing of all creation, then surely too this includes the healing of time as well, such that the rising and setting of the sun and the presence of a glowing moon reflect not simply the mere passing of days, but the gift of living in time in the presence of God and all the saints.

TERESA AND ECCLESIAL TIME

We can now look more fully at how Teresa's castle is a way of describing time. She famously begins *Interior Castle* by saying, "I began to think of the soul as if it were a castle [*castillo*] made of a single diamond or of very clear crystal, in which there are many rooms [*aposentos*], just as in Heaven there are many mansions [*moradas*]."[36] Teresa's opening words relate to John 14:2: "In my Father's house there are many dwelling places. If it were not so, would I have told you that I go to prepare a place for you?" At first glance, Teresa might appear to endorse an otherworldly view of the Christian life. Her castle could appear to be about time after this life: the place one goes only after death. On the other hand, as noted in chapter 1, some readers assume Teresa is writing strictly about the inner life of the soul, a timeless interior state also detached from any earthly time.

Yet Teresa vividly continues, "For we ourselves *are* the castle: and it would be absurd to tell someone to enter a room when he was in it already!"[37] *Castillo* (castle), *aposentos* (rooms or dwelling places), and *moradas* (mansions) all refer to spaces where we now are. At this point, Teresa makes a crucial observation: "But you must understand that there are many ways of 'being' in a place." This point underlines the fact that Teresa's dwellings are not primarily about one's physical location but first of all have to do with how one dwells *in time*. People can be in close physical proximity and yet dwell in different worlds. For example, someone is talk-

36 Teresa, *Interior Castle*, 3.
37 Ibid., 6; my emphasis.

ing to friend while the friend is thinking about her time in Hawaii. There are many ways of being in a place. Teresa also tells her sisters, however, that they are *already* in a castle. At face value, this might seem absurd, like telling folks today that they somehow are already in a luxury mansion off the coast of Florida. Such dwellings are only for the most wealthy, the highest class, as the medieval castles that housed the most wealthy would have been in Teresa's day. If we shift the image, however, from that of physical space to time, then the meaning becomes more theologically coherent. Teresa is saying that we are in a dwelling of great beauty because God already dwells with us *in time*.

As Teresa describes the diamond castle more fully, it has seven vast clusters of mansions (each with hundreds of rooms). Christ dwells in the center, and can be seen—however dimly—from the furthest outposts. In the first mansions, Teresa thus states, "You must note that the light which comes from the palace occupied by the King hardly reaches these first Mansions at all." This is not "because of anything that is wrong with the room, but rather (I hardly know how to explain myself) because there are so many bad things—snakes and vipers and poisonous creatures—which have come in with the soul that they prevent it from seeing the light."[38] Teresa's image nonetheless indicates that new creation is already present; we (meaning all of humanity) are *already* in the dwellings that constitute God's new creation. The number seven signifies the fulfillment of God's creating Word. Teresa's use of a single diamond points to the wonderful beauty and harmony of this fulfillment. That we are *already* within the castle further underlines the conviction that humans cannot *not* be a part of God's good creation being renewed through Christ. As Teresa puts it, "Would it not be a sign of great ignorance, my daughters, if a person were asked who he was, and could not say, and had no idea who his father or his mother was, or from what country he came?"[39] To forget that one is a creature made for communion with God is like suffering a kind of amnesia. True, one might well know certain things and even have a vast amount of knowledge, but such knowledge will be incomplete and distorted if one does not truly know who one is.[40]

38. Ibid., 17.

39. Ibid., 4.

40. Those who reject communion with God entirely can certainly know things, but they will know them without reference to God who calls them into being and sustains them. Paul Griffiths, to whom I am indebted to this point, develops the idea of knowledge as *studiositas* (knowledge as participation, ultimately in God) in contrast to *curiositas* (knowledge as possession and control) in *Intellectual Appetites*.

We can helpfully compare Teresa's placement of Christ at the center of the castle/creation with Irenaeus' well-known description of Christ recapitulating all of creation. Irenaeus uses "recapitulation" to describe how Christ repeats and fulfills creation. As indicated in Romans 5, Christ "repeats" Adam (like Adam, Christ is human); at the same time, Christ recapitulates Adam by bringing to completion the purpose for which humanity is created which is to love and serve God. In this sense, "Christ [goes] over the human process again, being victorious where Adam failed."[41] This recapitulation culminates in the resurrection, Christ's victory over death. Such recapitulation is not, however, simply over and done. As Teresa acknowledges in her varied descriptions of the different dwellings, Christ continues to recapitulate and heal humanity, offering forgiveness and grace in order to transform our sins and failures, enabling us to share in Christ's gift of salvation. To understand what Irenaeus means by "recapitulation" is to see that salvation in Christ entails a cosmic drama: whereas Adam and Eve were first in original creation, Jesus repeats this genesis, but now makes possible new creation and thus new life. "So if anyone is in Christ, there is a new creation: everything old has passed away; see, everything has become new!" (2 Cor 5:17). Time itself becomes something other than it was. No longer is time homogeneous or simply the space of self-creation. Time is now "simultaneous": Christ is present now, *in time* simultaneously with generations who have gone before, making possible God's new creation of a people. J. Kameron Carter emphasizes that this recapitulation begins with a particular people: "In short, Christ's fleshly recapitulation of all nations and languages—indeed, his recapitulation of creation as such—is concentrated in his recapitulation of Israel as the people of YHWH's covenant."[42] As Carter emphasizes, Christ in recapitulating Israel recapitulates all nations. As we will see, such a claim embodies a politics that reveals the inadequacies of all other politics.

Recapitulation is another way of describing time as both simultaneous and abundant, filled with God's mighty deeds, with the presence of Christ, and with the now and not-yet of God's reign. Even the enemy death cannot defeat time. As Stanley Hauerwas and Samuel Wells emphasize, God gives us all the time we need.[43] Death might and does often cut short a particular life; even death at the end of a long life is a deep trag-

41. Kurz, "Gifts of Creation," 119. In this excellent article, Kurz relies upon Terrence L. Tiessen, *Irenaeus on the Salvation of the Unevangelized*.

42. Carter, *Race*, 31.

43. Hauerwas and Wells, *Christian Ethics*, Part I.

edy. As Irenaeus and Teresa indicate, however, such loss cannot deny the abundance of time made possible by the One who has defeated death and remains present in time.

SUFFERING TIME

Yet, it remains the case that time is filled with tragedy, brokenness, depression, failure, sin, and on and on. All of this could easily make one conceive of time as not only empty (homogeneous) but also meaningless. Most of us have had periods of darkness. Teresa, in fact, tells of a vision she has of the dwellings/castle covered in mud and filth. One of Teresa's former confessors, Fray Diego, writes, "While [Teresa] was wondering at this beauty, which by God's grace can dwell in the human soul, the light suddenly vanished. Although the King of Glory did not leave the mansions, the crystal globe was plunged into darkness, became as black as coal, and emitted an insufferable odour, and the venomous creatures outside the palace boundaries were permitted to enter the castle."[44] Such a description captures the loss of light, beauty, and harmony that can easily characterize our lives and the manifold tragedies in the world. When sin and death seem to reign, time appears to lack abundance. Teresa thus registers how sin and darkness can eclipse the light of Christ. While this darkness can be devastating, especially in situations of profound tragedy, the darkness does not ultimately determine Christ's presence in the castle, according to Teresa. The King (Christ) does not leave the mansions, despite the "insufferable odour, and the venomous creatures." Teresa thus acknowledges that even when time seems empty and dark, it is not ultimately so.

Paul Griffiths captures something of this shift between light and darkness when he writes,

> To the extent that light is obscured, the world appears not as delightful gift, but as constrictingly repetitive burden whose days and nights pass with the rapidity and numbing sameness of the weaver's shuttle, a region of desolation and hunger composed in equal measure of pain and boredom. But the world of light, harmony, and liberating order, the real world, that is, rather than its negative image, its dark twin, appears as gift that delights when it is welcomed and embraced.[45]

44. As cited in Teresa, *Interior Castle*, x–xi.
45. Griffiths, *Intellectual Appetites*, 51.

Like Griffiths, Teresa sees in darkness a "negative image" of the created world where Christ dwells. Even though such darkness is an "image," the suffering that it can inflict is no less real.

Teresa even refers to a kind of suffering that comes from being in the presence of Christ. In one scene in Teresa's own life, for example, it was her encounter with a statue of the suffering Christ that enabled her to see how Christ needed her to share in his suffering.[46] Even beyond this call and identity with the wounded Christ is a suffering that comes, for lack of a better description, from a kind of fear or even terror before God. This suffering results from simultaneously encountering God, on the one hand, and, on the other, being in complete darkness. Scriptural accounts of this kind of dwelling include Moses frightened before the burning bush or Mary terrified before the angel Gabriel. It is a kind of "dwelling" in which, to cite Flannery O'Connor, Christ has "thrown everything off balance."[47] This seeming break in reality is terrifying because it destabilizes one's world. Moses, however, comes to see that Yahweh desires to save a people. Mary comes to understand her unique role in God's plan. The break is ultimately, then, not a break in one's self but a place or way through which God's deeds on behalf of a people can come to fruition. The frightening presence of God gives way to a realization that God is working through particular persons on behalf of a people (Israel and the church) and the world.

For Teresa's part, she writes about the "excessive torment" she suffered when she thought the favors the Lord was granting her would become public. "The disturbance reached the point that . . . it seemed to me I was more willing to be buried alive then have these favors made known publicly."[48] She describes this as a temptation. This could sound to modern ears as an indirect way of boasting. It is more accurate to say, however, that Teresa feels shame and fear because she is in a kind of darkness. She is afraid that others will criticize her and perceive her as placing herself above them (which had in fact happened). Teresa even considers moving to another monastery. Teresa eventually, however, comes to see a truth that, she says, the Lord taught her: "That I should be determined and certain that His favor was not some good thing belonging to me but that it belonged to God; that just as I wasn't sorry to hear other persons praises

46. I discuss this encounter more fully in chapter 5.

47. O'Connor, "Good Man," 131.

48. Teresa, *Book of Her Life*, 217.

. . . I should neither be sorry that His works be shown in me."[49] The fact that time is simultaneous and Christ is present where we are (sometimes in strange ways) does not negate the deep suffering that can occur from living in a church and world not yet fully healed. Dwelling with Christ involves a willingness to complete "what is lacking in Christ's afflictions for the sake of his body, that is, the church" (Col 1:24).

What does this willingness to suffer with Christ say about our ecclesial dwellings today? First, it suggests that the wounds of the church (its divisions, sins, and so forth) *can* become places of grace, or openings through which identification with Christ's suffering becomes a source of healing. Paul's well-known statement, "my grace is sufficient for you, for power is made perfect in weakness" (2 Cor 12:9), indicates how times of apparent weakness or dryness can in fact become places of Divine grace and healing.[50] Teresa herself acknowledges how periods of dryness or suffering can intensify desire for unity and for Christ. In reflecting on how our lives are gardens, Teresa notes that dryness "amounts to an authentic weeding and pulling up of the remaining bad growth by its roots . . ." The dryness can produce humility, Teresa emphasizes, because it enables the soul to trust God more fully.[51] Ephraim Radner draws the following conclusion for how a willingness to suffer relates to ecclesial division and to "staying put": "*Accept suffering*. Let the fool be prepared to suffer in patience the effects of the gospel's contradiction in our midst."[52] Such suffering is not for its own sake, but for the sake of participating in Christ's own cruciform way in the world, as Teresa herself so vividly saw before a statue of Christ suffering.

Secondly, periods of suffering and darkness are signs that creation itself is still in travail: "we know that the whole creation has been groaning in labor pains until now; and not only the creation, but we ourselves, who have the first fruits of the Spirit, groan inwardly while we wait for adoption, the redemption of our bodies" (Rom 8:22–23). While the church is called joyfully to receive the first fruits of the Spirit, it is also called to exercise both patience and hope in the midst of ecclesial darkness and disunity. One of Teresa's key ways of articulating this hope was to remind her

49. Ibid., 218.

50. As Lohfink so vividly describes this point: "Paul developed a whole theology of the superabundant grace of God that appears precisely in the weakness and distress of the faithful in order that it may be clear that the overflowing fullness of glory comes not from human strength, but from God alone" (*Does God Need the Church?*, 150).

51. Teresa, *Book of Her Life*, 85.

52. Radner, *Hope*, 212.

sisters that God knows their needs and provides the means to meet these. Movement through Teresa's dwellings can be read as a way of describing how the church can more fully desire and receive what God already offers. Even when time seems short, division insurmountable, or particular gestures insignificant, Teresa offers this wisdom: "but during the whole of this short life, which for any one of you may be shorter than you think, we must offer the Lord whatever interior or exterior sacrifice we are able . . . and His Majesty will unite it with that which He offered to the Father for us upon the Cross, so that it may have the value won for it by our will, even though our actions in themselves may be trivial."[53] Even though our efforts may seem weak and ineffective in the darkness of ecclesial division, Teresa's counsel is nonetheless to understand that Christ, now present in time, unites our meager offerings with his own and offers them to the Father. That is, Christ intercedes for us, uniting our prayer and worship to his own intercessions (Heb 7:26–27). Rightly understood, no prayer or worship is ever ineffective. The Spirit "helps us in our weakness . . . [interceding] with sighs too deep for words" (Rom 8:26). This is yet another way of saying that Christ transforms time: no time, prayer, or deed is insignificant or without hope when offered to God.

DWELLING: A SCRIPTURAL FIGURE

Teresa's use of "dwellings" derives ultimately from Scripture. It is because of this that Teresa can imagine with such conviction that our time now is continuous and depends upon both the past (beginning with Israel) and the future (the eschaton). To dwell with God is to dwell in God's time rather than only one's own. It is learning to see one's life as providentially part of a people.

In the Old Testament, the dwelling identified most fully with God is Zion. Zion is beautiful because this is where God reveals himself in glory: "Out of Zion, the perfection of beauty, God shines forth" (Ps 50:2). Zion is identified as "the very center of the world" (RSV), "the joy of the earth," "the city of the great King" (Ps 48:2). While God "shines forth" out of Zion, God's name and praise reach "to the ends of the earth" (Ps 48:10). Out of Zion, God gathers a people (Israel) who both rejoice and fear the presence of God in time and space. There is fear because, before God, they see the depths of their own uncleanness. As Isaiah cries out, "Woe is me! I am lost, for I am a man of unclean lips and I live among a people of unclean

___
53. Teresa, *Interior Castle*, 238.

lips; yet my eyes have seen the King, the Lord of hosts!" (Isa 6:5). God's dwelling humbles his people. Yet it is also *through* this particular Divine dwelling on Zion that Israel knows "the earth is the Lord's and the fullness thereof, the world and those who dwell therein . . ." (Ps 24:1, RSV). God's dwelling with a particular people makes possible an understanding of how the whole world dwells with God.

Teresa's dwellings, like Zion, are also beautiful, made of a single diamond. Like Zion, too, they are a dwelling for God, where Christ shines forth. Further, God's presence in the dwellings gathers a people. In fact, for Teresa, everyone already dwells with God (though if different ways). Like Isaiah, Teresa responds with humility before the living God and emphasizes that "humility must always be doing its work like a bee making its honey in the hive; without humility all will be lost."[54] Such humility is at the heart of self-knowledge. True humility differs from false humility because it is rather rooted in the truth of one's self before God, like the prophet Isaiah before Yahweh.

The invitation to dwell with God is at the same time an invitation to enter renewed time. Through their covenant with Yahweh, Israel comes to know that time itself is part of God's good creation. Not only does God establish patterns in time that culminate in the Sabbath, but time itself becomes framed in the context of promise and fulfillment. "[My word] shall accomplish that which I purpose, and succeed in the thing for which I sent it" (Isa 55:11). As Heschel emphasizes, Sabbath keeping becomes a way of sanctifying all time by receiving time as a gift. Time is holy not because people do exceptionally good things, nor even because particular times are set aside as holy, important as this might be. Rather, time is holy because God enters time, making it possible for Israel and the church to relate all time to God.

In the New Testament, the book of Revelation describes the holy city, Jerusalem, made of beautiful jewels; "the wall is built of jasper, while the city is pure gold, clear as glass" (21:18). Joseph Mangina comments about this city that "we should perhaps picture a translucent golden cube . . . with the city's towers and dwelling arranged in a kind of latticelike structure inside . . ."[55] The similarity with Teresa's castle is hard to miss. In fact, contemporary artists have depicted her castle in ways that bear a striking resemblance to Mangina's description: multiple transparent cubes

---

54. Ibid., 13.

55. Mangina, *Revelation*, 241.

resting at odd angles on top of others, creating a labyrinthine effect.[56] In the midst of the holy city, a voice from the throne cries out, echoing Isaiah, "See, the home (or dwelling place) of God is among mortals. He will dwell with them as their God; they will be his peoples, and God himself will be with them . . ." (Rev 21:3–4, RSV). Though this dwelling might appear to be only about a future hope, Teresa—like Israel and the church that forms her—assumes it is already present. The tabernacle of God is among mortals. This tabernacle becomes a "castle" in Teresa's medieval imagination, a dwelling that is no timeless reality but a new creation: a gathering of God's people into the life of Israel and church such that seemingly inconsequential women in sixteenth-century Spain can become disciples alongside the Apostles, members one of another in this grand communion.[57]

Finally, "dwellings" as a scriptural figure comes into focus most fully in the Word that "became flesh and lived [tabernacled] among us" (John 1:14). This Word is not "mere" speech, but the agent of all creation, thus fully divine, the One through whom "all things came into being . . ." (John 1:3). What exactly does this mean? Human words can also create. A word makes a world appear, for example, when a couple says, "I do" in a marriage service. Or a parent says, "I forgive you" to a remorseful child, and the child's bad deed no longer stands between them. In these and other ways, human speech can create new worlds. But this ability to speak new words, to bring forth new worlds, is itself a gift from God. Humans are given the gift of speech, a gift that can and is misused, but is a gift nonetheless, one that reaches perfection in the Word that is Christ. Christ is the new creation that makes renewed speech possible: words of forgiveness and promise, words spoken over the sacraments, words that preach good news, etc. This Word that dwells with us is thus both *agent* of creation and at the same time *within* creation. John 1:14 can be translated to say that the Word "pitched his tent" among us—the Word became fully human. The Word dwells with us, Teresa emphasizes, so that he is closer to us than we are to ourselves.

56. See especially Parker, "Interior Castle (Revisited)," 1989, discussed more fully in chapter 4.

57. As noted in the discussion of words as deeds in chapter 1, Teresa tells her sisters that they are *included* in Jesus' prayer for the Apostles, that "they might be One with the Father and with Him. . . . We shall none of us fail to be included here . . ." (*Interior Castle*, 218). Such a conviction also reflects the kind of bending of time that I am here discussing. The Apostles are not simply figures from long ago; they are contemporaries with Christ now and so also with us.

Much more, of course, could be said about "dwellings" in Scripture. To understand Teresa is to see how Scripture fired her imagination such that key figures such as "dwellings" shaped her life and theology, particularly her understanding of and reliance upon time as a gift from God.

IS EVERYONE "ON GOD'S TIME"?

The response to this question seems to be a clear no. After all, I have been arguing that our dominant politics relies on homogeneous, empty time, time that contradicts providential, ecclesial time. Yet, Teresa's description of the diamond dwellings indicates that *everyone* inhabits this time/space. Thus, one could well ask Teresa, does the fact that Christ already dwells where we are not conflate the now and not-yet of God's time? If the answer is yes, then Teresa's depiction of Christ already dwelling with us seems to short-circuit human agency or, even more, the church. Doesn't one need to have faith, participate in the sacraments, or be a member of a church to dwell in both the now and not-yet of God's kingdom?

Douglas Harink sheds light on this question in his discussion of 2 Corinthians 5, which he translates as follows: "For the love of Christ urges us on, because we are convinced that one has died for all; therefore all have died. . . . From now on, therefore, we regard no one from a human point of view. . . . So if anyone is in Christ, there is a new creation: everything old has passed away; see, everything has become new!" (5:14, 16, 17). Harink notes that these verses have often been interpreted as being about the state of the individual. He argues, however, that

> the new creation being asserted here is not a claim about the state of the Christian; it is a claim about how the world and in particular the other human being, must be acknowledged as new creation by the Christian, who knows that the old creation has been invaded, challenged and judged, in the death of Christ . . . The other who stands before me is already cosharer in that new creation; the task of the Christian in the face of this other is to call attention to that fact.[58]

In Teresa's depiction of persons as diamond castles, where Christ dwells, she is stating that all persons are already sharers in Christ's new creation. Such a portrayal of others relies upon the conviction that God has entered and transformed the time in which we now live. This is not

---

58. Harink, *Paul among the Postliberals*, 252–53.

to say that all persons are Christians, but rather to emphasize the renewal of all creation in and through Christ, who has "invaded" the old creation through death and resurrection. God, uniting himself to creation in Christ, exposes sin and death in their defeat as well as the magnificent beauty of new creation. As David B. Hart states, ". . . Christians are bidden to see in Christ at once the true form of God and the true shape of humanity, and to believe that the Father sees with pleasure his own very likeness in Jesus of Nazareth, even him crucified, and furthermore, consents to view *all of humanity* as gathered into the beauty of his Son."[59]

One hardly needs to point out that humanity, in many ways, is not beautiful. It is thus difficult to see all of humanity as gathered into the beauty of the Son. Wars, hatreds, jealousies and innumerable petty sins can make talk of beauty seem almost obscene. Teresa registers this fact in her own way when she describes those who have grown so accustomed "to living *all the time* with reptiles and other creatures to be found in the outer court of the castle that they have almost become like them . . ."[60] In her account, reptiles are ominous figures related to Teresa's own vivid sense of the "dark depths of the demonic world."[61] The soul, says Teresa, separates itself from God by preferring to give pleasure to the devil; "and, as the devil is darkness itself, the poor soul becomes darkness itself likewise . . . producing nothing but misery and filth."[62] Living all the time in the outer courts of the castle, however, does not negate God's dwelling in the castle: God's presence to and with each creature. As Teresa states, "This palace, then, as I say, is God Himself. Now can the sinner go away from it in order to commit his misdeeds? Certainly not; these abominations and dishonourable actions and evil deeds which we sinners commit are done within the palace itself—that is, within God."[63] God is ever-present, though the Divine presence may be differently received: as judgment, offense, consolation, forgiveness, and so forth.

59. Hart, *Beauty of the Infinite*, 336; my emphasis. Hart describes this restoration of human beauty again when he states, "In Christ God brings about a return of the gift he has given in creation by himself giving it again, anew, according to that Trinitarian dynamism in which donation and restoration are one; Christ effects a recapitulation . . . that refashions the human after its ancient beauty and thus restores it to the Father" (325).

60. Teresa, *Interior Castle*, 7.

61. Du Boulay uses this phrase in telling about Teresa's dreadful vision of hell in *Teresa of Avila*, 72.

62. *Interior Castle*, 10.

63. Ibid., 194.

In this sense, then, everyone lives in God's time; all creatures are in the dwellings, though in different ways. Teresa's effort to chart the movement to the center (the seventh mansions) is a way of acknowledging that people can move at different paces.[64] Even so, providential time is time that participates in God's abundance.[65] Such time is, above all, marked by communion and dwelling with God.

MEMORY

The way that I am interpreting Teresa has to do with remembering truthfully, remembering how to dwell faithfully in time. The question of time, then, cannot be separated from that of memory. As Heschel noted, the Sabbath makes it possible for Jews to remember that all days are not simply interchangeable. The Sabbath is a day set apart, without which time would not be holy. The Sabbath is thus a sign of contradiction to market time, where stores open around the clock could easily lead Jews as well as Christians to forget who they are.

Teresa herself heard and learned Scripture by inhabiting scriptural time. As noted in the previous chapter, this learning took place in the rhythmic monastic gathering for prayer and worship. Personal (mental) prayer and study were also formative. In chapter 1 we saw how Augustine's *Confessions* had a deep influence on Teresa. She would have been familiar with his description of memory in book 10, where Augustine asks, "What am I, then, O my God? What is my nature?" He responds, "it is teeming life of every conceivable kind, and exceedingly vast. See, in

64. While Teresa allowed for this variation in pace, she also encouraged her sisters not to be overly "rational" or orderly: "You need never fear that they [carefully ordered persons] will kill themselves: they are eminently reasonable folk! Their love is not yet ardent enough to overwhelm their reason. How I wish ours would make us dissatisfied with this habit of always serving God at a snail's pace!" (*Interior Castle*, 45).

65. Levering contrasts a purely linear, historical understanding of time with participatory time. Thus, to read Scripture as not merely a record of the past "requires the sense that all human time participates metaphysically (order of creation) and Christologically-pneumatologically (order of grace) in God's eternal Providence and therefore no historical text or event can be studied strictly 'on its own terms'" (*Participatory Biblical Exegesis*, 18). Levering is describing sympathetically the position of Catholic exegete and theologian Francis Martin. More broadly, Levering's description of participatory exegesis is a wonderful account of how modern understandings of "time" have skewed theological readings of Scripture. Levering traces this loss of participatory exegesis to late medieval nominalism, beginning as early as the fourteenth century.

the measureless plains and vaults and caves of my memory, immeasurably full of countless kinds of things . . ."[66] Augustine describes the memory as a "treasure-house" and a "vast, infinite recess. . . . Who can plumb its depth?"[67]

The vast treasure house of dwellings is similar to (and no doubt influences) Teresa's manifold dwellings through which the soul can wander. Augustine too confesses, "You have honored my memory by making it your *dwelling-place* . . ."[68] In one of the most famous passages from the *Confessions*, Augustine describes God's dwelling with him as follows:

> Late have I loved you, Beauty so ancient and so new,
> Late have I loved you!
> Lo, you were *within*, but I *outside*, seeking there for you . . .
> You were with me, but I was not with you.
> They held me back far from you,
> Those things which would have no being
> Were they not in you.[69]

If we read this passage through the lens of providential time, we can see that Augustine is remembering his life in a new way. It is not that he was without God but that God's light illumines his darkness. He now sees and remembers time differently.

As has been the case with Teresa, some modern readers have interpreted Augustine as an early inventor of the modern self, anticipating a Cartesian turn to the subject. Michael Hanby observes, however, that the constitutive role of memory is "a feature notably absent from the Cartesian *cogito* who only surely is in the moment of his self-assertion."[70] The Cartesian *cogito* relies not upon memory but upon homogeneous, self-originating time. Although Descartes is often interpreted as rigidifying an Augustinian dualism between mind and body, says Hanby, his understanding of mind is symptomatic of an altogether different break already well underway by the seventeenth century. "Now the individual will— distinct and separated from the love of beauty, the longing for God, or the

---

66. Augustine, *Confessions*, 254. Marveling at the capacity of human memory, Augustine exclaims, "O my God, profound, infinite complexity, what a great faculty memory is, how awesome a mystery! It is the mind, and this is nothing other than my very self."

67. Ibid., 246.

68. Ibid., 261.

69. Ibid., 262; my emphasis.

70. Hanby, *Augustine and Modernity*, 24.

praise of Christ—becomes a will to power, and it is set over against *God's* body, which must be placed under house arrest."[71] Hanby's emphasis on God's body is significant because this body, rather than the individual will, mediates Christ who makes possible renewed time. As Hanby points out, Augustine's self-presence requires "the gift of a mediator."[72] Augustine's emphasis on Divine mediation means that "the same cosmological time which is the vehicle for dissipation and loss can become the vehicle for restoration, for creation, for receiving oneself as gift."[73] Christ's mediation makes it possible for Augustine, and Teresa after him, to understand the self as always dependent upon the prior presence and gift of Christ and the body of Christ. As Hanby states,

> To the extent that our knowledge, memory, and love of our-selves turn out to have been true, we recognize that this self-giving love has been there all along, going before us. This is the heart of Augustine's Trinitarian theology, his Christology, and his doctrine of grace. This insight penetrates to the depths of what it means for Augustine to exist in time, to remember, to know, and to will.[74]

Memory, then, is not dependent on the individual, nor is it dependent on just any community. For Augustine, as well as Teresa, memory is related to grace, to the gift of the Spirit. We remember well to the extent that we remember through Christ in light of God remembering us. For Teresa, Christ remembers us even before we have any awareness of him at all. For Augustine too, memory is a gift that God gives to enable us to speak truthfully: to speak the gospel. To remember well is to live in time providentially, dwelling with Christ and the body of Christ, remembering in our bodies how the church dwells in a past, present, and future not its own. As Gerhard Lohfink states,

> The assembly is the place where the Church's memory is kept alive. . . . In the memorial celebration of the Eucharist it is ob-vious that salvation and liberation do not happen, ultimately, through moral appeals or instruction, or through free-form meditation or mysticism falsely understood, but through a precise salvation history that is 'called' into the memory and by that very means brings the Church together and builds up

71. Ibid., 178.
72. Ibid., 146.
73. Ibid., 25.
74. Ibid., 146.

community. Ultimately, the liturgy contains everything the Church needs: there is its *genuine* memory.[75]

TERESA'S DWELLINGS AS A POLITICS

God's dwelling on earth calls into being a people who remember that they are a "nation," to live as a light for all other nations. This "nation" is unlike all others because it is defined not by geographical or temporal borders but by the Word of God. We are now in a position to see more fully how Teresa's dwellings embody a political alternative to the politics of both empire and nation. As we have seen, Teresa's account of time is not purely historical, nor is time determined by a Lockean "punctual self" who exists as a blank slate (*tabula rasa*). There is rather a Divine "weight" in time drawing creatures toward the bountiful space of God's love, in order to make of them a people dwelling together in unity.

From this perspective, politics is not the so-called "public" time of nations, elections, voting, and so forth, which sequesters religion to the private time of families, extracurricular activities, and personal choice. Rather, to dwell in time with God and God's people is *already* to be political: to live in the time of God's inbreaking kingdom. In the movements through the seven dwellings, Teresa is describing ways to live with God who is always present in time. Such time is not internal (the soul) over against external (the body, the political). Rather, God's deeds, words, and sacraments in the midst of a people make providential time possible. Teresa wants her readers to learn to dwell in *this* time, and so be a visible alternative to other political bodies, including the this-worldly power politics of the day.

David Hart contrasts this ecclesial politics with a "gnostic politics" of "spiritual hygiene practiced only within the walls of the basilica," which does not "intrude upon the world about it."[76] Hart continues, "The church is no less (as Origen knew) than a politics, a society, another country, a new pattern of communal being meant not so much to complement the civic constitution of secular society as to displace it."[77] Language of "displacement" might raise concern for some. It could be interpreted to mean that the church must coercively take over secular politics. Yet, this politics

---

75. Lohfink, *Does God Need the Church?*, 252.

76. Hart, *Beauty*, 340.

77. Ibid.

of simultaneous (ecclesial) time versus homogeneous time *disrupts* any politics that requires violence. It understands justice rather as "bearing one another's burdens, forgiving even the debt truly owed, seeking reconciliation rather than due retribution . . ."[78] This politics is ultimately possible through Christ, who reconciles, forgives, and bears not only our sins and burdens but also, *through us*, those of others as we learn to dwell with Christ. Certainly those who are not Christians may share in something like this politics, most especially (and sometimes more fully) in practices of forgiveness, reconciliation, and so forth. One thinks of someone like Ghandi and those who participated in his political alternative. What makes this ecclesial politics distinct, however, is the worship of the Triune God, who is within time, transforming time into the time of Christ.

A new pattern of communal living comes into view when the church and her members dwell in providential time. In a well-known passage from Teresa's seventh mansions, she writes, "Martha and Mary must work together when they offer the Lord lodging, and must have Him ever with them, and they must not entertain Him badly and give Him nothing to eat."[79] Such an interpretation can sound quaint and apolitical, especially when Teresa uses "entertain." Yet Teresa understands that hospitality requires ordering the life of a community around a common good. Embedded in Teresa's wisdom is a classical understanding of politics and *polis* that has to do with the art of living together in light of a shared good or purpose. Teresa will typically describe this common good as "His Majesty," a political title. In her context, "His Majesty" was reserved for the most powerful political entity in the land: the Spanish monarch. By identifying Christ as King, Teresa is therefore acknowledging that she serves his kingdom.[80] Furthermore, her descriptions of Mary and Martha are implicit references to contemplation and action; both activities are needed to participate in the politics of His Majesty. Finally, as she will repeatedly stress, Christ's kingdom is not determined by wealth, pure blood, prestige, or geographical boundaries.

A story from Teresa's life is particularly revealing in this regard. In 1570, Teresa attempted to found a convent in Toledo. She met with

78. Ibid.

79. Teresa, *Interior Castle*, 236.

80. As Hauerwas and Baxter state, if "Christ became one of us, then he (like us) was embodied; and if Christ is king, then his kingdom is embodied as well" ("Kingship of Christ"). The authors are describing the rationale in *Quas primas* by Pope Pius XI for the establishment of Christ the King Sunday, a rationale resting ultimately on the Nicean doctrine of the Son's consubstantiality with the Father.

considerable opposition because of the *converso* background of her principle backers. *Conversos* were those Jews who had forcibly converted to
Christianity, often after violent pogroms. Teresa's grandfather, the reader
will remember, was a *converso* who had been accused of secretly practicing
Jewish customs. Toledo was the city where her grandfather had had to do
public penance for such judaizing, as it was called. Some *conversos* had,
over the years, married into old Christian families, though they were still
considered not to have *limpieza de sangre*, or pure blood. Jewish blood
was rather regarded as a "stain."[81] That Teresa met opposition because of
the *converso* background of many of her supporters reveals how deeply
concepts of pure blood dominated society.

This opposition extended to not allowing *conversos* to be buried in
the monastery. Teresa was told that she should not give a burying place to
anyone who did not belong to the "old nobility" (which would not have
included *conversos*). In the midst of this, Teresa writes,

> While I was at the monastery in Toledo and some were advising
> me that I shouldn't give a burying-place to anyone who had not
> belonged to the nobility the Lord said to me, 'You will grow very
> foolish, daughter, if you look to the world's laws. Fix your eyes
> on me, poor and despised by the world. Will the great ones of
> the world, perhaps, be great before me? Or, are you to be es-
> teemed for lineage, or for virtue?'[82]

What is so extraordinary about this passage is that Teresa, in a few strokes
so to speak, describes a shared life at radical odds with the aggressive political ideology of her day, a politics build on the erasure of Israel and thus
also on the forgetting of the *fullness* of providential time. Christian community as Teresa understands it is not determined by false and corrupt
understandings of such honor and politics. "Virtue" rather than "lineage"
establishes politics and community. "Virtue" is another way to describe
living and dwelling with Christ. Herein lies true honor. "Fix your eyes on
me, poor and despised by the world." As Paul states, "But God has so arranged the body, giving the greater honor to the inferior member, that
there may be no dissension within the body, but the members may have
the same care for one another" (1 Cor 12:24–25). Honor is a byproduct of
serving Christ, especially in those who are weaker. Teresa espouses a kind
of reverse hierarchy on honor to that of her day. The radical nature of this
reversal can only fully be understood against the background of nobility

81. Bilinkoff, *Avila of Saint Teresa*, 21.
82. Cited in ibid., 130. See also Teresa, *Collected Works*, 3:175.

and pure blood. In Teresa's day, Archbishop Rowan Williams observes, honor was "'objectified' as a matter of supreme public interest in such a way that an affront to one's public dignity or standing in the eyes of society becomes something worth killing for."[83]

Talk of such "honor," "nobility," and "blood" can easily seem disconnected from our contemporary understandings of politics. These ideologies are part of a medieval world long gone. Perhaps systems of honor and nobility live on in Mafioso-style politics or inner city gangs, where violations of honor are worth killing for. Such hierarchically ordered honor seems decidedly undemocratic.

Even in Teresa's own day, Cervantes' *Don Quixote* debunks the illusions and follies of honor associated with chivalry. Yet, as Peter Berger asks, what did this kind of debunking reveal? Don Quixote is ultimately a tragic figure. Berger draws a connection between Quixote and "modern man." He states, "Modern man is Don Quixote on his deathbed, denuded of the multicoloured banners that previously enveloped the self and revealed to be *nothing but a man*: 'I was mad, but I am now in my senses.'"[84] Berger notes, "It is important to understand that it is precisely this solitary self that modern consciousness has perceived as the bearer of human dignity and of inalienable human rights."[85] Berger's point is that honor, associated with socially obliged roles or norms, has been replaced by the self as such, the bearer of dignity and individual rights. One would not want to return to the system of honor grounded in "nobility" and "pure blood," but Berger sees the stripping of the solitary individual down to "rights" and "dignity" as no less a distortion of a true politics.

The replacement of dignity and rights for honor is good to the extent that personal worth is no longer defined (at least theoretically) in terms of blood and so forth. Yet, the loss of honor also has a downside. As J. Kameron Carter, among others, has argued, the invention of the modern, universalized, and rational "individual" continues to depend, albeit in a different way, upon the erasure of the Jews who are considered irrational and unenlightened.[86] The politics of honor/blood thus parallels that of the

83. Williams, *Teresa*, 25. For a fuller discussion of honor see 24–34.

84. Berger, "Obsolescence," 152.

85. Ibid., 153.

86. Carter gives an extensive account of how the project of modernity depends upon "dejudaization," and the elevation of whiteness, which he identifies with the universal. For example, "Kant's ultimate concern is with the success of the universalist project of modernity, the project of whiteness as the advance of cultured civilization (which is the advance toward the perfect race of humans" (*Race*, 95). The body politic

individual/rights in the sense that both rely upon distortions of time, and both distort (though in different ways) providential time.

By contrast, for Teresa, politics is a community *dwelling* in friendship with God in God's time. "Do you know when people really become spiritual?" Teresa asks. We could paraphrase this: "Do you know when people really become political?" Teresa responds, "It is when they become the slaves of God and are branded with His sign, which is the sign of the Cross, in token that they have given him their freedom."[87] In this alternative politics, one does not secure freedom but rather gives it up—a concept that might sit uneasily with citizens formed by the politics of the nation-state. Teresa, however, is only acknowledging that all politics serves someone or something; all politics is willing to sacrifice freedom for a higher good, whether that good is "individual rights" or defense of "pure blood." What the politics of Teresa's figural dwellings reveal is that the Good can be none other than Christ, who honors the least among us including all those with impure blood.

Such politics requires not the greatness of empire or the success of the nation-state, but faithfulness. In a poignant passage at the end of *Las Moradas*, Teresa imagines her sisters saying back to her, "[we] are unable to teach and preach like the Apostles." A current version of this might be, "we cannot change society," or "we do not have the great gifts of the saints." With irony, Teresa counsels, "instead of setting our hand to the work which lies nearest to us, and thus serving Our Lord in ways within our power, we may rest content with having desired the impossible."[88] In this final dwelling, Teresa emphasizes a willingness to do the small thing that lies in front of us, but with great love. This is not the politics of "being important," where one is always at the mercy of a system of power and reward, but rather a politics of faithful gestures flowing out of friendship with God and others. Teresa is well-known for her saying, "the Lord also walks among the pots and pans . . ."[89] Dwelling with Christ and his

---

becomes the state because religion is no longer seen as that which binds people to the material order. "Christianity is reimagined as 'racially' severed from and ethnographically triumphant over its oriental Jewish roots" (107). As a revitalized gnosticism, "Christianity, reconstituted as the moral religion par excellence of reason, extols a Jesus who, rather than disclosing YHWH or the God of Israel as the ground of redemption for Jews and Gentiles alike, instead affirms what the human species 'can or should make of itself'" (107).

87. Teresa, *Interior Castle*, 234.

88. Ibid., 237.

89. Teresa, *Collected Works*, 3:120.

body through prayer, Word, Sacrament, and humble service make the body politics of Christ visible in a way it cannot be when other political arrangements dominate.[90]

POLITICS AND UNITY

Stanley Hauerwas has made the observation that when Christians kill one another they are committing suicide. Of course, to accept this as true one must also accept the conviction that the church *is* one body, despite its many divisions. It is more likely in our context, however, for Christian citizens to believe in the unity of the United States than that of the church. I recently visited Pearl Harbor and heard of the horror and death that resulted from the Japanese attack some sixty years ago. That day "lived in infamy," in the famous words of President Roosevelt, because our country was threatened; hundreds of lives were lost. More recently, the images of 9/11 continue to be vivid and horrible reminders of a devastating tragedy. At the time, much debate surrounded the question, "Why do they hate us so?" Given these horrifying events, the providential politics that I attribute to Teresa and for which I argue can seem like a weak reed. Such politics cannot defend our country, or any country for that matter. One often hears the point that if not for our military, Christians and others would not have the freedom to worship as they do. Such a statement appears to make the nation's military necessary for the church to survive.

To begin to reimagine politics, however, means also learning new habits of being. As Teresa emphasizes throughout the dwellings, God knows what we need. She often makes this comment after discussing some particular grace (such as the grace of receiving visions), emphasizing that not everyone will receive the same kinds of gifts. While Teresa's point might seem far removed from the nation's military might, Teresa is nonetheless describing a central virtue for living together as God's people. That is, we do not need to defend ourselves; God will defend us. God knows what we need to live lives of faithfulness, and even more, God desires to give us gifts that will build up the entire body.

It still, however, can seem difficult to imagine a different politics. More often than not, our church can seem weak and compromised. It can easily seem as if God is *not* protecting the church. The question we need

90 At this point, we can see Teresa retrieving the politics and practices of the early church as described in Acts 2:42: "They devoted themselves to the apostles' teaching and fellowship, to the breaking of bread and the prayers."

to attend to, however, is, "What habits of being can help us imagine otherwise?" To return to my discussion of time, a crucial habit to cultivate is learning to live in time differently than that of our dominant culture. Time is neither homogeneous nor empty, the place of self-origination. Rather, the Sabbath, the liturgy, and the practices of forgiveness, prayer, and reconciliation are all ways that time is reconfigured. We do not live in inner/spiritual versus outer/political time. Rather, we live in the now and not-yet of God's time, in which Divine patterns shape all our days.

How does this contribute to the unity of the body of Christ? In my view, unity breaks apart on the rocks of homogeneous time, on the politics that would have us believe in time as strictly linear and thus, in a sense, always new. On this view, there can be no communion with the saints, nor any vision of Israel and the Church across time. It is easy to forget the wider communion in Christ. It thus becomes easier to kill other Christians.

Teresa's dwellings, however, as figures of God dwelling with us in time—transforming creation, ourselves and time from within—help us imagine more fully what it means to live liturgical, political lives without defense and without fear. Dwelling with Christ, we are bound to his body, but this is a bondage that frees. We are free to love and serve the other, whether the other is a separated Christian, a neighbor, or an enemy.

On a final note, does the politics Teresa offers require joining a monastic community? There has been an intriguing revival of monasticism recently, particularly amongst Protestants.[91] This impulse toward Christian communal living in small groups has been affirmed and encouraged recently by Pope Benedict: "Maybe we are facing a new and different kind of epoch in the Church's history, where Christianity will again be characterized more by the mustard seed, where it will exist in small, seemingly insignificant groups that nonetheless live an intensive struggle against evil and bring the good into the world—that let God in."[92] I return to this question of monastic and communal living in chapter 6. For now, however, I will say that the ecclesial way of being, of dwelling, that Teresa describes can take different shapes. Just as in Teresa's many mansions, however, all ecclesial shapes will seek to live in time providentially, and thus embody a politics in contrast with that of any empire or nation.

91. For an example, see the New Monasticism movement at http://www.new monasticism.org/index.php.

92. Ratzinger, *Salt of the Earth*, 16.

3

Divine Marriage and an Economics of Abundance

With zeal I have been zealous for the honor of my spouse, Jesus Christ.[1]

What freedom is and what love is, we have to learn from [God].[2]

MARRIAGE IS ABOUT UNITY. But what kind of unity? Couples come together for a variety of reasons: similar interests, same social class, common life goals, shared pleasures, and so forth. As a scriptural figure, marriage is also about unity, but specifically the unity between Christ and the church. This ecclesial unity generates and relies upon a particular economics, one grounded in God's extravagant abundance rather than the scarcity of human rivalry and competition. This economy of abundance locates unity not in the competition for and accumulation of financial wealth, but in a common life sustained by God's own non-competitive giving in Christ through the Spirit, which is itself the true wealth.

In this chapter, I look at how Teresa uses the figure of Divine marriage to describe the abundance that flows from the unity between Christ and the church. In this economics, the unity and abundance of a shared life is always a gift of the Holy Spirit, and scarcity a refusal to receive. In what follows I look more deeply at 1) Teresa's scriptural use of marriage as a figure for life with God, 2) how marriage and economics are intertwined,

1 The opening antiphon for St. Teresa's liturgy, cited in Boyce, *Praising God*, 355.

2. Barth, *Dogmatics in Outline*, 39.

and 3) how Teresa's use of this figure provides healing for ecclesial wounds sustained by an economics of scarcity.

THE DIVINE LOVER

"May You be blessed and praised forever, for You are so good a Lover,"[3] Teresa declares in her commentary on the Song of Songs. "I am only making a rough comparison," she writes elsewhere, "but I can find no other which will better explain what I am trying to say than the Sacrament of Matrimony." In these and other passages, Teresa portrays God as a Divine Lover inflaming her soul so that "for her part she does her utmost not to thwart this Divine betrothal."[4]

Teresa is quick to add that this betrothal is not only for a few. It is not only for select individuals. While she does recall well-known saints who were Divinely betrothed (Saint Ursula, Saint Dominic, and Saint Francis, for example), Teresa emphasizes that all who allow themselves to be "wooed" will know themselves loved by God, and can become united with Him. "Oh, my daughters, how ready this Lord still is to grant us favours, just as He was then!"[5] Furthermore, Teresa assures her readers that oneness with God does not require "great favours," or exceptional experiences of God. This is because "he has given us all we need in giving us His Son to show us the way."[6] The love of God in and through Christ is already abundantly available. Christ is already present as Divine spouse, waiting for Teresa's sisters—and more broadly the church—to enter into this communion. Teresa relates this divine marriage to such well-known passages as "to me, to live is Christ; and to die is gain" (Phil 1:21, RSV) and "he who is joined to the Lord becomes one spirit with him" (1 Cor 6:17, RSV).[7]

In the final three mansions of *Interior Castle*, Teresa famously describes most fully a process of union with God using the figure of marriage. In the fifth mansions, she notes that the union has "not yet reached

3. Teresa, *Song of Songs*, in *Collected Works*, 2:249.

4. Teresa, *Interior Castle*, 108, 109.

5. Ibid., 110. She reminds her sisters, though, that "if she is neglectful, however, and sets her affection on anything other than Himself, she loses everything . . ." (109).

6. Ibid., 102.

7. Both passages are cited in ibid., 217. Benedict XVI likewise references this latter passage is his discussion of how "God's *eros* for man is also totally *agape*," and that the unity with God is one "which creates love, a unity in which both God and man remain themselves and yet become fully one" (*Deus Caritas Est*, ¶ 10).

the point of spiritual betrothal, but is rather like what happens in our earthly life when two people are about to be betrothed."[8] While Teresa portrays God as wooing his beloved in the fifth mansions, in the sixth mansions this Divine pursuit gives way to engagement. In these mansions, trials as well as favors can awaken the soul to the Divine Lover. I write "can" because movement toward divine marriage is not robotic or automatic for Teresa; it is rather a way of opening her readers' imaginations to the providential possibilities and reality that lie before them.

In the seventh mansions, marriage is a figure for unity between the soul and God. Teresa registers the difference between betrothal and marriage in the following way: "there is the same difference between the Spiritual Betrothal and the Spiritual Marriage as there is between two betrothed persons and two who are united so they cannot be separated any more."[9] Whereas Spiritual Betrothal is still to some degree transient (like two candles that can still be separated), Spiritual Marriage is permanent.

> But here it is like rain falling from the heavens into a river or a spring; there is nothing but water there and it is impossible to divide or separate the water belonging to the river from that which fell from the heavens. Or it is as if a tiny streamlet enters the sea, from which it will find no way of separating itself, or as if in a room there were two large windows through which the light streamed in: it enters in different places but it all becomes one.[10]

There is a strong experiential aspect to Teresa's description of such marriage. For example, she writes that the soul at times experiences "certain secret aspirations, that it is endowed with life by God . . . very forcibly."[11] Such vivid experiences, however, always relate back to the Word who is Christ, the ever-faithful Spouse. The effects of unity with this Spouse include not only particular experiences that shape human affections but self-forgetfulness, a "great desire to suffer" (but, Teresa adds, "this is not of such a kind as to disturb the soul, as it did previously"), and an "equally strong desire to serve Him."[12]

---

8. Teresa, *Interior Castle*, 108.

9. Ibid., 215.

10. Ibid., 216–17.

11. Ibid., 217.

12. Ibid., 223.

ROMANTICISM?

"Spouse," "Lover," and "Betrothed" are all terms that come easily to Teresa's pen in a way that might seem rather alien to the modern reader. This kind of nuptial imagery might even seem distasteful when applied to God. As discussed in the first chapter, such imagery can easily be read as a Freudian projection of unconscious desires: Teresa and her sisters in the monastery did not have *real* spouses so they turned Jesus into their "spiritual" spouse; consequently, they projected onto him their unfulfilled romantic and sexual longings.[13] As Teresa herself notes, she was familiar even as a young child with the medieval myths of romance and chivalry.[14]

Not only is this romantic projection a concern, but the image of marriage—when applied to Christ—can seem highly privatized. Before the betrothal occurs, Teresa in fact describes a "short meeting" between the soul and future Spouse, when the soul is given certain desires. "All giving and taking have now come to an end," she writes, "and in a secret way the soul sees Who this Spouse is that she is to take."[15] This apparent clandestine rendezvous between Christ and his chosen spouse seems disconnected not only from the wider church, but also from engagement with the world.

If one interprets the figure of divine marriage in these ways, it will provide little insight into healing wounds of division on the body of Christ, economic or otherwise. In what follows, however, I want to show how Teresa's use of marriage challenges the story of romanticism by providing a richer way to imagine the shape of covenant love and the kinds of lives such love makes possible. I use the term "romantic" not simply to describe that "special" love between a couple, but more fully to name a particular story that informs a dominant understanding of marriage and love today.

In *Love in the Western World*, Denis de Rougemont analyzes romanticism by looking at the classic twelfth-century tale of Tristan and Iseult. In the story, Tristan, after defeating the Irish knight Morhold, goes to Ireland for the fair maiden Iseult. Tristan's charge is to bring her back to his uncle, King Mark, so that the two might become husband and wife. En route,

13. As mentioned earlier, this is no doubt the way many interpret Bernini's famous statue of Teresa.

14. Teresa describes in her autobiography how, at age seven, she and her brother, Rodrigo, ran off on a chivalrous, romantic adventure to fight the Moors, and possibly become martyrs. As might be expected, they traveled only a quarter of a mile before their uncle discovered them.

15. Teresa, *Interior Castle*, 109.

however, Tristan and Iseult inadvertently take a love potion and fall madly in love with each other. Iseult goes forward with the marriage to King Mark, but the potion "forces" her and Tristan into adulterous relations. Endings of this tale vary, but it is typical that either Iseult dies (of mortal wounds from a poison lance) or Tristan dies (of grief).

A key romantic feature of this tale is that Tristan and Iseult "fall" in love because of a potion. They are thus helpless before the moral consequences of their deeds. As de Rougemont states, "like all other great lovers, they imagine that they have been ravished 'beyond good and evil' into a kind of transcendental state outside ordinary human experience . . ."[16] In this sense, romantic love is otherworldly. Such a claim might sound counterintuitive. Why could be more "worldly" than their passionate secret love? De Rougemont points out, however, that "*what [Tristan and Iseult] love is love and being in love.*"[17] This can be seen most clearly in the fact that the potion causes them to fall in love; it is not a personal, committal act. The fact that such love is ultimately otherworldly means that it cannot be attained in this world. Romantic tales typically end in the death of one or both of the lovers, which is the only way to make such love last. De Rougemont describes this love as Manichean (or gnostic) in that it requires escape *from* the world. "The fundamental dogma of all Manichaean sects," he writes, "is that the soul is divine or angelic, and is *imprisoned* in created forms—in terrestrial matter, which is Night."[18] From this perspective, the fulfillment of love (or *eros* so understood) "is the denial of any particular terrestrial love, and its Bliss of any particular terrestrial bliss."[19] As de Rougemont succinctly states about Tristan and Iseult, "They love, but not one another."[20] Such romantic love thus survives by fleeing the world for an ideal, infinite love.

The plotline of the romantic myth continues today: fall in love, get married, and live happily ever after. John McFadden and David McCarthy observe that we see this myth in "TV images where married people are usually shown alone (or with children) romping on the beach when young or holding hands on a front porch in advanced years." They suggest that we contrast this with single people who are always shown in groups, "sharing laughter and adventure with a community of other persons. Their

16. Rougemont, *Love in the Western World*, 39.

17. Ibid., 41.

18. Ibid., 65; my emphasis.

19. Ibid., 66.

20. Ibid., 39.

community is based in leisure activities and indulgent pleasures . . . when a couple marry they 'graduate' from a community they no longer need, because the love they share is *sufficient unto itself*; their new 'community' will be made up of one another, and later, their children."[21] The private, personal fulfillment of the spouses is adequate. As McFadden and Mc-Carthy observe, the popular mindset is that the married couple is now free from "community."

Romanticism, so understood, shares key plotlines with a market society. For example, both use strategies of "non-stop seduction."[22] In Tristan and Iseult, the potion is the means of irresistible seduction in a way that is similar to the incessant manipulation of desire by the market. Furthermore, both romanticism and consumerism involve the fiction of finding oneself through union with a "real" that is unattainable.[23] The capitalist market relies upon the creation of needs and desires that can never be fully satisfied; the consumer must keep buying products to reach that ideal image of the self. So also in romanticism, the lovers imagine they will find themselves through the fiction of an idealized other. The other is unattainable not simply because he or she is already married, though this is often true as in the case of Iseult. Such love is unattainable because it requires for its very existence a false sense of self. One has to have the other to be complete, just as one needs to consume to be fulfilled. The fiction of the romantic-consumer myth centers on the fact that desire can never be satisfied precisely because such desires both create and arise from a false self, a self that seeks completion through love of an impossible, otherworldly ideal. As we will see more fully, this myth continues in manifold ways to imagine the lives of many today.[24]

21. McFadden and McCarthy, *Preparing for Christian Marriage*, 2; my emphasis.

22. This term is from Gilles Lipovetsky, cited in Gallagher, "Tone of Culture."

23. Kettle, *Western Culture*, 219–44. Kettle, analyzing the myth of Narcissus and modern narcissism, states, "Narcissus may seem at first sight to be too full of himself, to the exclusion of all others, but the deeper story is of a personal lack and of a futile longing" (230). The real is "unattainable" in modern consumerism because the consumer can never be fully satisfied or else he or she would not need to keep buying the latest products. At the same time, such striving for the unattainable reveals not true self-love but a sense of lack, and even "self-hatred" (231).

24. I gleaned this way of putting the matter from Micheal Warren, who writes about youth ministry that part of the trouble in the world of media images is that "young people are continually having their lives imagined for them" (cited in Gallagher, "Tone of Culture").

As is perhaps already obvious, to read Teresa through the lens of this romantic love is to misread her. From the perspective of romantic love, the marriage between the soul and God will be seen as more pure, more ideal than the all too worldly ecclesial institution. On this view, as indicated, one leaves behind the ecclesial community, or any community for that matter, for life with the Divine Other. Teresa, by contrast, situates her understanding of divine love and marriage within the Carmelite community of sisters, and more broadly, within the life of the church. This Divine love does not call lovers to leave their ecclesial place behind, but rather to immerse themselves more deeply in it through a particular kind of life together. If, as noted earlier, "God walks amid the pots and pans," then God is present in the ordinary, mundane activities and places of daily life. The point is not to amass "wealth," i.e., more and better pots and pans, but to use our possessions to build a common life with God.[25] It is precisely this kind of common life that, for Teresa, can be illumined through the figure of divine marriage. As de Rougemont states so powerfully in his analysis of Christian love, "The symbol of Love is no longer the infinite passion of a soul in quest of light, but the marriage of Christ and the Church." Thus human love, "being understood according to the image of Christ's love for His Church . . . , is able to be truly mutual."[26] It is precisely Christ's love for the church, and thus the possibility of mutuality between God and humanity, that forms Teresa's own convictions about Divine love.

In terms of "love" leaving community behind, however, one might rightly wonder how this relates to the familiar passages from Scripture, which states that a man should "[leave] his father and his mother and [cling] to his wife, and they become one flesh" (Gen 2:24, cited in Eph 5:31). How does this differ from the leave-taking that constitutes the romantic myth? Most obviously, the leaving described in Scripture is for the purpose of being bound together in the covenant of marriage. It is not Manichean: a couple does not leave for an idealized otherworldly realm. Even more, the possibility for the condition of marriage is Christ's love for the church. That is, a couple can be in covenant with each other because the possibility of such covenant is revealed and made possible in Christ's

---

25. I would also make a similar point about "experience," as this is often understood in some denominations and non-denominational churches. The point is not to amass personal experiences of God (where this is equated with uplift in mood and good feelings) but to allow ourselves to be formed by God's Spirit through Word, Sacrament, and other Christian practices.

26. Rougemont, *Love in the Western World*, 68.

relation through the Spirit with church. Human marriage is thus related analogously to the marriage between Christ and the church.[27]

In fact, the whole church is *already* married to Christ, who has taken the church as his spouse. But the church is divided and split in so many ways that it easily seems as if Christ has many spouses, not one. Such division, however, is sin. It reflects our own brokenness, not the desire of the Divine Spouse for many partners. Teresa portrays Christ as always a source of unity for the communities she has established, but this unity requires a willingness to please and serve God and your companions.[28] In her own way, Teresa is reflecting the conviction that unity is both a gift and a task.

A reader might rightly puzzle, as well, at Teresa's use of "secret" to refer to the growing unity between the soul and her Spouse. Is this not the epitome of a private, anti-institutional (anti-ecclesial) romanticism? Could this not be read as a kind of gnostic secret knowledge, one that underwrites a dualism between the body/world and the soul/heaven? Teresa's use of "secret," however, should not be read as meaning merely private but rather as referring to Divine mystery. It is, in fact, from this perspective that Teresa refers to God approaching Moses in the burning bush, who was then given "courage to do what he did for the people of Israel." In this encounter, Teresa writes, God reveals "*secret* things to his soul in such a way as to make him *sure of their truth* . . ."[29]

The juxtaposition, in Teresa's words, between "secret," "assurance," and "truth" is fascinating in that it challenges modern assumptions that relate "secret" to "private." Teresa is describing something other than

27. Paul writes, "This is a great mystery, and I am applying it to Christ and the church" (Eph 5:32). On the face of it, this passage could sound as if Paul is applying human marriage (of which he has prior knowledge) to Christ and the church. I am arguing the other way around, however. It is precisely Christ's love for the church that enables Christians to know what marriage looks like. In fact, in the wider context, this is also what Paul is arguing—"Husbands, love your wives, just as Christ loved the church . . ." (5:25). Some worry, rightly, that such passages can be used in ways that shore up male domination. The wider context that Paul is imagining, however, has to do with the *holiness* of the church. Both husbands and wives are to be holy (set apart) as are all Christians so that the church may be Christ's visible bride.

28. In one of many instances of this conviction, Teresa writes, "Therefore, sisters, if you wish to lay good foundations, each of you must try to be the least of all, and the slave of God, and must seek a way and means to please and serve all your companions. If you do that, it will be of more value to you than to them and your foundation will be so firmly laid that your Castle will not fall" (*Interior Castle*, 234). Being a slave to Christ unites the communities.

29. Teresa, *Interior Castle*, 145; my emphasis.

simply "private." Her use of "secret" rather describes an assurance from God that enables a person (in this case Moses) to lead a community (the Hebrew people) to their longed-for hope (freedom, the promised land). The assurance of God's mysterious truth is precisely what enables Moses to participate in God's visible deeds in the world, in spite of his profound misgivings. Thus, Teresa's use of "secret" is related to Divine assurance, an assurance that shapes both her description and experience of divine marriage. The church, like Israel, can trust that it belongs to God and that God is faithful. Christ will not abandon his spouse. Teresa refers to Jesus' prayer that his disciples might become one with Him, even as the Son in one with the Father (John 20:19, 21). She then adds, "How true are these words. . . . The words of Jesus Christ our King and Lord cannot fail . . ."[30] Such an emphasis describes the faithfulness of the Divine Spouse even in the midst of human failure. This is a long way from the self-consuming romanticism of Tristan and Iseult.

CREATED FOR LOVE

For Teresa, the figure of marriage means that humans are created for love. Augustine famously states at the beginning of the *Confessions*, "Our hearts are restless until they rest in Thee, O God."[31] The influence of Augustine on Teresa can be seen in the fact that she too begins *Interior Castle* with an image of the self or soul being created for and drawn to something beyond itself. Teresa's initial focus is not so much the "restlessness" of the soul as it is the presence of Christ in and with the soul, a Christ who can be seen—though perhaps barely—through the diamond walls of the castle.[32] To catch even brief glimpses of Christ is to desire more.

Like Augustine, too, Teresa portrays humanity as already *inside* a drama that it did not initiate. The drama begins with creation and with the conviction that humans are created *for* something. To ignore this fact is to live in the dark, an opaque shadowy half-life of the kind that C. S. Lewis describes in *The Great Divorce*. When the narrator in Lewis's story

30. Ibid., 219.

31. Maria Boulding translates this as follows: ". . . you have made us and drawn us to yourself, and our heart is unquiet until it rests in you (*Confessions*, 39).

32. This difference in initial emphasis may reflect in part their biographies. While Augustine narrates his journey in search of God with the Manicheans, the Platonists, the struggles of his flesh, and so forth, Teresa already as a young child had a devotion to Christ (though this is not to deny that her own journey had a wide range of trials, dryness, and so forth).

leaves the joyless city and takes a bus that arrives at the joyful city, he discovers he cannot walk on the grass because it is painful. Everything is more solid and real precisely because it is participating in God's good, renewed creation. Teresa's way of narrating this grand drama is to use not only the figure of a majestic diamond castle but also that of marriage and communion; travelers, or better, pilgrims, become more solid, more real the closer they get to God. To be created for love is the initial context for Teresa's figural use of divine marriage.[33]

This figural marriage is no otherworldly bliss. Teresa writes in the sixth mansion (where the soul is engaged to God), "This great God *desires* us to know that He is a King and we are miserable creatures—a point of great importance for what follows."[34] From the perspective of the romantic myth, knowledge of the other or the self as a "miserable creature" would be incomprehensible. For the romantic, the lover is prince charming or Cinderella. There can be no acknowledgement of "sin" precisely because the romantic myth is itself an escape *from* the sinful world. As we saw, deceit, selfishness, betrayal, and so forth are therefore justified for the sake of the ideal love.

The language of "sinner" or "miserable creature," however, is not a threat in the great drama of divine marriage. "Sin" does name the broken-ness between God and humanity—between the Lover and the beloved—but it is a brokenness *already* healed in and through Christ, even though the soul may be suffering great darkness. In the sixth mansion, Teresa describes "many things which assault [the] soul with an interior oppression so keenly felt and so intolerable that I do not know to what it can be compared, save to the torment of those who suffer hell, for in this spiritual tempest no consolation is possible."[35] Far from a rosy romanticism, Teresa is narrating a profound and mysterious darkness into which the soul simply falls. The seduction of the market, of course, offers no consolation: "So do not suppose, sisters, if you even find yourselves in this condition, that people who are wealthy, or free to do as they like, have any better remedy for such times."[36] Teresa further explains that for a person suffering in this

---

33. Pope Benedict XVI shares Teresa's understanding when he writes, ". . . you are not built as an island whose only foundation is itself. Rather, you are built for love, and therefore for giving, for renunciation, for the pruning of yourself" (Ratzinger, *Salt of the Earth*, 168).

34. Teresa, *Interior Castle*, 124; my emphasis. Teresa is here describing periods of great dryness or emptiness when neither solitude, prayer, nor company seem to help.

35. Ibid., 123.

36. Ibid., 124.

way, "solitude is still worse for her, though it is also torture for her to be in anyone's company or to be spoken to; and so, despite all her effort to conceal the fact, she becomes outwardly upset and despondent, to a very noticeable extent."[37]

I have quoted Teresa at length because these passages show how she is not describing a marital ideal, but rather Christ's faithfulness even in the midst of our darkness. Teresa does not explain this suffering, reflecting the Augustinian emphasis that evil has no explanation. Since it is the negation of created being, it is ultimately absurd. Teresa does, however, offer the following advice: "The best medicine—I do not say for removing the trouble, for I know of none for that, but for enabling the soul to endure it—is to occupy oneself with external affairs and works of charity and to hope in God's mercy, which never fails those who hope in Him."[38] Teresa thus returns to the faithfulness of the Divine Spouse and to participation in works of charity. Even though one may be in darkness, the Divine Spouse gives his beloved the grace to participate and share in works of charity. It might well be that as one comes closer to the light of Christ one perceives the darkness of the world more readily (recall that Teresa is here discussing the sixth mansions). Teresa's important counsel is not to flee the world but to engage it with external acts of love. In this case, even though the soul is in darkness, the bond of love nonetheless enables it to extend Christ's love to others. The darkness is no barrier to Christ's presence.

True, we can and often do place ourselves through our sins at a far distance from God, but it is exactly this distance that Christ overcomes. The point of Teresa's placement of Christ in the center of the diamond castle highlights that God in Christ is with us even though we are not with him.[39] Divine marriage is a possibility not because of where we are or how we are able to position ourselves to attract the Other, but because of who and where Christ is.

Teresa's path to marriage as one moves through the fifth, sixth, and seventh mansions (through engagement, betrothal, and marriage) is, in a vital sense, about learning to be loved. Pope Benedict XVI describes this as follows: "The core of faith rests upon accepting being loved by God, and therefore to believe is to say Yes, not only to him, but to creation, to creatures, above all, to men, to try to see the image of God in each person

37. Ibid.

38. Ibid., 125.

39. When we look at Hosea, we will see the persistence of God as Divine Lover even in the face of tremendous unfaithfulness.

and thereby to become a lover."[40] Pope Benedict's use of "lover" illuminates Teresa's own application of the figure of marriage to the Christian life. The figure of divine marriage has to do at its core with accepting being loved by God. This is different from Paul Tillich's well-known "accept that you are accepted," where he argued that the courage of faith involved moving beyond meaninglessness to a feeling of acceptance "by that which is greater than you, and the name of which you do not know."[41] For Teresa, rather, to accept and receive God's love is necessarily to enter a particular kind of life, one that involves, as I will discuss, a particular kind of economics.

MARRIAGE AS SCRIPTURAL FIGURE

First, though, I want to look more fully at the figure of marriage in Scripture as a way 1) to undergird Teresa's understanding; and 2) to display how it is a figure of abundance. I will do so by focusing on select passages from Revelation, Hosea, and the Song of Songs.

Revelation

In Revelation 21 we read,

> Then one of the seven angels who had the seven bowls full of the seven last plagues came and said to me, "Come, I will show you the bride, the wife of the Lamb." And in the spirit he carried me away to a great, high mountain and showed me the holy city Jerusalem coming down out of heaven from God. It has the glory of God and a radiance like a very rare jewel, like jasper, clear as crystal. (vv. 9–11).

These verses vividly describe a diamond dwelling and divine marriage—figures, as we have seen, central in Teresa's theology. Joseph Mangina, in his commentary on these verses, emphasizes that the "trope of bride and bridegroom runs throughout scripture and can be read at multiple levels." In Song of Songs, for example, Mangina states that Jewish and Christian

---

40. Ratzinger, *Salt of the Earth*, 117.

41. Cited by Gomes, "Introduction," in Tillich, *Courage to Be*, xxii. This is Tillich's popular classic, and his emphasis on the virtue of courage still resonates today, as Gomes points out. As is well known, Tillich seeks to avoid the word "God," speaking instead of a ground of being and of an ultimate concern. He moved in this direction because he wanted to avoid objectifying God, thereby making him all-powerful, possibly turning God into a tyrant.

tradition "have always found in the lovers . . . a figure of YHWH's marriage to Israel or of Christ's love for the church." There is a frustrated longing on both sides that "may be understood as the energy that propels the whole biblical narrative." Thus, "God loves his people, but is rebuffed and rejected; the people long for God, but foolishly lose their way . . ."[42]

In romantic myths, as we saw, there is also a frustrated longing as lovers "magically" fall in love but are often prevented from consummating their passion due to family, tradition, moral laws, and so forth. They must therefore escape their past—often through death, as in Romeo and Juliet—or create their own "moral universe" in order to be free to love. In the scriptural figure of marriage, however, the movement of love flows in the opposite direction: not toward escape but toward engagement and repentance. Israel, God's own people, must repent of their disobedience in the past and of their unfaithfulness to the moral law in order to be free to worship and love God. Similarly, while Christ's love for the church never wavers, the members of Christ's body enter communion not by fleeing their past but by acknowledging their own brokenness and frailty, turning from their sins, and entering more fully God's new creation/order.

Hosea

Scripture, of course, registers time and again how God's chosen people turn from God in order to follow their own malformed desires. The book of Hosea portrays God as an ever-faithful Spouse even though Israel is repeatedly faithless. The prophet Hosea thus writes, "The Lord said to me again, 'Go, love a woman who has a lover and is an adulteress, just as the Lord loves the people of Israel, though they turn to other gods and love raisin cakes'" (3:1). The marriage between God and Israel means that idolatry is like adultery. In addition, Israel's lack of faith and loyalty is manifested in its way of life: swearing, lying, stealing, and "bloodshed [that] follows bloodshed" (4:2). Even the land mourns; the birds of the air and the fish of the sea are languishing (4:3). While the wrath of God is against Israel, ultimately God "cannot forget the first love."[43] "When Israel was a child, I loved him, and out of Egypt I called my son. . . . How can I give you up, Ephraim? How can I hand you over, O Israel? . . . My heart recoils within me; my compassion grows warm and tender. I will not execute my fierce anger . . ." (11:1, 8, 9). While the infidelity of Israel has consequences, God,

42. Mangina, *Revelation*, 240.
43. Lohfink, *Does God Need the Church?*, 98.

the Divine and ever-faithful Spouse, relentlessly pursues his chosen ones. He will not let Israel go even though she has been faithless many times over. Hosea ends by relaying how the love of the Divine Spouse will heal Israel: "I will heal their disloyalty; I will love them freely . . . They shall again live beneath my shadow, they shall flourish as a garden; they shall blossom like the vine, their fragrance shall be like the wine of Lebanon" (14:4, 7). God's healing will result in a flourishing life that can be seen, smelled, and even tasted. It thus reverses the languishing of the land and animals resulting from Israel's earlier faithlessness; Israel shall again become a fragrant garden.

In the book of Hosea, the reality of marriage between God and Israel both reveals false desires and creates true ones. When Israel turns away from her Beloved Spouse, her desires become idolatrous and she turns to deception, bloodshed, and division. God longs for the return of love from his beloved (Israel) even though she has wandered far from him. But, how can Israel desire God when she has become corrupted by false desires? Only God, the one true God of Abraham, Isaac, and Jacob, can overcome Israel's faithlessness and heal their faithless ways.

It might be tempting to dismiss Hosea's description of Israel as a harlot (practicing idolatry) as relevant to the stubborn Israelites a long time ago but of little practical relevance to the church today. Ephraim Radner reminds us, however, that scriptural figures such as divine marriage are not literary metaphors that bring some deeper meaning to the intellect when attached to another image. That is, the image of divine marriage is not simply taken from human marriage. It is not as if humans invented marriage and then thought it would be interesting to apply it to God. Rather, as Radner states, "a figure is a form that God actually makes historical experience fit, like some providential mold. . . . In God's providence, sacraments [which are also scriptural figures] shape history according to God's plan."[44] To make historical experience fit a scriptural figure is not to say that human existence is determined in a way that denies human agency and freedom. As Hosea narrates, the Israelites freely abandoned their covenant with God. God does not coerce Israel's love but rather refuses to abandon her.

Radner is describing how God providentially creates, orders and redeems the world in a way that can be discerned in particular patterns. These patterns might indeed be difficult to see, more so in the midst of faithlessness, division, and bloodshed. Israel, for example, in her unfaithfulness,

44. Radner, *Hope*, 126.

is unable to call the Lord "my husband," but instead says "my Baal" (Hos 2:17). Because of her idolatry, the figure of Divine marriage appears incoherent; "there is no faithfulness or loyalty, and no knowledge of God in the land" (Hos 4:1). This ignorance and blindness, however, does not thwart the providence of God, the Divine Spouse. For, as Radner puts it, marriage, like baptism and the Eucharist (sacraments tied to the very shape of Christ's own life), is an act that in God's providence conforms the church, "whether she likes it or not, recognizes it or not, to the prophecies of Scripture fulfilled in Jesus Christ."[45]

This does not mean that such Divine patterns or figures can be woodenly applied to particular contexts. Rather, they are the means through which God draws his creatures to dwell in the Truth of who he is. Doing so is a thoroughly human process that calls for the formation of a people into a history shaped by God's deeds and faithfulness. From this standpoint, human marriage is a kind of participation in Christ's marriage to the church where, through Word and Sacrament, we enter into communion with God. Divine marriage is a supreme sign of God's love (as in Hosea) and Christ's self-giving to the church on behalf of the world. Hosea thus points to a pattern of human faithlessness and evasion, and of a Divine love that will not let us go.

The Song of Songs

As noted above, Teresa wrote a commentary on the Song of Songs, a book that profoundly shaped her understanding of divine marriage. Teresa reminds her sisters, in fact, that many of the antiphons and readings in the Office of our Lady ("which we recite each week") are taken from this book.[46] While her commentary focuses on only a selection of verses from the Song, she uses these to develop what it means to call the Lord "Spouse." Mary's question to Gabriel, "How can this be?," becomes a kind of refrain. How is it possible, Teresa asks, to say with the Song of Songs, "Now I see, my Bridegroom, that *You are mine*" (Song 2:16; Teresa's emphasis).[47] "How can I be Yours, my God? . . . Why does a Lord so powerful need [me]?"[48] Would not such need reduce God to human level?

45. Ibid.
46. Teresa, *Song of Songs*, in *Collected Works*, 2:253.
47. Citations from the Song of Songs are from the translation that Teresa used.
48. Teresa, *Song of Songs*, in *Collected Works*, 2:250–51.

Whether Teresa is explicitly aware of it or not, she is struggling with questions that have some age-old theological histories. To say that God creates out of need obscures the fact that creation is pure gift. God does not have to create; God creates out of freedom and love. At the same time, "need" can be used to signal other crucial theological points. Gerhard Lohfink, for example, titles one of his books *Does God Need the Church?*, to which he gives a definitive yes. Aquinas, registering these different uses of "need," describes at least two different ways that "need" might be used in reference to God: strict need and convenient need. Strict need emphasizes that God is perfect and complete. In this sense, God does not strictly need anyone or anything. Aquinas employs the notion of convenient necessity, however, to describe how God is not bound to a particular way of acting but in freedom acts in a way that is most delightful and pleasing, most fitting and convenient. In other words, God could act in some other way, but acts in a particular, contingent way that most fully unfolds God's goodness and extravagant love for the world.[49]

This all-too-brief background provides a framework for understanding Teresa's response to whether or not God needs us. She writes that God "gives us permission to think that He, this true Lover, my Spouse and my God, needs us." Such a resolution will be unsatisfactory if we interpret Teresa as saying that God is simply pretending to need us but in reality does not. Rather, Teresa emphasizes again and again how God really desires to have people who truly love him. "God would never want to do anything else than give if He could find receivers. And as I have said often—I want you never to forget, daughters—the Lord is never content with giving us as little as we desire . . ."[50] Such a statement suggests a kind of need on God's part; not by any means an absolute need but rather a contingent one: God has freely desired to enter into communion with creation and thus "needs" our response and reception. God would still be God even if we never acknowledged him. At the same time, as Teresa notes, God needs us (and grants us permission to respond to this need) in the sense that the Bridegroom needs and loves the Bride. So understood, the Divine Lover pursues the Bride across time and space (even into the depths of hell).[51]

49. Barron, *Thomas Aquinas*, 46–47.

50. Ibid., 250–51.

51. As Thompson's poem "The Hound of Heaven" so vividly states, "I fled Him, down the nights and down the days; I fled Him, down the arches of the years; I fled Him, down the labyrinthine ways . . ."

Teresa's meditation on the Song of Songs emphasizes not only the Divine Lover pursuing us but also the extravagance of Divine provision. God "is manna, for the taste we get from Him conforms to the taste we prefer."[52] Later Teresa writes, ". . . for the Lord gives from the apple tree (to which she compares her Beloved) the fruit already cut, cooked, and even chewed."[53] The nearness of God leads the soul to say, as does the Song of Songs, "Your breasts are better than wine" (1:2). Teresa describes images of abundance not so much in terms of amount but rather in terms of how perfectly God provides exactly what we need, even more fully than we are able to imagine. Abundance, in other words, is not having a lot of stuff, but a kind of human flourishing sustained by the grace of God. Thus, Teresa emphasizes that God knows what we need to live and grow in faithfulness. It is in this light that Teresa discusses the verse, "He brought me into the wine cellar; set charity in order within me" (Song 2:4). She adds, ". . . much is contained in what the bride says. He brings her into the wine cellar so that she may come out more abundantly enriched."[54] That is, human flourishing has to do with a particular kind of life lived in response to Divine extravagance.

Teresa characterizes life with God, the Divine Lover, as not only extravagant but also one in which desires are "inflamed." The King, according to Teresa, wants us to "drink in conformity with [our] desire and become wholly inebriated, drinking of all the wines of God's storehouse."[55] The advice to drink in conformity with one's desire seems rather hazardous, as does becoming "wholly inebriated." But Teresa is reflecting on "the wines of God's storehouse," an image of the many delights that God provides. Teresa later emphasizes that God showers these delights in such a way that the wonderful extravagance of God's giving is magnified for all. Thus, Teresa writes about the favors of the Lord:

> . . . to one He gives a little wine of devotion, to another more, with another He increases it in such a way that the person begins to go out from himself, from his sensuality, and from all earthly things; to some He gives great fervor in His service; to others, impulses of love; to others, great charity toward their neighbors.[56]

52. Teresa, *Song of Songs*, in *Collected Works*, 2:248.

53. Ibid., 2:249.

54. Ibid., 2:251.

55. Ibid.

56. Ibid. In her own case, Teresa writes that "for to a soul as poor and wretched

Such a passage echoes 1 Corinthians 12 with its emphasis on shared gifts for the purpose of building up a common good. Such an economy prioritizes being over having.

To return to the question that Teresa herself cites numerous times in this commentary: "How can this be?" or "How is this divine extravagance possible?" As Teresa reminds her readers, the response to Mary's question is, "The Holy Spirit will come upon you; the power of the Most High will overshadow you."[57] It is the gift of the Spirit that makes possible the mysterious abundance of God. This is no ephemeral, otherworldly reality. The Spirit rather is the bond of unity that enables communion with God through Christ and with one another. The Spirit makes room for and enables humans to participate in the communion between the Son and the Father.[58]

Teresa's commentary on the Song shows more fully how her use of the figure of marriage is not simply a "spiritual" one divorced from material living. She is rather describing, in a wonderfully vivid way, a particular kind of human flourishing. This flourishing is characterized by abundance, delight, and extravagance—only these terms do not have the same meaning as typically used today, at least in Western culture. "Extravagance" does not refer to property, lifestyle, or a lavish amount of money. It is not an economic term in this sense of referring to a person's "net worth." Teresa however, is describing an alternative economy grounded in a particular way of life. To say that this is an "economy" might strike the reader as rather odd, since, to contemporary ears, "economy" has to do with markets, money, employment, and so forth. But this assumption typically rests on a division between the material and spiritual world. Teresa, however, rejects this dichotomy. For her, Divine abundance is at once about communion with God, the Divine Lover, and about the ordinary ways the church lives out of this abundance. We will return to this understanding of economy

---

and without merit as mine, for which the first of these jewels was enough, and more than enough, He desired to grant more riches; more than I knew how to desire" (*Book of Her Life*, 55).

57. Teresa, *Song of Songs*, in *Collected Works*, 2:253; see also 248.

58. "For you did not receive a spirit of slavery to fall back into fear, but you have received a spirit of adoption. When we cry, 'Abba! Father!' it is that very Spirit bearing witness with our spirit that we are children of God, and if children, then heirs, heirs of God and joint heirs with Christ . . ." (Rom 8:15–17a). For the concept of making room applied to the Trinity, see Jenson, *Systematic Theology*, vol. 1, where he states that ". . . God can indeed, if he chooses, accommodate other persons in his life without distorting that life. God, to state it as boldly as possible, is *roomy*" (226).

below. For now, however, let us examine in more detail how dominant images of "economics" easily shape our lives.

ECONOMICS AS WE IMAGINE IT

When most of us hear "economics," we think about the volatility of the market, employment prospects, how much money we make, how much savings we have or have lost, and so forth. We might worry about the sufficiency of our income or the meager savings of our parents or in-laws. Economics, in this dominant framework, has to do with money, competition, efficiency, a solid work ethic, investments, and so forth. But where did the idea that economics is primarily about earning, saving, and spending money come from? This is no doubt a large question. I do not pretend to have a full response to it. I will examine, however, some of the *theological* assumptions that have shaped this modern view.[59]

To do this, I turn to Max Weber's classic *The Protestant Work Ethic and the Spirit of Capitalism*, focusing on one of his key points: his analysis of the advent of capitalism in light of the Reformation, particularly Calvinism and its Puritan offspring.[60] His theory, simply put, is that the Puritan work ethic emphasized work itself as a *vocation*. In doing so, the Puritans provided the theological leverage for an intense disciplined work ethic. Work became a *duty* one gave to God, expecting nothing in return. Such an understanding of work led to frugal habits of consumption. No human work, however good, could earn one salvation. Rightly understood, salvation was always a gift of God's grace. The blessings of work, however, along with an intensely disciplined way of life, were signs that one was indeed chosen (or predestined) by God. To imagine otherwise would be to compromise a key Protestant conviction: *sola fides*, faith alone saves. As Christopher van Ginhoven puts it, "The doctrine of *sola fide*, as is well known, implied a rejection of the soteriological merits of works, of what

59 Weber's thesis has been criticized in a variety of ways. Davide Cantoni, for example, using population data from 1300–1900, argues that Protestantism had no effect on economic growth ("Economic Effects of the Protestant Reformation"). Political theorist Murray Jardine, while accepting the general direction of Weber's thesis, states that Weber oversimplifies. Jardine argues that "the culture of compulsive work, and later consumption, that has developed in modern societies is due at least as much to the secularized version of the work ethic developed by early liberalism as to the Calvinist conception of predestination." Jardine adds: "Weber's argument, however, is essential as a starting point" (*Making and Unmaking*, 208).

60. See especially Weber, *Protestant Work Ethic*.

one did and could do in this world." [61] A key point of Weber's argument is that the emphasis on disciplined work as vocation along with habits of frugality contributed greatly to the invention of industrial capitalism.

What happens when future generations inherit this work ethic without its theological underpinnings? Weber famously argues that without the inspiration of vocation, this "Protestant work ethic" easily becomes an "iron cage."

> The Puritan wanted to work in a calling; we are forced to do so. For when asceticism was carried out of monastic cells into everyday life, and began to dominate worldly morality, it did its part in building the tremendous cosmos of the modern economic order. This order is now bound to the technical and economic conditions of machine production which today determine the lives of all the individuals who are born into this mechanism, not only those directly concerned with economic acquisition, with irresistible force. . . . In [Richard] Baxter's view the care for external goods should only lie on the shoulders of the "saint like a light cloak, which can be thrown aside at any moment." But fate decreed that the cloak should become an iron cage. [62]

According to Weber, as the Protestant work ethic becomes secularized, it becomes an almost unbearable, unchosen burden. No longer restrained by Puritan virtues, the work ethic with its the inevitable creation of wealth unleashes market forces across society. [63] "[This] work ethic," political theorist Murray Jardine notes, "is what tends to turn the market into an all-consuming force," [64] or what Weber famously calls an "iron cage."

61. Ginhoven, "Theurgic Image," 19. The author is following the work of Georges Bataille.

62. Weber, *Protestant Work Ethic*, 181.

63. Rodney Clapp describes how aspects of modern consumerism grew out of Protestant practices such as revivalism. Advertising testimonials, for example, drew their inspiration from evangelical testimonies, and John Wanamaker, founder of Wanamaker department stores, commodified Christian holy days, particularly Christmas. Clapp also points out, following the work of British sociologist Colin Campbell (*Romantic Ethic and the Spirit of Modern Consumption*), that for the Puritans "experience" increasingly also became of sign of true faith. Hence there was a growing focus on an intense, inward experience as the measure of grace. Campbell relates this phenomenon to Puritanism giving way to an eventually secularized Romanticism (nineteenth century). Thus Campbell states, "One way of looking at this change is to regard the Puritans as having developed a 'taste' for the strong meat of powerful religious emotion, and when their convictions waned, seeking alternative fare with which to satisfy their appetite" (quoted in Clapp, "Theology of Consumption," 179).

64. Jardine, *Making and Unmaking*, 142.

A helpful way to recognize the effects of this "cage" in our late modern time is to understand the difference between a *market economy* and a *market society*. A market economy is one that makes extensive use of markets, whereas a market society is completely dominated by market forces. In a market economy, the market is not *the* overriding force. In a market society, however, all human relations are reduced to contract, destroying the longer-term bonds needed to sustain human society. Jardine notes that in some cultures various communal bonds or concerns might override market values. In such an economy, for example, people might

> buy from a merchant who charges higher prices out of a sense of personal loyalty . . . more efficient producers may refrain from putting less efficient producers out of business by limiting their own production. They may do this because they feel it would be uncharitable to destroy the livelihood of others or simply because they feel that they already have enough wealth and don't need any more, preferring instead greater leisure time. This type of behavior was quite common in Europe before liberalism became dominant . . .[65]

According to Jardine, a secularized Protestant ethic in a bourgeois culture—a culture that is both highly individualistic and concerned with material wealth—is what produces a market society. Liberal capitalism takes the market as the model for all of society. Having enough wealth is an alien concept in a *market society*, where the market dominates, producing a ruthlessly fierce competition. The market society is Weber's iron cage.

The point of Weber's overall thesis is not that Luther or Calvin themselves argued for what Weber famously calls the "Protestant work ethic," but that certain distorted theological strands came to dominate the public imagination. Work and economics, practices that were regarded (at least in the West) as part of a wider Christian framework, migrated into their own sphere. This is not to deny, of course, that greed, theft, and many other economic abuses have plagued Christian living in its various manifestations. But it is to say that theological convictions were at least in place that made the unchecked pursuit of wealth problematic. Perhaps best known of these convictions was the idea that one should not make money with money, a conviction almost inconceivable to us today. Yet up through the Middle Ages (including Martin Luther), charging interest on loans (usury) was deemed unjust, a sign that one served mammon rather than God. As Weber indicates, however, *sola fide*, taken in a certain direction,

65. Ibid., 132.

can easily divorce faith from other spheres of life. Ginhoven states, for example, that "rather than emptying action of value, [*sola fide*] had the effect, as many have argued, of endowing action with a certain *autonomy*, in ways that made it possible to think not only of something like work for its own sake, but also of an orientation of productive energies towards the expansion and perpetuation of the process of production . . ."[66] Whatever the no doubt complex history of interpretation of *sola fide*, modern references to "faith and economics" typically rely upon the conviction that faith is in a separate, more private sphere and must be brought in the already public domain of economics.

Philip Goodchild describes this economic shift that occurred in modernity as "the reorganization of society according to the ideal of the self-regulating market. Indeed, the *separation* of the economic sphere of life from the political and religious spheres is what the notion of a self-regulating market means."[67] Just as the apparent independent order of nature is the basis for a science separate from faith (and so also, Goodchild notes, the theoretical condition of atheism), "the independent sphere of the market is the practical condition for atheism."[68] So understood, the market, like nature, has its own laws, which the science of economics analyzes and understands. On this view, Christian faith resides in a different sphere, the private sphere of the subject, not the outer real world sphere of economic and scientific analysis.

Given its own sphere, work often becomes utilitarian: the ends of making money justify the means of working, or the ends of making a profit justify the means by which that profit is made. Work becomes the means to earning one's "worth" or "net value." The "chosen," so to speak, are the wealthy, the successful, and the ones who have been able to make the system work for them.

This is ironic because this secularized "Protestant work ethic" is the opposite of Martin Luther's original emphasis. As is well known, Luther stated that worth cannot be earned but is always a gift *already* given in Christ through the Holy Spirit.[69] Human worth is discovered through

66. Ginhoven, "Theurgic Image," 19.

67. Goodchild, *Theology of Money*, xiii; my emphasis.

68. Ibid.

69. One of Luther's key theological concerns is that humans can not earn righteousness before God. In his famous treatise *The Freedom of a Christian*, Luther emphasizes that right relation with God is always a gift to be received. The Christian does not have to be forever anxious about whether he or she is loved by God. Christ mediates this love already through his death and resurrection, the forgiveness of sins,

salvation and as such always flows from the gift of communion with the Triune God. Luther thus describes faith as "passive" in the sense that it is the receptive organ of God's free and unmerited grace.

While Luther did maintain a strong place for "works"—as the spontaneous overflow of faith in Christ and as necessary habits for restraining the former self—he disallowed any "soteriological merit" to work because of his emphasis that salvation cannot be earned, an emphasis that rightly describes the heart of the gospel.[70] This separation between salvation and work, however, can lead to potential difficulties when it comes to thinking about how Christians are to sustain a life together economically, politically, and so forth. It is absolutely crucial to affirm that salvation is the gift of God in Christ. It is also crucial, however, to give a christological account of work and economics. Luther's emphasis on the "spontaneity" of good works is powerful to the extent that he emphasizes how what we do flows from our being in Christ. While an important theological emphasis, is "spontaneity" adequate enough to give a sustained account of human work and economics as these are a part of Christian living? Luther also describes "works" as necessary habits or disciplines that shape us such that we do not fall into the desires of the flesh. While Luther's emphasis on the spontaneity of works and training the "flesh" is important, it will be helpful for my purposes to consider ways we might add to Luther so as to allow for a more robust theological account of work and economics.[71]

Salvation given in Christ is, of course, once and for all; humans do not merit or earn this gift in any way, or else it would not be a Divine gift. At the same time, faith in necessarily bound up with both hope and love. True faith—faith that receives God's gift of salvation through Christ—will in fact be a faith made operative in love. Moreover, such love is only

---

the restoration of communion, and the ongoing gift of new life given in and through the Body of Christ. Luther depicts the role of works in two complementary ways. First, he maintains that *good* works flow from our reception of Christ. Like a cup filled with water, one who receives Christ will naturally, or "spontaneously," do good works. Good fruit will naturally grow when the roots are well planted. Luther's second use of "good works" refer to habits that assist us in growing in Christ. The old self has not yet died; the new self is not yet fully alive in Christ. Habits such as prayer, Eucharist, proper control of the body, confession, and so forth are good works in that they form us to receive Christ more fully. Luther emphasized, however, that these works do not earn God's favor since that favor is already present as gift.

70. On the topic of faith, salvation, and justification in Lutheran-Catholic theology today, see the *Joint Declaration on the Doctrine of Justification*.

71. Most recently, D. Stephen Long has addressed theology and economics in depth in his fine book, *Divine Economy*.

possible when practiced in light of the reality of resurrection hope. But am I not repeating what Luther said, at least in his famous treatise *The Freedom of the Christian*: namely, that faith comes before love and gives spontaneous birth to love? Whether or not Luther intended it, a kind of autonomy tends to hover around his understanding of faith. If it is true that faith, hope, and love are inseparable, as I believe to be the case, then it is a mistake to single out one of the three theological virtues. To the extent that faith is separated from hope and love, then to that same extent it becomes easier to separate faith from economics and other spheres of life. Karl Barth rightly describes the unity of these theological virtues: "This 'we with God' enclosed in the 'God with us' is Christian faith, Christian love, and Christian hope. These are the magnifying of the grace of God which still remain to us—and remain to us as something specifically human, as the greatest thing of all, as action in the truest sense of the word.[72] Barth emphasizes that Christian faith, hope, and love are dependent upon the faith, hope, and love of Christ, all of which name the fact that God in Christ is with us. For our part, this "God with us" is the fulfillment of human being "by participation in the divine being which comes to him by the grace of God."[73]

It is in light of the unity of faith, hope, and love of Christ, and our participation in it, that we can begin to imagine work and economics as more than either spontaneity or duty, much less as competition over scarce goods. Economics is always first an *invitation*. Christian practices of economics and work are invitations to participate in God's new creation made possible through Christ. We alone do not create wealth; rather, mutual reception of the Spirit and participation in the life of the Spirit generate wealth. From this perspective, God invites us into economic practices that embody love and friendship. Such friendships make possible faithful economic practices. If we do not have resurrection hope, then such faith and love unravel, making it difficult to see God's alternative economy of abundance.

This might sound ideal, and thus ultimately irrelevant, to our daily lives, deeply formed as we are by the "real" world of the market economy. As Goodchild succinctly describes this ideal/real contrast, "Where God promises eternity, money promises the world. Where God offers a delayed reward, money offers a reward in advance. Where God offers himself as grace, money offers itself as a loan. Where God offers spiritual benefits,

72. Barth, *Church Dogmatics*, IV/1:15.
73. Goodchild, *Theology of Money*, 18.

money offers tangible benefits . . ."[74] I do not wish to deny how deeply embedded this picture is in our imaginations. One of the myths, surely, of a market society is that this way of being economically is the only economics that will enable us to flourish. Nor do I wish to deny all the ways in which work seems uninviting. Work can be a means simply to make ends meet. Work can become sheer drudgery. Work can be demeaning. We can be helplessly without work, joining the long lines of the unemployed.

This is a bleak, if not despairing, portrait of our contemporary economic situation. If we are so deeply mired in a market society, can we even begin to extricate ourselves from this economic web of competition and profit? Most of us have benefited from this kind of market economy, and we often do not want to look too closely "behind the scenes," i.e., at the workers in Indonesia laboring long hours for practically nothing or the immigrants working in slaughterhouses in unsafe conditions. If we do look, we often feel helpless to do much about it.

Yet, one of the economic gifts that God gives is that we do not have to live at the mercy of systems of power that demean and diminish human life. We can accept, even if in small ways, the Divine invitation—always open—to practice a different economics, one that Teresa both describes and shares. To do this, we need to look more fully at how to desire what God desires.

DIVINE MARRIAGE: DESIRING WHAT GOD DESIRES

If scriptural figures are divinely given ecclesial patterns, then marriage continues to be a scriptural figure forming the life of the church today. The question is not *whether* but *how* marriage shapes the life of the church. As Gerhard Lohfink emphasizes, the story of Israel is our story. What is narrated in the stories of the wilderness, for example, is the "tale of our own resistance to the history of God's guidance; concretely it is the story of our resistance to exodus from the Egypt of our *desires* and projections and to entry into the land God has promised us."[75] Perhaps more than any other scriptural figure, marriage highlights the centrality of desire for life with God. As Teresa emphasizes so well, life with God is not about the eradication of desire but allowing the Spirit to inflame the right kinds of desires.

Paul Griffiths argues that desires "can be directed to anything at all. But desire never seeks anything at all, but rather always something

74. Ibid., 11.

75. Lohfink, *Does God Need the Church?*, 96; my emphasis.

in particular."[76] His point is that humans are born with an excess of desire; in our fallen world, however, that excess is not directed at God, but aims in many directions. The superfluity of desire means also that desire, apart from resting in God, is never satisfied.[77] Griffiths argues that desire is not "natural" in the sense that we do not naturally desire God. Griffiths cites Shakespeare as illustrative of his point: "This is the monstrosity in love, lady," Troilus tells Cressida, "that the will is infinite and the execution confined, that the desire is boundless and the act a slave to limit." If desire is both unlimited yet always particular, then, as Griffiths notes, this means that desires are always being catechized, disciplined, and enclosed. Children, for example, are disciplined in some tastes (fried chicken) rather than others (squid). More seriously, desires are configured "for political action or for the deployment of violence." Our desires are thus open to "formation in any possible direction." Thus, Griffiths states, "every formed and configured desire is a local gift, which may participate in or remove itself from God's fundamental and universal gift."[78]

For my purposes, Griffith's analysis is important for two reasons. First, like Teresa, he shows that Christianity is not about the suppression of desire. If that were true, then spousal imagery and the figure of marriage would make little sense of Christian life. Secondly, Griffiths relates bodily formation to desire. While certainly the transformation of desire is ultimately the result of the grace of God, this grace comes through catechesis, and catechesis involves bodily formation and discipline. Various habits and rituals that form our bodies can often be very subtle. The formation of desire often takes place below the radar, in ways that we are not explicitly aware.[79] Yet desires, in fact, are *always* being disciplined and enclosed in one direction to the exclusion of others.

Such an emphasis can shed new light on the enclosed Carmelite monasteries that Teresa founded and formed. A typical modern response

76. Griffiths, "Deranged Desire."

77. Augustine shares this conviction since he believes that our loves must be rightly ordered. For Augustine, we love others not simply for their own sake but in relation to God. To love someone for their own sake, in Augustine's schema, would be to worship the creature rather than the Creator.

78. Griffiths, "Deranged Desire," 7.

79. This is true of both good and bad formation. The liturgy, for example, can "mark" us in ways that we might not realize until years after the fact. The Lord's Prayer, when one is a child, might seem like simply memorized words. Later, however, say in a tragic situation, it is there for the child-now-adult to pray when words might be difficult to find.

to this kind of life is, "Why enclose a community instead of being 'out in the world'?" Yet, is it not the case that all communities or groups are enclosed in some way or another? As Griffiths indicates, the desires of particular communities, groups, and even cultures are always disciplined, often unknowingly, by certain ideologies or practices. The deeper question for the church and particular congregations is to discern what kind of disciplines and enclosure best form them to be living witnesses to God.

Kyle Potter identifies one of our late modern desires as the desire to "make a difference." He notes:

> Suburbanites like to feel they are accomplishing great things by their efforts, and if not, they become restless. The ethos of a consumer society has taught people that the solution to a lack of results is to quit and try something else, rather than continuing what might be the right thing to do for a long time. We pursue significance rather than obedience to God and the tradition of the church because we have chosen to separate ourselves from suffering in favor of religious experience.[80]

The desire to make a difference, to be significant, and to see results is a desire catechized by a consumer society. This might seem odd since "making a difference" sounds like a good thing. The ideology of a market society (a society in which all areas of life are dominated by market forces, competition, and contract) trains people to place their self-defined and chosen needs at the center of their identity. While the "need" to make a difference might seem laudable, on closer inspection, it can easily conflict with learning to have one's own needs transformed by Christ. Christian catechesis aims not for making a difference, but for faithfulness and obedience. The delight of desire thus rests not in results but in life together in Christ. True desires aim not at what I as an individual can accomplish but how we can mutually submit ourselves to Christ and, as the body of Christ, to one another. The focus is thus not on results that an individual can control, but on the surprising ways that a mustard seed produces a mighty tree. The mustard seed parable is about human response to what God is already doing in the world (in ways often not seen) rather than predicable results through human effort.

Further, we can see how a market society trains desire by making a buyer feel significant through his or her particular purchase. The habit of expecting quick results, and knowing what these results are ahead of time, easily malforms desire. Scripture testifies that faithfulness to God need

---

80. Potter, "Encountering the Christian Colony," 52.

not, and in fact seldom does, conform to human expectations. Predictability can easily suffocate the surprising ways that God's kingdom manifests itself. By contrast, ecclesial formation trains participants to wait (Advent, Lent), to watch for Divine surprises (the resurrection), and to "feel significant" through becoming part of a communion in Christ who desires to heal the world.

MALFORMED DESIRES

Gerhard Lohfink states that Israel subjected its own history to revision by acknowledging that it was a history of resistance and rebellion against God, and so also opened up a will to repent. In Hosea, as we saw, Israel narrates herself as an unfaithful spouse, and God as Divine Lover. Israel could thus see her own idolatry and adultery. By contrast, Lohfink states that the church in the late twentieth century is dissolving "almost without resistance." "The rescue of the people of God from the old society and its travels through the wilderness to the land of promise are something in the dim and distant past, but no longer a present reality." There are, he writes, at least in Europe, "countless gods but no longer a history with the biblical God."[81]

Some might observe that the church in the United States is better off than the church in Europe, at least numerically. Yet, as has often been noted, the church that flourishes in the U.S. is often the church as consumer option, attracting customers through programs and packages. People are seldom surprised when members change churches and even denominations, often, as one might change jobs or school. Is this a kind of adultery in which the ecclesial consumer is looking for more satisfaction? If the new lover becomes boring or no longer pleasing, then should one feel obligated to remain? Certainly, there might be justified reasons for leaving a particular church or church tradition. It is not easy to remain in a place, when everything about our economy indicates that moving for financial gain, bigger and better programs, more opportunities, and so forth might be necessary. In light of our current situation, the figure of marriage—of faithfulness to a people and place—can seem more like a "ball and chain." Why stay in one place, one church, or one denomination when things look more promising elsewhere? Indeed, some churches are better than others, whether liturgically or financially or in terms of teaching, preaching, or service. Some embrace this ecclesial diversity as a good because it allows

81. Lohfink, *Does God Need the Church?*, 96.

people more choices and freedom to figure out the kind of church that best fits them.

Such division makes it difficult to know how to be faithful. Yet, the brokenness of the body of Christ, on scriptural and theological grounds, cannot be celebrated. The prayer of Jesus in John 17 links Christian unity to mission and witness in a particular way: "I in them and you in me, that they may become completely one, so that the world may know that you have sent me and have loved them even as you have loved me" (v. 23). Apart from the unity of the church in Christ, the world cannot fully know the love of God in Christ. Lohfink thus rightly states, "The condition of Christianity at the present time, is nothing like a colorful field in which wheat is growing and poppies and cornflowers are blooming; it is rather like a broken mirror that distorts the image of Christ."[82] Yet division has come to seem natural, a phenomenon as we have seen shaped in part by our dominant economics. As the authors of *In One Body Through the Cross: The Princeton Proposal for Christian Unity* state, division seems to be "the natural expression of a Christian marketplace with churches representing different options for a variety of spiritual tastes."[83] The authors rightly add, "Consumerist values and an ideology of diversity can anesthetize us to the *wound* of divison."[84] Division in the church is thus easily legitimated by a market ideology. Why not provide a variety of options and styles that meet the needs of different kinds of Christians? Even within a particular congregation, it has become commonplace to have different services that meet the needs of different generations, i.e., contemporary, traditional, blended services, and so forth. The result, of course, is that such a market approach to church maintains the very kinds of division that prevent the church from being an alternative to the world: divisions between old and young, divisions between Republicans and Democrats, divisions between races and so forth replicate the kinds of divisions that are in the world.

The argument in favor of a market-style evangelism is that more people will be brought into the church. This approach thus has to do with meeting people where they are, similar to the Apostle Paul, who says he seeks to be all things to all people for the sake of the Gospel: "To the Jews I became as a Jew, or order to win Jews. To those under the law I became as one under the law . . ." (1 Cor 9:20). Paul, however, is not supporting

82. Ibid., 298.

83. Braaten and Jenson, *One Body*, 43. The authors state, "But friendly division is still division."

84. Ibid., 43; my emphasis.

a strategy of dividing the church in order to reach others. Rather, he is describing a discipleship marked by service and submission for the sake of the gospel. To be made part of this story is to learn to live the unity that Christ freely gives. It is from this perspective that the Princeton Proposal states, "However loudly our rhetoric insists that Christian discipleship is not a matter of consumer choice, the point will be made effectively only when potential believers encounter all around them Christian communities united in shared disciplines of faithfulness to the apostolic word."[85]

To the extent that the church is divided in so many ways, then the figure of marriage registers a *negative* image; like Israel as portrayed in Hosea, the church has gone after many lovers, resulting in division and idolatry. It could easily appear that Christ does not have one bride but many. To the extent that the scriptural figure of God desiring a single people is denied or simply ignored, then human desire is malformed. Marriage thus figures the church by illuminating her sinfulness against unity in Christ.

Such a judgment is harsh. After all, the church continues to do many good things: baptize converts, gather for worship, serve the community and beyond, etc. These can certainly build up the body of Christ and witness to God's kingdom in the world. At this same time, however, "deranged desires" prevent the church from seeing the expansion of commercial logic into her very life.

MARRIAGE, UNITY, AND ECONOMIC DESIRES

In what ways, then, can the figure of marriage, when tended to in the life of the church, transform desire? How might bodies be retaught such that marriage and church are not relegated to consumer options that meet one's needs? Finally, how does Teresa's use of the figure of marriage in her life and that of the reformed Carmelites of her day provide any guidance?

I will begin to address these questions by returning to Griffiths' argument that desires are always being catechized. Human desires are limited because our desires are always trained in a particular direction. From this perspective, the idea that marriage inevitably inhibits freedom fails to see how all paths are limited. The key question, rather, is whether the particular enclosure of desire fosters the love of God and neighbor.

In this light, we can turn more fully to monastic enclosures. Teresa had come to see that the Convent of Incarnación (which she entered in 1535) often lacked spiritual vitality. Some of the wealthier nuns had

85. Ibid., 42.

personal servants, others spent long periods away from the community on visits, and many (including Teresa herself) spent long hours entertaining friends and guests in the parlor. Teresa came to advocate a way of life more closely eremitical, the kind "their holy forefathers on Mount Carmel had embraced."[86] She summed up her vision in a letter to her brother, Lorenzo, in 1561: "To found a monastery where there will be only fifteen nuns and no possibility for any increase in numbers. They will practice a very strict enclosure and thus never go out or be seen without veils covering their faces. Their lives will be founded on prayer and mortification."[87]

Some could interpret Teresa's reform as a turn away or withdrawal from the world. This understanding, however, fails to see how Teresa is rather discerning between different kinds of "enclosures." Living according to standards of honor (based on social status), wealth (accumulation of property), and attraction (external appearance, especially for women) were themselves an enclosure that, she rightly saw, drew her and her sisters away from life with God. On the other hand, a communal life sustained by the Word, the Eucharist, prayer, and good works provided an enclosure that fostered faith, hope, and love.

In this light, the monasteries that form Teresa—and which she in turn reforms—can be best understood as schools of charity. Teresa stands in the tradition of St. Benedict (sixth century) as well as St. Bernard of Clairvaux (twelfth century), both of whom described the monastery as a *schola caritatis*, a "school of charity." By this description, they understood that worship, contemplation of God, and service all work together in *schooling* one's desires away from the idolatrous, false loves of the world and toward the true love of God. "The term *caritatis*, or charity, not yet entirely co-opted by the market and state to signal a tax deduction, meant 'love of God' or 'love of the things God loves.'"[88] The aim for Teresa was to provide schooling into a way of life more open to receiving and practicing God's abundance. This involved a particular way of living in time, of relating to one's possessions, of dressing, of praying and so forth. This way of being and living enabled Teresa's communities to desire more fully what God desires.

---

86. Kavanaugh and Rodriguez, "Introduction," in Teresa, *Collected Works*, 3:23.

87. Ibid., 24. As Kavanaugh notes, the use of veils would have been a common custom for women, a practice inherited from three civilizations (Jewish, Greek, and Roman). While the veil fell into disuse in the West, it was still very current in sixteenth-century Spain, especially where the Moorish influence was strong (ibid., 27).

88. Gulker, "Schola Caritatis," 6.

We are now in a position to see how the scriptural figure of marriage is a way of naming and imagining an alternative economics grounded in charity. Marriage is learning to love the one (or ones) with whom you are in covenant. When well schooled, the love between husband and wife overflows into love for others: children, of course, but also love of the stranger. Likewise, as Teresa so vividly describes, learning to participate in divine marriage is not a solitary process between the self and God. To learn to be a faithful spouse involves, or rather requires, being in community and communion with the body of Christ above any other bodies or gatherings. This body generates a particular kind of economics that reflects and embodies the faith, hope, and love of Christ.

Catholic theologian David Schindler describes the particularity of this economics in a recent interview. When asked whether capitalism was not a healthy alternative to Marxism, Schindler responds: "We have to order our economy within this call to love. The fact that Marxism-Leninism has been eliminated does not mean that the only alternative is a capitalism to which the Church must provide a moral correction. The Church proposes something *different* from both—namely, communio."[89] By "communio," Schindler is referring to participation in the Trinitarian communion of love within God through Jesus Christ. This is not an abstract concept but ushers in concrete ways of living, "a culture of being rather than having." He continues,

> In other words, the call to sanctity should form what we do in our economy. So, with a notion like self-interest: Of course we can't suppress that impulse forcibly; if we try, we end up in totalitarianism. But that doesn't mean we should bless it as a virtue of necessity. The call to sanctity requires a transformation of self-interest and its replacement, insofar as possible, with love.[90]

Schindler is describing what could be called an "economics of love," one that rests primarily in a way of being marked by communion, love, and holiness. An economics of love creates bonds of unity as a way of living in the love of Christ.

Some might see this kind of economics as impossible in our world today. The global economy is too far-reaching, too determinative of our lives. We cannot control the fact, for example, that exploited Chinese or Indonesian workers make the shirt that we buy. Similarly, though on a different scale, Teresa could not control in her day how wealth determined

89. Schindler, "'Threads' interviews David Schindler."
90. Ibid.

status and prestige. Yet, from a Christian perspective, our lives as Christ's body are never so overly determined that we have no freedom. This is not freedom of consumer choice (in a culture of having). Schindler rightly describes this as false freedom: "we have the illusion that we're free because no one tells us what to do."[91] An economics of love begins, by contrast, with the acknowledgement that we do not choose God; he chooses us. This initiative from the Divine Spouse is the source of true freedom because we are freed to live lives of faith, hope, and love. An economics of being in communion, of love, frees our imaginations as it did Teresa's. Contemporary reforms will not take the exact shape that Teresa's did, but they will follow similar providential patterns.

However, where are our bodies habituated into this economics of communion, this economics of love? Where are we trained to live out of the acknowledgment that God chooses us, and that our freedom lies precisely in receiving what God desires to give? Where are our desires, economic and otherwise, formed so that they flow ultimately in response to God's desires for us?

One could say "going to church," and certainly allowing God to gather us at particular times and places is crucial. But, as suggested earlier, it is easy in our context to go to church in a way that is similar to going to a mall or to a restaurant. That is, one goes for the experience or for the "feeling." Yet this understanding reinforces "the religious domain in the sphere of worldly autonomy, a religious domain that is de-institutionalized, subjective and focused on the emotions."[92]

We can begin to shift bodily, however, when we substitute "going to church" with "being the church." Granted, this is a small linguistic change, but nonetheless one that can open a wide door. The figure of divine marriage, after all, does not describe a spouse (the church) that chooses certain times to be married (to Christ). Rather, it describes the reality of already being pursued and chosen by Christ. The church is not to flee or go after other gods, but to rest and receive its true status as the bride of Christ. This is first of all a way of being, which can usher in, as Schindler says, a culture of being rather than one of having (whether one seeks to have experiences, wealth, or other possessions).

91. Ibid.

92. Lipovetsky, *Hypermodern Times*, 64. Lipovetsky adds, "We need to think of hyperconsumerism as an emotional rejuvenating experience, one that can start all over again an indefinite number of times" (52). This habit becomes possible, according to Lipovetsky, because time has shrunk.

But the question still remains: how does and can the church practice a way of being in unity with Christ? A contemporary example of this economics of ecclesial being can be found in the life of Englewood Church in Indianapolis, Indiana. A church that suffered "urbanization," the loss of members, and a struggle to survive financial freefall, Englewood was able to survive by a slow and at times painful reformation of desires. They gathered every Sunday evening, allowing three scriptural convictions to guide their path to renewal and dialogue: 1) the church must pursue one mindedness; 2) assembly is for the purpose of edification; and 3) godly discernment must take place in assembly. The eventual result was that Englewood became a vibrant congregation and presence in their neighborhood.[93] Michael Bowling, Englewood's pastor, states that they seek to practice an "economics of love." This means that their economic focus is not on getting rich people to give money but on how you envision the kingdom of God in the concrete place where you *are* (thus the emphasis on being). The practice of being together in assembly around Scripture and seeking one-mindedness no doubt shaped the members to seek the desires of the whole body. It also shifted economic practices from the dominant ones of getting and having to envisioning God's kingdom in their midst, and pursuing how they could extend that in their neighborhood. While the figure of divine marriage is not explicitly used (to my knowledge), the community's "economics of love" is grounded in the love of a Divine Spouse who pursues and loves us in all the broken places of our lives, seeking to heal us so that we may more faithfully be Christ for the world.

THE FIGURE OF DIVINE MARRIAGE: TRAINING IN UNITY

But this "economics of love" can still seem abstracted from the various ecclesial contexts in which we exist. God's abundant love in Christ might be a belief we easily accept, but it can seem far removed from buying groceries, paying bills, caring for our children, and so forth. We often struggle along in our families and personal lives, seeking, understandably, for security for ourselves as well as the future of our children.

93. Even a partial list of the community projects supported by Englewood is remarkable: a lawn care business, bookkeeping and PC repair services, and a bookstore with online ordering capability. All of these benefit their neighbors in the streets around the church. Their largest area of outreach has been in the housing sector, where they have helped over twenty-five householders become homeowners in their neighborhood. See their website at http://www.englewoodcc.com for more of their story.

Where does this leave us? Christians are called to *be* a people of hope. In Revelation 21, the renewal of all creation is associated with a wedding feast, specifically with a bride: "Then I saw a new heaven and a new earth; for the first heaven and the first earth had passed away, and the sea was no more. And I saw the holy city, the new Jerusalem, coming down out of heaven from God, prepared as a bride adorned for her husband. And I heard a loud voice from the throne say, 'See, the home of God is among mortals...'" (vv. 1–3). Revelation portrays an image of unimaginable abundance: a new creation, a new earth, and a fantastic city (New Jerusalem) adorned as a bride, the dwelling of God, where death, mourning, and pain will be no more. This eschatological city does not scatter humanity (as in Gen 11:1–9, when humans attempted to build a tower to the heavens) but gathers it. The "bride" signals the *unity* and gathering in of the church, a unity that testifies to God's extravagant abundance in new creation.

Yet such abundance is not only a description of heaven; it is describing who God is now, already in our time. God provides manna for the Israelites. Christ turns water into wine. The wildest excess of God's provision is the Father sending the Son and pouring forth the Spirit. The abundance of God is both promise and reality. The fundamental contrast, therefore, is not the real versus ideal, but the eschatological now and not-yet.

Such an eschatological understanding of God's abundance involves the realization that the joy of the reign of God comes with persecution and suffering.[94] An "economics of love" involves a willingness to suffer. A key emphasis in Teresa's own understanding of Christ our Spouse is that a willingness to suffer is a way to embody and extend God's love.

Such a conviction relates to the unity of the church since the thirst for oneness involves the willingness to suffer the brokenness between brothers and sisters in Christ. This involves both a willingness to repent and to share the burdens of division. We must, as Ephraim Radner states, be willing to remain wherever we are in the brokenness of God's church "[b]ecause it is the most evangelical thing to do, witnessing not to weakness, not to compromise, not to disingenuity, but witnessing to the reality of the power of the cross of Jesus Christ in history. . . . Truth itself is more clearly magnified and more divinely potent through its suffering contradiction within a wayward people than otherwise...."[95] Radner's theological

94. Lohfink cites Mark 10:30, where Jesus says that there is no one who left family or fields for my sake who will not receive "a hundredfold now in this age—houses, brothers and sisters, mothers and children, and fields with persecutions—and in the age to come eternal life" (quoted in *Does God Need the Church?*, 150).

95. Radner, *Hope*, 210–11.

rationale for being in a place of ecclesial brokenness involves seeing the church now as a figure of Israel (especially in its waywardness). Teresa, too, emphasizes that our waywardness is ultimately no obstacle to Christ's love. To see this truth in a posture of repentance is to witness to the cross of Christ, and ultimately to the abundance of God's love for the world.

4

On Pilgrimage

A Unity both Visible and Hidden

Make me know your ways, O Lord; teach me your paths . . . All the paths of the Lord are steadfast love and faithfulness, for those who keep his covenant and his decrees. (Ps 25:4, 10)

IN THE PREVIOUS CHAPTERS, I have described how Teresa's use of the scriptural figures of dwellings and marriage helps us reimagine time and abundance, and in so doing provides us with a different way of seeing both politics and economics. In this chapter, I turn to Teresa's reliance upon *pilgrimage* as a way to reimagine ecclesial space. I use the term "pilgrimage" because Teresa charts a journey to a holy place, even though she is well aware that her sisters will unlikely be able to travel to any holy site, as so many Christians had done in the preceding centuries. Yet one does not have to travel to be on pilgrimage. Gregory the Great captures a more ancient usage when he observes, "pilgrimage is our present life."[1] From this perspective, we can think of life itself as pilgrimage. Such a use relies upon the grand sweep of scriptural tradition: Abraham responding to a calling from God, the Israelites wandering in the wilderness for forty days and nights, the Hebrew people's exile and return from Babylon. For those grafted onto this tradition, pilgrims and pilgrimages "do not belong simply to the external forms of Christian piety, but are signs of an important characteristic of the *Church*, signs of the messianic people of God,

---

1. Morris, "Introduction," 2.

who draw near to their Lord."[2] So understood, pilgrimage pertains to the whole church, even at it wanders in our present wilderness, thirsting for living water, and hungering for the bread of life.

If pilgrimage does not necessarily involve moving across geographical space (though it may, of course), then it can invite us to think differently about space. We can find analogies for different conceptions of space in the scientific world. Einstein, for example, has shown more fully how time and space are intimately intertwined. According to physicist Alan Lightman, Einstein enables us to understand why "the angles of a triangle no longer add up to 180 degrees, and clocks tick more slowly the closer they are to a gravitational mass like the sun."[3] For non-scientists, such apparent bending of "normal" space-time is counterintuitive. How can clocks actually slow down? Yet, in our everyday lives a kind of space-time bending can occur quite often. The clock ticks more slowly as we sit anxiously at the fourth stoplight, late for an important meeting. Someone says, "I need some space; leave me alone," meaning not primarily geographical space but psychological or emotional space. Such examples illustrate that space is more than "a world of moving bodies which have a totally 'objective' existence apart from any human observer."[4] In what follows, I consider how Teresa's use of pilgrimage can transform space into a renewed ecclesial place at once visible and hidden.

ON PILGRIMAGE IN A FOREIGN LAND

In its original Latin, *peregrinus* can mean "traveler, stranger, alien, or immigrant."[5] It has also been associated with "wanderer." Teresa uses this sense of wandering when she writes, "Since God has given [the soul] such

2. Engender, cited in ibid., 2; my emphasis.

3. Lightman, "Relativity and the Cosmos." Lightman describes this phenomenon more fully: "If gravity is equivalent to acceleration [he gives the example of how an elevator, when pushing a person upward, feels like gravity pulling one to the floor], and if motion affects measurements of time and space (as shown in special relativity), then it follows that gravity does so as well."

4. Newbigin, *Other Side*, 10. Newbigin is describing a typical Enlightenment view of the "real world." The examples that I give might seem more psychological, unlike the examples from Einstein, which are grounded in the physical world. Yet the distinction between psychological and physical relies on a split between mind (psyche) and body (physical), often accepting the physical as real space in a way that the psychological is not.

5. Morris, "Introduction," 1.

dignity, it must be allowed to roam through these mansions—through those above, those below and those on either side."[6] Such wandering as pilgrims rests upon a freedom in the Spirit. We may not know the exact shape of our destination, but God does, and Teresa assures her readers many times over that God knows what they need to be faithful. Teresa herself roamed the Spanish countryside, often in the face of incredible odds, in her efforts to establish Carmelite convents. She had no way of knowing if these convents would survive or flourish. On numerous occasions she was met with hostility. The end of Teresa's pilgrimage was not in full view to her. She had no way of seeing, for example, that she would become a doctor of the church or that her monasteries would continue to flourish over four hundred years into the future. In this sense, pilgrimage can be hidden, because we do not have eyes fully to see how God will bring our lives and those of others to fruition.

As Teresa discusses, there are risks to being on pilgrimage. Pilgrims can wander in the wrong direction; they can become distracted, bored, overly cautious, fearful, hopeless, and so forth.[7] The real danger, however, is not that one will take a wrong turn and meet hardship. One could argue that taking a wrong turn is part of the risk of being on pilgrimage and, further, that one can learn about holiness by going in the wrong direction. Even apparent failure can lead a person or a people toward God. The real hazard is that pilgrims will *remain* stuck in a place, thus ceasing to be on pilgrimage.

In many ways, this is the position of the church, at least the Western church, in late modernity. It has accepted dwelling in distorted space— space made possible in part by disunity in the church. Christopher Dawson relates secular space and Christian disunity as follows:

> The secularization of Western Christendom, for example, involved first the *loss of Christian unity*, which was itself due not to secularism but to the violence of religious passion and conflict of rival doctrines. Secondly, it involved the abdication by Christians of their responsibilities with regard to certain fields of social activity, so that we may say that nineteenth-century England was still a Christian society, but a Christian society that had diverted its energies to the pursuit of wealth. And finally it

6. Teresa, *Interior Castle*, 13.

7. Teresa describes ways in which pilgrims can lack courage. They are "glancing around and saying, 'Are people looking at me or not?' 'If I take a certain path shall I come to harm?' . . . 'Will people think better of me if I refrain from following the crowd?'" (*Interior Castle*, 15).

involved a loss of belief, which was to a certain extent involuntary and inevitable, since the stability of faith had already been undermined by the two processes which I have mentioned.[8]

According to Dawson, the loss of Christian unity contributed to a secularization by narrowing Christianity to a sphere of life. This narrowing has led, eventually, to "involuntary" unbelief. One might argue that such secularization was good to the extent that, as Dawson himself implies, the violence of religious passions and rival doctrines were not allowed to undermine or disturb the unity of the public sphere. Yet, as we will see more fully, this privatization of religious conflict rendered invisible the Christian pilgrimage toward unity.

William Cavanaugh supplements Dawson's observations by arguing that the creation of "religion" correlates with the rise of the nation-state.[9] The "wars of religion," he argues, were not simply about theological doctrine. If this were entirely the case, Cavanaugh points out, Catholics would not have fought against Catholics, or Protestants against Protestants. These so-called religious wars display instead how Christian loyalty to particular nations or princes can supersede loyalty to the body of Christ.[10] In the name of the nation, Christians come to accept division as necessary and, even more, the necessity of fighting other Christians in the name of national ideology. It is from this perspective that Talal Asad states, "Scholars are now more aware that religious toleration was a political means to the formation of the strong state power that emerged from the sectarian wars of the sixteenth and seventeenth centuries rather than the benign intention to defend pluralism."[11] Religious toleration became a tool to shore up

8. Dawson, *Christianity and European Culture*, 8–9; my emphasis. Dawson also names other complex factors that have led to new understandings of space: science, Cartesian philosophy, Galileo's heliocentric discovery, and so forth.

9. Cavanaugh challenges the common claim that the enlightened state came into being in order to stop the wars of religion. On this view, the state is thought necessary to put on end to religious conflict and fanaticism; it prevented Catholics and Protestants from killing each other over doctrinal loyalties. Cavanaugh describes this standard story of the nation-state as a "soteriological story" because it is told in such a way that it makes the state *necessary* to save us from religious conflict and violence. As a result, religion becomes a "set of beliefs . . . [as arising more or less out of] personal conviction and which can exist separately from one's public loyalty to the state" (Cavanaugh, *Theopolitical Imagination*, quote on 31, see 31–42). See, more recently, Cavanaugh, *Myth of Religious Violence*.

10. Cavanaugh argues that these wars are better described as the birth pangs of the modern nation in *Theopolitical Imagination*, 22.

11. Cited in Kenneson, *Beyond Sectarianism*, 54–55; my emphasis.

the unity of the nation-state, which redefined religion as belief or personal sentiment. The problem is not that religious violence was shunned (as it should have been), but that Christians violently participated in the breaking of Christ's body in order to shore up the unity and protection provided by the state. This pattern continues. As Lesslie Newbigin puts it, "In the twentieth century we have become accustomed to the fact that—in the name of the nation—Catholics will fight Catholics, Protestant will fight Protestants, and Marxists will fight Marxists."[12]

J. Kameron Carter contributes another dimension to this analysis. He argues that the modern nation-state was made possible by a gnostic—and thus supersessionist—telling of the Christian story. Gnosticism relies upon a separation between the spiritual (the realm of religion) and the material (the realm of the body and the state). Carter argues that modernity severed Christ from his Jewish identity by inventing a purely rational and autonomous individual. Carter calls this the embodiment of "whiteness," a term that he uses not simply to refer to skin pigmentation but to a complete sociopolitical way of being. Like Cavanaugh, Carter argues that the disinterested nation-state becomes the necessary corollary to the autonomous, disinterested individual. Carter adds, however, that "religion conceived of in terms of beliefs . . . gets ordered according to a hierarchy of rationality that coincides with a hierarchy within the human species itself. This hierarchy within the species is the hierarchy of races."[13] Carter thus ties the creation of rational political space to race, and even more to a hierarchy of races.

Dawson, Cavanaugh, and Carter all point to a heretical ordering of space, one that creates such dichotomies as nation-state/religion, public/private or citizen/alien. The unity of the nation supplants the unity of the body of Christ. The church, at least in the West, is now on pilgrimage in this "foreign land." To the extent that it accepts these dichotomies and this disunity, the church, like Israel, has allowed itself to be taken captive by alien powers, only not yet to the point of weeping. In fact, many are quite content to live ecclesial lives that are "separate but equal." Some are indeed asking, "How can we sing the Lord's song in a foreign land?" (Ps 137: 4, ESV) But many of us have enjoyed the foreign land too much, enamored

12. Newbigin, *Other Side*, 15.

13. Carter, *Race*, 393–94. He adds: "The most rational or reasonable religions are those that habituate the rational races toward loyalty to the state as its Ecclesia or what ensures humans' natural redemption or salvation and safety in a dangerous world. The irrational religions are those that do not so habituate the irrational races into citizens of the state . . ."

by its wealth, power, and success. The seduction can be overwhelming, like the poppy field in *The Wizard of Oz*. Why can't we just stay, and even eventually fall asleep?

FOREIGN RITUALS OF SPONTANEITY AND CHOICE

The challenge of reimagining space can be daunting given our dominant late modern landscape. Shopping malls "reminiscent of cathedrals" populate our cities and towns. Shopping windows display "products as if they were sacred treasures for veneration."[14] The land itself is easily seen through the lens of development and profit rather than care and creation. Daily rituals are more likely to include Facebook, email, and TV rather than prayer, hymn, and Communion.

If the Cartesian moment is that moment when the self is imagined apart from the body, then it is also the moment when it is imagined apart from ritual. The Enlightenment, states William H. Poteat, has given us a modern suspicion of ritual and myth as "meaningless residues of a tradition that we wish to abandon. At the same time, however, the Enlightenment has intimidated us with its impeachment of myths, all the while preserving and fashioning myths of its own."[15] That is, the modern self rejects ritual and tradition all the while failing to see how she is *in fact* participating in certain rituals, not the least of which are those determined by a culture of market capitalism.

Lori Branch in *Rituals of Spontaneity* describes how, as the Cartesian *cogito* came to dominate the social imagination, rituals underwent a transformation. Branch uses the phrase "rituals of spontaneity" to describe a shift from outer ritual to inner sentiment. As Branch states, "the Reformation religious subject gradually became less a participant in communal, bodily ritual action, and more and more the Cartesian *cogito*, an individual, inward looking possessor of knowledge drawn from evidence and analysis."[16] Even though one participated less in certain ritual action,

14. Kettle, *Western Culture*, 145.

15. Poteat, *Philosophical Daybook*, 71. Hauerwas makes a similar point when he states, "[The project of modernity] is the attempt to produce a people who believe that they should have no story except the story that they choose when they had no story. That is what Americans mean by freedom. The institutions that constitute the disciplinary forms of that project are liberal democracy and capitalism" ("America's God").

16. Branch, *Rituals of Spontaneity*, 37. Branch's work focuses on England during the seventeenth and eighteenth centuries as a window into modernity, ritual, and spontaneity.

Branch argues that rituals in and of themselves did not cease. They instead came to rely on spontaneous emotion, and in fact emotions were taken as evidence of one's conversion. Rituals did not disappear, but were instead transformed, now geared to promote spontaneity.

Branch further shows how spontaneity became linked with novelty and market rationality. That is, the market seeks to create spontaneous emotion in order to sell its products. Seventeenth- and eighteenth-century literature that embraced "the new value for spontaneous emotional feelings resonate[s] with the languages of experimental discovery and with mercantile and emerging consumer discourses of being current and up-to-date."[17] So understood, the market place comes to generate its own rituals. Branch notes, "The structures of subjectivity and desire generated in the marketplace nonetheless organize rituals of daily life, through behaviors like money exchange that seem inevitable and desires that seem spontaneous."[18] Rituals of spontaneity and novelty both mimic and make possible those of the market.

One implication of Branch's analysis is that memory ceases to be carried in the ecclesial body and instead migrates to the individual subject. It can be liberating to shed old, archaic rituals in some instances. A sense that certain ecclesial rituals had become inauthentic and even dead no doubt influenced the rise of spontaneity. A growing number of Protestants became convinced that the liturgy, holy days, and most of the church calendar represented a betrayal of authentic Christianity.

To the extent that religious ritual space becomes marked by spontaneity and novelty, however, it becomes disconnected from the past and the future. Spontaneity after all is fleeting. The Spirit is here and then she is gone. From this perspective, continuity will appear to limit the Spirit's freedom. Scripture affirms, of course, that the Spirit is indeed free. "The wind blows where it chooses, and you hear the sound of it, but you do not know where it comes from or where it goes. So it is with everyone who is born of the Spirit" (John 3:8). Scripture also suggests that rituals can become dead, disconnected, or even contradictory to a faithful way of life. "I hate, I despise your feasts, and I take no delight in your solemn assemblies. Even though you offer me your burnt offerings and cereal offerings, I will not accept them, and the peace offerings of your fatted beasts I will not look upon" (Amos 5:21–22, RSV). Yet the way to abandon dead

17. Ibid., 4. The kind of formation that leads to the desire for spontaneity and novelty, whether in prayer or commerce, is not necessarily explicit.

18. Ibid., 6.

ritual, and to become more open to the Spirit, is not through spontaneity in and of itself. Rituals of spontaneity easily replace "chains of memory"[19] with rituals of forgetting. It is the exactly the loss of memory—of God's justice and mercy—that Amos is addressing. And Jesus is challenging Nicodemus to remember himself truthfully by being born of "water and the Spirit." Changing a particular ritual can be a way to strengthen the "chain of memory." The challenge, however, is learning to discern and practice those rituals that can reform a people to remember God faithfully, rituals that participate in the redemptive deeds of God for the sake of the world.

Branch's analysis addresses in part the question, "What story is determining the church's sense of place?" Stanley Hauerwas adds to Branch's analysis by focusing not so much on spontaneity but on freedom and choice. He argues throughout his many writings that the story of the church has become deeply implicated in the story of America. "More Americans may go to church than their counterparts in Europe, but the churches to which they go do little to challenge the secular presumptions that form their lives or the lives of the churches to which they go. For the church is assumed to exist to reinforce the presumption that those who come to church have done so freely."[20] The freedom to choose one's church and identity seems natural to most Americans. We know we do not want the opposite, i.e., being forced to go to a church or be something that we do not want to be. Such volunteerism seems necessary in order to protect us from coercion.

The language of "choice," however, easily undermines the Christian pilgrimage, particularly when one understands that the pilgrimage is not about the individual self but about God's gathering of a people. True, Christ does not use violence or coercion when he calls the disciples. At this same time, the disciples did not choose their own calling. They were drawn through the power of the Holy Spirit to follow a Messiah that they did not even begin fully to understand. In a similar way, Israel was not a voluntary gathering but a people called into being by God. As Scott Bayer-Saye states,

> Israel did not arise out of a collection of autonomous indi-
> viduals who agreed that their self-interest would be furthered

19. Ibid. The term "chain of memory" comes from the title of a book by Hervieu-Léger.

20. Hauerwas, "America's God." Hauerwas adds, "The church's primary function, therefore, is to legitimate and sustain the presumption that America represents what all people would want to be if they had the benefit of American education and money."

by entering into a political alliance. Nor did the people qua people exist as a prior political entity which God then elected as God's own. Rather, Israel became a people by God's action and remains a people by God's continually welcoming new generations into the covenant of their ancestors. Chosenness calls forth existence.[21]

If it is true, as John Inge states, that places are storied spaces,[22] then we see in Israel the pilgrimage of a people gathered by God. They are free to the extent that they are faithful. Freedom is thus a byproduct as they allow themselves to be re-created through covenant with God and one another. When Israel is unfaithful, they end up worshipping false idols, with the result that they are no longer truly free.

Hauerwas points out that the inability to distinguish between the American story and the church's story makes the nation-state (America) seem necessary to ensure the health of the church. In fact, the state becomes more necessary than the church. He states, ". . . Americans continue to maintain a stubborn belief in a god, but the god they believe in turns out to be the American god. To know or worship that god does not require that a church exists because that god is known through the providential establishment of a free people. This is a presumption shared by the religious right as well as the religious left in America. Both assume that America is the church."[23] The religious right seeks to elect its candidates and to prop up that nation as Christian. The religious left, while also seeking to elect its candidates, typically embraces "diversity" and "pluralism," arguing that these are essentially Christian values.[24] Both sides in different ways remember the nation's story as the story of Christianity, a remembering that leads eventually to the invisibility of the body of Christ. This is because the reality of God calling and gathering a people beyond that of any nation fades from the ecclesial memory.

This is not to say that coercion becomes the alternative to voluntarism. We imagine it is the only alternative because we are so captivated by freedom of choice; either the will is free to do what it wants or else it is coerced. Yet to conceive of the will in this way is to imagine it floating in space, as does the Cartesian *cogito*, with no body that inevitably shapes the

21. Bader-Saye, *Church and Israel*, 35.

22. See Inge, *Christian Theology of Place*.

23. Hauerwas, "America's God."

24. I discuss the challenges of pluralism and diversity more fully in Newman, *Untamed Hospitality*. See especially chapter 5, "The Politics of Higher Education."

will. Such a view can easily blind us to the ways in which dominant forces such as the market are in fact forming our wills in ways we do not choose. To conceive of freedom and will in this Cartesian way is to remain in the storied space of late modernity.

The cure to these distortions begins with a willingness to leave modern space so conceived behind and go on pilgrimage to another place. In other words, it involves a willingness to see pilgrimage as a providential figure through which God forms a people. "Israel" itself names a people who knows its identity cannot be understood only in relation to itself, or even to its own family. Abram was called by God to leave Ur of Chaldees. Ruth was a Moabite whose love for her mother-in-law led her to journey and made her part of God's people. In his faltering attempts to be faithful, Jacob mysteriously wrestled God. "Israel" comes to name a people who, while on a covenant journey, strive with Yahweh, a God who has called them into being as a people.

Teresa, of course, lived before the full emergence of this modern spacial configuration. The nation-state had not yet come to be. Many of us today would regard the Spanish (Catholic) monarchy as inferior to our modern politics. Not only was this the time of the Inquisition (which Teresa herself was subject to), it was also, more deplorably, at we noted in chapter 2, the time of the expulsion or forced conversion of Jews to Christianity. Teresa's own grandfather, we can recall, was a *converso*. We see in Teresa's time, then, a Catholic Christianity that sees the Jew as alien and other, a threat to its own identity (at least in Spain). Muslims too were expelled during this time. In this space called the Spanish Empire, we see an effort to embody and contain pure blood, through maintaining its borders and extending its colonial powers. Our modern nation-states are an advance over this in that we do not have the Inquisition or the medieval code of honor. Moreover, all citizens, regardless of their religion, have certain rights.[25] At the same time, the modern nation-state is similar to the medieval empire in some ways. Both entities are there to protect the identity and way of life of a people. The nation-state, like the empire, is willing to use violence against the "other" or the "alien" in order to shore up its way of life. While the church is not as *visibly* implicated as it was in the Spanish Empire, the nation-state is also an entity that requires ultimate public allegiance in order ultimately to survive. As Newbigin puts it, the charge of blasphemy today is considered quaint and anachronistic, "but

25. Though, as debates surrounding immigration show, who gets counted as a citizen is contested in ways similar to the contesting of citizens in Teresa's day.

the charge of treason, of placing another loyalty above that to the nation state, is treated as the unforgivable crime."[26]

Teresa, as we have seen, resisted any notion of *limpia sangre* (pure blood), a political ideology deeply tied to the creation of the Spanish Empire. For her, the Christian pilgrimage is about being grafted into the life of God's people, which inevitably leads to "mixed" blood. For Teresa, then, what unites people is the fact that they are on the same pilgrimage with and toward Christ. The pilgrimage has Christ as its goal even as it enables pilgrims to see all others as those with whom Christ is present, thus opening for the world a fuller vista to God. Ultimately, Christian pilgrimage is about allowing God to heal the church so that it might be more fully Christ's body in its very flesh. Rightly understood, it involves reimagining space so that the shards of late modern space no longer define it.

REIMAGINING SPACE

Reimagining space is thus a process of relearning to see and to say. The reader is likely familiar with pictures where one can see, for example, either a young woman or an old woman. One of these images dominates such that the viewer is unable to see the other. In many ways, the way we see space is like this. Paul Cézanne once described his way of painting as follows: "I wait until the landscape thinks itself in me." What does he mean? Cézanne's description of how he paints differs from the usual expectations many of us have about how artists paint. He is not relying upon an objective gaze, nor is he simply painting his own point of view. Cézanne is rather waiting for the landscape to become part of him.

William H. Poteat observes that Cézanne, in fact, began an "assault upon Renaissance linear perspective by painting still lifes that simply didn't 'look right.'"[27] The space inside the frame was more "ambiguous, polycentric, resisting closure; the beholder's position in relation to that space became equivocal . . . there is no (perspectival) center from which the eye can achieve a (perspectivally) visual closure on the whole."[28] Cézanne thus relocates the modern observer. Poteat further notes that as one observes the painting, "any moment may yield a fluent organizing gestalt . . . the center now becomes the tonic, ductile mindbody of the viewer

---

26. Newbigin, *Other Side*, 15.

27. Poteat, *Recovering the Ground*, xv.

28. Ibid.

himself."[29] Cézanne is reimagining ways to occupy space. His paintings invite the viewer to inhabit a world without a central, "God's-eye" perspective, but rather to dwell in spaces as these relate to other objects, and thus potentially to inhabit many spaces.

In a similar way, Teresa's description of the diamond castle reconfigures space. The seven mansions that Teresa describes each contain hundreds of rooms that overlap. To revisit a passage cited earlier: "You must not imagine these mansions as arranged in a row, one behind another ... Since God has given [the soul] such dignity, it must be allowed to roam through these mansions—through those above, those below and those on either side."[30] The artist Temple Lee Parker, in his painting *Interior Castle (Revisited)*, depicts the many rooms as transparent cubes, capturing Teresa's description of the castle as crystal. The cubes overlap such that one can (counterintuitively) be in many rooms at one time. For example, one can simultaneously be in the first mansions (particularly the rooms of humility and self-knowledge) and the seventh mansions (united with Christ). Parker depicts Christ at the center by leaving space in the shape of a cross. No matter where the pilgrim dwells, he or she can see the cross even if it is not readily apparent how to get there.[31]

Both Cézanne and Teresa, different as they are in both time and medium used, highlight the fact that all spaces are storied. The story that has dominated our modern conception of space is that of a static eye looking upon objects.[32] A looking eye in *static time* gives rise to the idea that space is constitutive of inert objects. The Cartesian God's-eye view, while criticized many times over, nonetheless continues to form the late modern imagination, not least of in the assumption that objectively measured space is more real than other kinds of space. As Neil Smith puts it, "In the advanced capitalist world today we all conceive of space as emptiness, as a universal receptacle in which objects exist and events occur, as a frame of reference, a coordinate system (along with time) within which all reality exists."[33]

29. Ibid.

30. Teresa, *Interior Castle*, 13.

31. Parker, "Temple's TangleWave Art."

32. Poteat, *Recovering the Ground*, 1. Poteat describes this space as a "theater of solitude": the "dominant epistemological paradigm of our philosophic tradition," that reduces the lively reality of our seeing and coming to know to "an abstraction wherein there can be clarity and distinctness for an inert eye gazing upon an immobile object in the stasis of a time that is an 'eternity.'"

33. Smith, *Uneven Development*, 95.

The beauty of a Cézanne painting is that it can challenge domesticated assumptions about what it means to "fit" spatially into the world. The viewer cannot simply look on in a rather detached sense at objectively measured objects. Rather she feels herself disoriented by the lack of expected patterns. The angle of the table and the location of the fruit are not as they should be. A different "story" is configuring Cézanne's visual, spatial world, a story that fractures standard forms.[34] When Cézanne states, "I wait until the landscape thinks itself in me," he is not just looking at the so-called real world and trying to copy it. Rather, he is seeing a different world.

In a similar sense, Teresa too is seeing a different world, one in which Christ already occupies space and transforms it. It is tempting to accept the way things are as the way they are supposed to be, whether we are thinking about the location of religion in a sphere or about the many divisions that continue to wound the body of Christ. These kinds of spatial configurations easily come to seem normal. Yet, to go on the kind of pilgrimage that Teresa describes is to discover in the process new spatial configurations. In Christ "there is no east or west, in Him no south or north." This grand view of Divine space relies upon the conviction that Christ already occupies our space while also transforming it. In other words, to describe Christ as the goal of pilgrimage does not negate the fact that Christ is *already* fully present in the world: he is the Alpha and Omega of all creation, the One through whom God created the world (John 1:3) and toward whom all of creation finds its fulfillment (Rev 22:13). Irenaeus of Lyons states that the Word of God, our Lord Jesus Christ, "did, through His transcendent love, become what we are, that He might bring us to be even what He is Himself."[35] To live in this particular kind of space is to inhabit an entirely different world than the one determined by a conception of space as emptiness.

To be on such a grand pilgrimage, then, involves allowing a different story to "think itself" in us. As Robert Jenson writes, "Not only is Scripture within the church, but we, the church, are within Scripture—that is, our common life is located *inside* the story Scripture tells."[36] We do not first

34. What is the story informing Cézanne's paintings? Cézanne is typically identified with the beginning of cubism, a mode of art that involves at one level a fracturing of form. But the fracturing is not simply negative or deconstructive. Its purpose is to see something not previously available by means of the standard form. As Picasso famously puts it, "Art is a lie that makes us realize the truth."

35. Irenaeus, *Against Heresies*, preface in book 5.

36. Jenson, "Scripture's Authority," 30. In a similar sense, poetry is not another

have to understand Scripture in light of modern science, a modern world-
view, and so forth. Rather, as Jenson states, we are to work the other way
around, "to salvage from other bodies of convictions what can be made
coherent with Scripture."[37] The categories of modernity (scientific, chronological, linear historical) need not, in the final analysis, define the space
in which we dwell. As we will see more fully, Teresa describes a pilgrimage
into occupied space, occupied by Christ who moves us through the Spirit
to places heretofore unimagined.

TERESA'S PLACE VERSUS MODERN SPACE

Thus far, I have been describing prominent features of modern space:
the relocation of religion to a private space, the substitution of ritual for
spontaneity, the Cartesian separation between the *cogito* and extended,
measured space, all of which constitute dominant plotlines of late modernity. A Christianity that journeys in these kinds of "storied spaces,"
however, will deeply compromise the visibility of the body of Christ. How
does Teresa's use of pilgrimage provide an alternative?

Toward the beginning of *Interior Castle*, Teresa writes, "But you
must understand that there are many ways of 'being' in a place."[38] In "our
beautiful and delightful castle," Teresa notes that some remain occupied
and distracted; others do not even know where they are. People can be in
different places, as noted earlier, even while occupying the same physical
space. Such observations set the stage for Teresa's description of journey
and pilgrimage. One's place (storied space) is not set or fixed, in contrast to
the modern self's "I think therefore I am." Postmodernity has often taken
this fragile stability (dependent on the self alone) to mean that the subject
in inherently unstable. The stability of the Christian pilgrim, however, is
not in the space of the inner self.

Must not the self, however, have some inner confidence and self-mastery in order to make his or her journey? Margaret Miles, in fact, states that
"devotional manuals have cumulatively formed modern consciousness to

---

version of the facts but a different way of seeing. I am grateful to Don Saliers for this
point.

37. Ibid., 32. Jenson exhorts, "do not when reading Scripture try to figure out how
what you are reading fits into some larger story; there is no larger story. Try instead
to figure out how American history or scientists' predictions of the universe's future
course or the travail of a family in your congregation fit into Scripture's story" (34).

38. Teresa, *Interior Castle*, 6.

such an extent that the favorite character in fiction, 'autonomous Western man,' has come into being."[39] Miles links devotional manuals to the modern autonomous self by arguing that both of these focus on the struggle and mastery of the inner soul/self. In *The Pilgrim's Progress* (1678), for example, images in the outer world are "externalizations of the pilgrim's inner struggles, temptations, comforts and assistance . . ."[40] The primary storied space lies within. If we were to apply this reading to Teresa's *Interior Castle*, we could conclude that the real journey of the Christian life is an internal one and the external spaces/places, such as Scripture, liturgy, and the visible Body of Christ, are merely secondary stage props.

Talal Asad helps us understand, however, how the interior/exterior dichotomy as we know it today would not have dominated the landscape of Teresa's "storied spaces." Asad notes that the distinction between feelings as private or intuitional and ritual as public and legible is a modern one. In his work on medieval ritual, Asad states that "the inability to enter into communion with God becomes *a function of untaught bodies*. 'Consciousness' becomes a dependent concept . . . an experience of the body becomes a moment in an experienced (taught) body."[41] Here we see a reversal of typical modern assumptions. The mind does not think independently of the body, but rather thinks after and with the body. In discussing *The Rule of Saint Benedict*, Asad further notes, "the liturgy is not a species of enacted symbolism . . ." The liturgy is "a practice among others essential to the acquisition of Christian virtues." Liturgical competence is bodily competence. Asad can thus conclude that "the things prescribed, including liturgical services, had a place in the overall scheme of training the Christian self . . . there could be no radical disjunction between *outer* behavior and *inner* motive, between social rituals and individual sentiments . . ."[42]

One might find this lack of distinction between ritual and feeling hard to imagine today. Yet Christian pilgrimage, in Teresa's view, relies upon and provides a kind of body training that is essential to the destination of the pilgrim. Whether the pilgrim physically travels or stays in one place, Christian pilgrimage rests upon and requires liturgical training. One might object, however, that surely a person can simply go through the external motions of a ritual, say a church service, all the while feeling

39. Miles, *Practicing Christianity*, 59.

40. Ibid., 51.

41. Asad, *Genealogies of Religion*, 77; my emphasis.

42. Ibid., 63.

sad or lonely or some other feeling incommensurate with what is going on externally. As we saw, Teresa herself acknowledges that there are many ways of being "in a place." The point that Asad is making, however—that our "inner life" is itself dependent upon the ritual training of bodies—still holds. If there are disconnects when we gather to worship, then we can take this as a sign that conflicting rituals and stories are forming us. For example, feelings of deep loneliness cay display how modernity's autonomous subject (and all the rituals that shape this subject as essentially competitive with others) might be more formative than the liturgical subject who sees herself as a vulnerable member of Christ's body.

Let us turn more fully to the theological contours that define Teresa's "storied space." The language of pilgrimage/journey rests most fully for Teresa on the conviction that God desires our presence and is, in fact, already present with us. As she states, "[W]e have our being from God. ... He created us from nothing and sustains us . . ."[43] Elsewhere she claims, "Your delight is to be with the children of the earth, O my Lord."[44] The editors note that this is an illusion to Proverbs 8:31, where we read that the Wisdom of God delights in all of creation. Teresa relates God's delight in being with us to God's presence in the sacrament: "How You desire, Lord, thus to be with us and to be present in the Sacrament (for in all truth this can be believed since it is so, and in the fullness of truth we can make this comparison) . . ."[45] She thus implicitly links creation and new creation as signs of God's delight in our presence. God is present in the sacrament because God desires our company.

Such convictions support Teresa's assurance that God sustains us on our journey. "Let His Majesty lead the way along the *path* He desires. We belong no longer to ourselves but to Him."[46] God desires that the soul "may become more courageous in following the *path* of the Lord, trampling under its feet all worldly things."[47] The journey is thus one of receiving God's presence and thus becoming God's people, which is to become holy, set apart in order to be God's love and presence for the world. The journey takes time. Teresa reassures her readers, "Have great confidence, for it is necessary not to hold back one's desires, but to believe in God that if we

43. Teresa, *Book of Her Life*, 55.
44. Ibid., 86.
45. Ibid.
46. Ibid., 64.
47. Ibid., 102.

try we shall little by little, even though it may not be soon, reach the state the saints did with His help."[48]

The sacrament that Teresa describes in relation to Proverbs is central because it mediates Christ. Her words in response are a prayer: "O my Lord and my God!"[49] That the sacrament mediates Christ rests upon the fuller conviction that Christ is both fully divine and fully human. As mentioned in chapter 1, some in Teresa's day—the *alumbrados*—were tempted to imagine that they were too spiritual to meditate on merely corporeal things.[50] They thus shared with gnosticism a sense that the journey took one beyond creation into a purely spiritual realm. One of the ways Teresa counters them is to say that Jesus "is very glad when we grieve for His afflictions . . ."[51] For Teresa, Jesus is present precisely as One who is fully human. One can be with Christ in his affliction, at the feeding of the five thousand, or at his feet with the disciples. This is not a matter of simply remembering past events from two thousand years ago. Rather, Christ makes possible ongoing patterns that give form to Christian pilgrimage in the lives of the faithful. Christ delights to be with pilgrims in Word and Sacrament as well as prayer, meditation, and good works. Seen in this light, our "space" in never simply ours but always also occupied by Christ, who does not compete to be where we are but is present, healing and renewing our lives.

What stabilizes this place, then, is not self-mastery but the love of God in Christ. I hasten to add that Teresa does describe a kind of instability that occurs as one journeys through the mansions. The self/community is destabilized in the sense that it sheds false identities. Teresa famously uses the metaphor of the silkworm becoming a butterfly to describe how earlier identities take new form. The worm, "which was large and ugly, comes right out of the cocoon a beautiful white butterfly."[52] One might think of this metaphor as overly childlike and sentimental. Yet Teresa is using the wonders of creation to display the wisdom of God. In so doing, she shows that earlier forms are not abandoned, but transformed through the Holy Spirit. The key scriptural passage that Teresa uses here is from

48. Ibid., 71.

49. Ibid., 86.

50. Teresa writes, "I think I have explained what it is well for you to know—namely that, however spiritual you are, you must not flee so completely from corporeal things as to think that meditation on the most sacred Humanity can actually harm you" (*Interior Castle*, 175).

51. Ibid., 175.

52. Ibid., 91.

Colossians 3:3: "I think I read or heard somewhere that our life is hid in Christ, or in God (for that is the same thing), or that our life is Christ."[53] In the language of "storied space," one's story is not erased but reimagined and retold in light of Christ. The same is true for ecclesial communities: their stories are not erased but healed in such a way that their lives in Christ become more fully visible.

At the same time, Teresa notes that our lives are "hidden." To be hidden with Christ is to be hidden with the resurrected Christ, to be hidden participants in what God is doing in the world. We can apply Reinhard Hütter's description of pneumatological eschatology to Teresa's understanding at this point. Such a pneumatology, says Hütter, sees that "the success of the church's faithful witness might be hidden in a twofold way: under the form of the cross and in the future of God's reign."[54] Even though possibly hidden from the world, God is nonetheless acting in Christ through the Spirit, who creates and sustains the church. We are like the silkworm whose tiny, hidden efforts can lead to amazing results. As Teresa states,

> The silkworm is like the soul which takes life when, through the heat which comes from the Holy Spirit, it begins to utilize the general help which God gives to us all, and to make use of the remedies which He left in His Church—such as frequent confessions, good book and sermons. . . . And, before we have finished doing all that we can in that respect, God will take this tiny achievement of ours, which is nothing at all, unite it with His greatness and gives it such worth that its reward will be he Lord Himself.[55]

The landscape is transformed, but not because we control our destiny or story, or because we finally arrive at a fixed destination. The place we journey is rather a way of life lived in the dynamism of the Spirit, who works in ways that we cannot fully see or even imagine. This is another way of saying that the "storied space" is not ours, but a Divine communion in which we participate.

53. Ibid., 92.
54. Hütter, "Ecclesial Ethics," 435.
55. Teresa, *Interior Castle*, 92.

THE LITURGY AS PLACE

As mentioned in chapter 1, Teresa inhabited a liturgical world. Her days were structured by prayer, reading and praying the Psalms, hearing the Word of God, and receiving the Eucharist. In other words, a "chain of memory" embodied in certain practices enabled Teresa and her communities to be *in* Scripture. Her life displays Eugene Rogers's point that "the Spirit's indwelling the heart, and socializing the body, are two sides to the same process."[56] Rogers importantly adds that "the second takes place visibly in space and time: it takes place in particular communities, at particular times, in particular locations, among particular people. We may sum up that it takes place *liturgically*, if that word is taken in the widest possible sense, to denote social formation that reaches a certain paradigm in the society of the church at prayer."[57] Such emphases help us understand how the liturgical rhythm of Teresa's world developed particular kinds of "taught bodies." The monastic order of the office involved chanting or singing the Psalms to ensure that all one hundred and fifty songs would be recited each week. Each day was divided into eight sections or hours. The Major Hours were Matins, Lauds, Vespers, and Compline, and the Little Hours were Prime, Terce, Sext, and None. Mass was celebrated daily. The Carmelite liturgical year included both a temporal cycle (following the church calendar with Advent, Easter, and so forth) and a sanctoral cycle, which celebrated the lives of dozens of saints, to which Teresa herself was eventually added. While this cycle of prayer has varied over the centuries in different Christian communions, it is based on a shared conviction that the Psalms are the prayer book of the Bible. These are the prayers of the whole people of God as well as Christ's own prayers on behalf of the church.[58]

To capture something of the liveliness of this liturgical world, I turn to a contemporary community: the Benedictine Abbey of Regina Laudis (Bethlehem, Connecticut). Even though separated by centuries, this community shares with Teresa's Carmelite community certain liturgical rhythms and practices oriented around Word and Sacrament. In a fascinating documentary, *Joyful Noise: Psalms in Community*, the Benedictine sisters reflect on how praying the Psalms daily shapes their life together, whether one is driving a tractor or trying to live in the tensions of

56. Roger, *After the Spirit*, 184.

57. Ibid.

58. For an excellent Protestant description of the Psalms as "book of common prayer," see Bonhoeffer, *Life Together*.

communal life. As the narrator notes, the Psalms "live within the memory, filling each day with musical expectation and leading to conversion of heart." One sister describes how when tensions arise in the community, one could easily say that a particular sister is never going to change. The sister adds, however, that it does not matter. The practiced rhythm and fluidity of saying the Psalms together means, "I have to change, to find another way to come at a problem or situation or even approach something that is good so that it has a new vitality. I can't be stuck in this. I have to try and look at it from another point of view."[59]

The ritual of chanting the Psalms day in and day out enables the sisters to live creatively in response to one another and God. The sisters testify that living the Psalms in this way actually fosters more imagination than they would otherwise have. The individual sister does not lose her uniqueness; she is not absorbed into a kind of groupthink mentality. Perhaps from an outsider's point of view, the same dress and the same repetitive gathering with the same forty women could seem like only a highly homogenized way of life. Yet the Psalms, as the narrator of the documentary states, call each sister to make her life a "new song." This "new song" is the "gospel song," the "'song of the Lamb' in praise of the slain and victorious Redeemer (Rev 5:6–14; 14:1–3)."[60] Different psalms "catch hold" of the sisters in different ways. In the film, several sisters describe the particular phrases that had come to live in them. For one it was, "My eyes look to the hills from whence cometh my help." For another, it was the word spoken before each psalm, *esculta* or "listen," which the sister notes refers to active listening. The words become "living memories" with layers of meaning, memories that have been handed over (tradition) from one generation to another in Israel and the life of the church. The "new song" that the sisters seek to become is not "new" in the sense of completely original. Rather, they join the multitude of singers/prayers who have lived and live on in the life of God. What is new is the re-creation taking place in the life of the community, a renewal that takes place within and not apart from the ongoing re-creation of God's own people.[61]

59. Fassler, *Joyful Noise*.

60. Wainwright, *Embracing Purpose*, 123.

61. The Psalms have been central to the life of Christian communities across time. Christ himself, as a faithful Jew, was deeply formed by the Psalms such that they were on his lips at significant moments. On the cross, for example, at the height of his passion, Jesus cites Psalm 22: "My God, my God, why hast thou forsaken me?" (Matt 27:46; Mark 15:34). As he is dying, Jesus commits his spirit into his Father's hands with the words of Psalm 31:5: "Father, into your hands I commend my spirit" (Luke 23:46).

There are, of course, differences between the Spanish Carmelite communities of the sixteenth century and religious communities today, but praying the Psalms also makes possible a deep continuity. This continuity is manifest most fully in the "internalization of [the liturgy and liturgical time's] specifically religious themes and patterns and their devotional elaboration in lay piety."[62] It is most fully manifest where there is no alternative ordering of time, no "secular reckoning of time." Eamon Duffy, in his discussion of Christianity in England from 1400 to 1580, describes the abundant evidence for this kind of liturgical internalization. Adults were obliged to fast almost seventy days of the year, dependent on the liturgical calendar. Forty to fifty days, depending on one's region, would have been feast days, when "total or partial abstention from servile work was required."[63] The seasonal pattern of the liturgy that shaped the days and lives of villages and communities would have been a universal feature of the late medieval landscape (though, according to Duffy, before the Council of Trent there would have been considerable variation depending on locale).

Today, such ways of being in time might seem unrealistic (unless one joins a monastery). From this perspective, it could seem as if Teresa is narrating a way of life—a liturgical pilgrimage—that is inaccessible to most. Yet, as we have seen, the liturgical journey is an embodiment and extension of the scriptural journey. The liturgy, and the "liturgy after the liturgy," is a way of embodying and extending the shared story of Israel, the first disciples, the early church, and the church across the centuries. A key question that Christians face today is how to see in one another the presence of fellow pilgrims on a shared journey. If the church is truly a "pilgrim people," then how does this shape and transform our understanding of shared place and destination? Further, how might the figure of pilgrimage help heal the wounds of division on Christ's body?

In 1980, Pope John Paul II wrote,

> Authentic knowledge of the God of mercy, the God of tender love, is a constant and inexhaustible source of conversion, not only as a momentary interior act but also as a permanent

---

In Acts, Peter applies three psalms (16:8–11; 132:11; 110:1) to Christ as a prophecy for his resurrection, his messianic enthronement, and his exaltation and heavenly sovereignty (Acts 2:22–36). What the Abbey of Regina Laudis is doing is continuous with Teresa's Carmelite psalmody, which is continuous with how the Psalms were incorporated in the life of the early church.

62. Duffy, *Stripping of the Altars*, 15.

63. Ibid., 42.

> attitude, as a state of mind. Those who come to know God in
> this way, who "see" Him in this way, can live only in a state of be-
> ing continually converted to Him. They live, therefore, in *statu
> conversionis*; and it is this state of conversion which marks out
> the most profound element of the pilgrimage of every man and
> woman on earth in *statu viatoris*.[64]

Here the process of conversion is linked to the designation *viatoris*, or
"wanderer," "walker," "wayfarer," or "pilgrim." To be on pilgrimage as God's
people is to be continually open to the ways that God might yet convert
us, making us more fully Christ's one body. Pope John Paul II continues by
describing "the *ecumenical* task which aims at uniting all those who confess Christ. As she makes many efforts in this direction, the Church confesses with humility that only that love which is more powerful than the
weakness of human divisions can definitively bring about that unity which
Christ implored from the Father and which the Spirit never ceases to be-
seech for us 'with sighs too deep for words.'"[65] So understood, pilgrimage
is a conversion toward love: toward participating in the love of Christ so
that divisions are overcome. Rightly understood, Christian pilgrimage is
not about trying to recreate the past or nostalgically return to a place that
never was. Nor is it pining for an idealized future. It is rather about allowing Christ, through Word and Sacrament, to become more fully a living
reality in our midst.

Nostalgia focuses on wishing for a dream or ideal in one's mind.
Dietrich Bonhoeffer describes this ideal as one that *we* create of what a
Christian community should look like. As Bonhoeffer notes, God "speed-
ily shatters such dreams."[66] Such disillusionment, he argues, fosters the
habit of gratitude; "we enter into that common life not as demanders but
as thankful recipients."[67] The problem with such nostalgia is that it locks
one into thinking that Christian community is a human ideal rather than
a divine reality. Yet, Christians do not have to be nostalgic because we are
free to trust that God desires to create communion in our time and place,
as fully as God worked in the past and will in the future. Stated christo-
logically, this means that Jesus Christ—and all those alive in Christ—are
not bound by time or space, whether by geography or the confinement of

64. Pope John Paul II, *Dives in Misericordia*, 13.
65. Ibid.
66. Bonhoeffer, *Life Together*, 27.
67. Ibid., 28.

the modern self. We already are members one of another across time and space; pilgrimage is about learning to live and move in this dynamic place.

TERESA'S PILGRIMAGE AS ECUMENICAL

Earlier I cited Gregory the Great's saying, "Pilgrimage is our present life." This "our," as I have noted, includes the whole church. If we are truly brothers and sisters in Christ, then we can be in a kind of communion together in our present time, even if it is incomplete. If we are brothers and sisters in Christ, then we can see the saints, even if from another time and place, as our friends. It is in this spirit that we can be in the company of Teresa herself, seeing her as a fellow pilgrim.

Teresa understands our pilgrimage as a grand one. To read *Interior Castle* is to be drawn into this magnificent pilgrimage, involving trails and aridity; places of silence, waiting, and prayer; gifts and graces to be received; and mysteries to behold. For Teresa, the journey itself is crucial, but it is always a journey toward an end or *telos* that is none other than being in communion with Christ and his body. For Teresa, the beauty of this life is seen not in the majestic castles that marked the Spanish countryside but in a eucharistic way of life marked by a humility, grace, and love capable of honoring and serving Christ.

John Kenney discusses the fact that, as Augustine saw it, the Platonists were "unable to provide [a] completion to the pilgrim's journey and to secure stable habitation in God."[68] Augustine, according to Kenny, comes to see that the "way which leads to the house of bliss" is not merely "an end to be perceived," but "a realm to live in." Not only, says Augustine, "is one admonished to see you, who remain ever the same, but also [one is] healed to make it possible for him to hold on to you."[69] Healing, habitation, and stability are provided through the grace of Christ. In a similar sense, Teresa too describes a journey that is healing so that a people might live in God's dwelling. For Teresa, God gives in a way that we might be able to receive him, most fully by becoming one of us.[70] The giving does not stop

68. Kenny, *Mysticism of Saint Augustine*, 69.

69. Cited in ibid., 70.

70. This language echoes that of Athanasius: "The Lord did not come to make a display. He came [to heal and to teach suffering men] . . . to put himself at the disposal of those who needed Him and to be manifested according as they could bear it, not vitiating (impairing, destroying) the value of the Divine appearing by exceeding their capacity to receive it" (*On the Incarnation*, 78).

with the "historical Jesus," but continues as God the Son, now resurrected, continues to give life through the Spirit. From this perspective, Teresa's pilgrimage can be described as first of all a descent: God comes to where we are in order to make a space for communion.

This healing pilgrimage follows providential patterns displayed in both the life of Israel and the church. The journey through the castle repeats in a sense the journey of the Israelites. The exodus relates to Teresa's time and place because God is still leading people from slavery to freedom, from captivity to salvation. *Interior Castle* thus describes an exodus from the outer court, from concerns about honor and reputation, and even from a zeal for perfection. The journey requires humility, which Teresa, as we have seen, relates to self-knowledge, but the only way travelers can gain self-knowledge is through seeking to know God: "we shall never succeed in knowing ourselves unless we seek to know God."[71] Just as the Hebrew people discover their identity—and even that they are a people—through their obedience to God, the same is true also for travelers through the castle. They come to know who they are in the process of exodus and pilgrimage. Among the many obstacles that pilgrims encounter are sloth, cowardice, and bondage to others' opinions. Such obstacles are a kind of aimless wandering in the desert. Teresa writes, "We shall always be glancing around and saying: 'Are people looking at me or not?' . . . 'Will people think better of me if I refrain from following the crowd?'"[72] Such words echo Moses' own response to God's call to lead the Hebrews out of slavery: "But suppose [the Israelites] do not believe me or listen to me, but say, 'The Lord did not appear to you'" (Exod 4:1). As individuals join on pilgrimage, God will recreate them together as a people, free from worldly worries and opinions.

Like the Israelites, Teresa's journey involves wandering in the wilderness or dry land. In the third mansions, Teresa tells her sisters to move through times of "aridity" and not "at a snail's pace."[73] There is a passing through waters and a raining down of manna. In the fourth mansions, Teresa discusses God's consolations as different kinds of refreshing waters. Like the waters of salvation (passing through the Red Sea), these are ways that God opens up a way forward where previously none existed, moving those gathered toward the promised land. In the fifth mansions, those journeying receive the commandments. Teresa refers particularly to the

71. Teresa, *Interior Castle*, 14.

72. Ibid., 15.

73. Ibid., 39.

command to love of God and neighbor.[74] Finally, there is an entry into the promised land, yet this is not otherworldly. In the seventh and final mansions, Teresa discusses what life lived in communion with God and others looks like, particularly as this applies to her monastic context.

To continue this figural reading, Teresa herself is a Moses figure, encountering God in dramatic burning bush–like ways (through locutions and visions), and leading her hearers to the promised land. This is not to say that Teresa would have self-consciously thought of herself in these terms. In fact, her own "inner theater" sometimes included self-doubt and, at times, belittling statements about herself and about being a woman. But the point is that the reader, perhaps more so than Teresa herself, can see scriptural patterns in Teresa's life and writings.

We can add another figural layer to Teresa's journey through the dwellings. Not only does it repeat, in a sense, the journey of Israel, it also loosely follows a liturgical pattern. There is an entrance, confession of sin, and listening to sermons (second mansions). The waters associated with prayer that Teresa describes so vividly (fourth mansions), like the waters of baptism, make possible a dying and rising with Christ: a new life heretofore unimaginable. In the sixth and seventh dwellings, Teresa describes betrothal and marriage to God (discussed in chapter 3), language that reflects an intimacy and friendship between God and his people, a union that is "material" in that it produces a eucharistic way of life. Augustine famously states that at the Lord's Table the normal pattern of consumption is reversed. "Other food is digested by Christian believers, but the Eucharist as a heavenly food digests its own communicants, making them immortal and giving them a share in resurrection life."[75] Teresa stands in this Augustinian eucharistic tradition of being "consumed" by Christ in order to become the body of Christ for the world.

This is an ecumenical pilgrimage because it follows Scripture's own providential patterns: calling, leaving a place, wandering in the wilderness, receiving living water, being fed with the bread of life, hearing God's word, repenting, and living lives of love and reconciliation in Christ. All

74. Teresa states, "The surest sign we are keeping the two commandments (love for His Majesty and love for our neighbor) is, I think, that we should really be loving our neighbour; for we cannot be sure if we are loving God, although we may have good reasons for believing that we are, but we can know quite well if we are loving our neighbour" (ibid., 103).

75. Steinmetz, *Taking the Long View*, 32. Similarly, Cavanaugh writes, "The individual consumer of the Eucharist does not simply take Christ into herself, but it taken up into Christ" (*Being Consumed*, 54).

are called, according to Teresa, to live into the providential shape of God's called-out people.

CHRISTIAN PILGRIMAGE TOWARD VISIBILITY

Such providential pilgrimage patterns radically challenge late modern conceptions of space, chief of which is the idea that the space I inhabit cannot be inhabited at the same time by another. Attempts to inhabit another's space typically result in competition or animosity. From this modern perspective of individual space, it is also assumed that Divine agency and human agency are thus in competition. Either the human controls his space or God does. Going down this mistaken trail, however, places divine agency in competition with human agency. From a theological perspective, humans compete with God only in their sin, a conviction displayed in Genesis 3.[76]

A more satisfying way of understanding agency is to see that God is always seeking our friendship and is, in fact, already where we are. Divine wooing is such that it never ceases. It is not in competition with human agency but seeks to orient human agency to its proper end, which is receiving the gift of communion with the Triune God. Such reception does not obliterate the will but rather completes it. We become more fully our true selves in communion with the One who makes such communion possible. It is in this light that Irenaeus of Lyons says, "The glory of God is a human being fully alive." The mystery of why some do not receive God's gift remains a mystery, even as we ourselves do not have a lucid perspective on why we turn away from God at various times in our own lives. As I described it in chapter 2, God's time is not strictly chronological. Eschatology points to the Divine Logos as one whose logic can bend time and space, such that the past (our pasts) can be redeemed and healed. This logic is made manifest most fully in Jesus Christ, whose presence in our time and space in no way locks him out of being present in the past as well as the future through the power of the Spirit. Such is the ground of hope to which the church bears witness: "at the name of Jesus every

76. The initial act that leads Adam and Eve to break God's prohibition is one of covetousness and envy. At the suggestion of the *serpent*, the command not to eat of the tree of knowledge becomes a sign for Adam and Eve that God is "*withholding* something of his being from humans." Such envy turns a prohibition that is given for human benefit into a sign of "divine *rivalry* . . . rather than divine *love* . . ." (Lohfink, *Does God Need the Church?*, 17). Envy and rivalry leading to death appear now to constitute the human lot.

knee should bend, in heaven and on earth and under the earth, and every tongue should confess that Jesus Christ is Lord, to the glory of God the Father" (Phil 2:10–11).

Teresa vividly describes the journey through the castle as one in which God's presence is pervasive. There is no room where God is not, even in the outermost courts, where travelers are overtaken by terrifying reptiles. God is present in these outer spaces as fully as God is present in the space of the seventh mansions, though it might well be that we experience God differently in different mansions. Teresa herself gives as one of many examples a description of a soul being consumed with grief in the second mansions because she is unable "to do His bidding immediately."[77] In this instance, a person experiences sadness in the presence of Christ because she is unable fully to extricate herself from that which prevents her from moving toward him. The beauty of Teresa's narrative is that she accepts all these vast places (mansions) as part of what can lead our ecclesial bodies toward God: the sadness, the remorse, the suffering for wrong things, the pettiness, the distractions and so on.

All of this is part of the pilgrimage of learning to be a people (or a community of sisters). The journey takes time; it calls for waiting but also learning how and when to continue. To cite Irenaeus of Lyons again: "People who do not wait for the period of growth, who attribute the weakness of their nature to God, are completely unreasonable . . . they are more unreasonable than the dumb animals. The beasts do not blame God for not making them human."[78]

Why is it that the pilgrimage takes time from a theological perspective? Irenaeus points in the right direction when he reminds us that we are creatures, part of God's good creation and that time and place are therefore gifts. Learning how to receive time (and place) as gifts is part of the process. Especially in our context today, time is often seen as the enemy: we do not have enough time, time is slipping away, and others are interruptions of "my" time. Similarly, it is easy to become impatient with the places where we are, i.e., why stay is this particular church when another one seems more appealing? Yet, to see our time and place on scriptural terms, as does Teresa, is to see that the places where we are and the pilgrimage that constitutes our lives are always gifts. The scriptural tradition being the lens, and thus the norm, "is not a Romantic return to scripture

---

77. Teresa, *Interior Castle*, 24.

78. Cited by Rogers, *After the Spirit*, 183.

but is a recognition that to live in the time and place God puts you is to live in that time and place in biblical terms."[79]

On biblical terms, God desires to transform our places of brokenness, not only for our own sake, but for the sake of the whole. "If one member suffers, all suffer together with it; if one member is honored, all rejoice together with it" (1 Cor 12:26). In terms of Christian unity, we are pilgrims together, and so share in the brokenness of the *whole* church. If one part of the church suffers, then so does the whole. The pilgrimage, in fact, providentially moves toward the brokenness of Christ (Eucharist), so that pilgrims might yet share in Christ's suffering: "completing what is lacking in Christ's afflictions for the sake of his body, that is, the church" (Col 1:24). This does not mean that Christ's cruciform sacrifice was incomplete or insufficient. It is rather pointing to the fact that the body of Christ will become Christ's body for the world as it follows the way of the cross.

The pilgrimage that Teresa is charting, then, is not one that seeks to leave the world. The Carmelite convents that Teresa founded were oriented around the contemplative life. From a modern perspective, this kind of life does not appear to be "in" the world. Thus, one might well wonder how the visibility of the church is constitutive of the journey that Teresa narrates. In some ways, it seems as if the rule required the sisters to become more *invisible*, i.e., wearing veils and living enclosed lives. The debate about whether or not, and to what extent, the church should withdraw from the world can easily frame our way of thinking about Teresa's journey. She can appear to end up on the high withdrawal end of the continuum. At the other end, we find a church highly engaged in the world: in ministries for the homeless, in advocacy efforts on behalf of the poor, and even through support of various political candidates.

Yet, the scriptural journey that Teresa describes does not imagine visibility in these terms. It is not about how much the church does in the world. On these terms alone, the Catholic Church in Teresa's day was highly visible. The Catholic monarchy in the persons of Ferdinand and Isabella had, in 1492, effectively reconquered the Spanish territories under Muslim rule, and were likewise effectively expanding the Spanish Empire around the globe. The point Teresa's own context raises is not whether the church is visible in the world, but *how* the church is visible.

Christian pilgrimage, Teresa would affirm, engages not only ecclesial brokenness but the sufferings and beauty of the world as well. In

---

79. Goodson, "Adoption of American Pragmatism," 8.

the Christian journey, God does not reject the city (world) but desires to repair it. The journey is *not* one where pilgrims seek escape from the world. Rather friendship, food, water, and words become the means through which God is present in the world, sanctifying the world from within. The liturgy, according to Mannion, "is the unification of the New Jerusalem and the human city, so that in the process everything human is redeemed."[80] God enters human space and time in order to repair it, and this repair requires a people. The people is rightly called "eschatological" because it acknowledges in a way no other people can that our time and space has been invaded by God; the kingdom of the cross is present in the world.

THE PILGRIMAGE AS VEILED

While I have been emphasizing that Teresa's scriptural pilgrimage is one that move towards visibility, I have also noted that there is an important sense in which it is also hidden. I find it necessary to emphasize "visibility" in light of the modern tendency to domesticate the body of Christ to a day (Sunday), a place (a church building), a feeling (in one's heart), or a set of beliefs (in one's mind). In addition, the pilgrimage easily gets off track, staying in a compartmentalized sphere separate from other spheres such as economics or politics. In the face of this, it is crucial to see that the figures Teresa employs are constitutive of a visible way of life.

Yet, it is also true that this life and the pilgrimage are "veiled." Since this is an ecclesial pilgrimage in response to God's good deeds in the world, we are never in a position fully to see how particular lives or churches will contribute to the building up of the whole body. It might well seem that, to state it colloquially, we are on the side of "the losers."

We can see a secular parable of "being on the losing side" in a story that Tracy Kidder tells about Paul Farmer, a Harvard-trained doctor who lives most of his life caring for the desperately poor in Haiti. On one particular occasion, his medical care team decided to fly a young boy diagnosed with cancer to Boston, where they had arranged for free medical care. By the time the boy arrived, and with the aid of more sophisticated medical technology, they discover the cancer had spread, and the boy died in a fairly short time. PIH (Partners in Health) had spent $20,000 on the flight. Kidder later asks Farmer whether the expense was worth it. Farmer initially responds by saying that if he had been in Haiti at the time he

80. Mannion, "Church and the City."

would not have stopped the process. No one knew until the young patient was in Boston that the cancer had spread. Farmer goes on to say, however, that there are so many different ways of describing this. "For example, why didn't the airplane company that makes money, the mercenaries, why didn't they pay for his flight? . . . How about if I say, I have fought for *my whole life* a long defeat. . . . How about if I said, That's all it adds up to is defeat?"[81] For Farmer, the practice of medicine involves a willingness to be with people who are on "the losing side."

In an analogous way, Teresa describes the pilgrimage as a willingness to be on the defeated side: with Christ in his woundedness. From a certain perspective, it could seem like a ridiculous waste of life: beautiful young women secluding themselves in a convent simply in order to give themselves to lives of prayer. A Harvard-trained doctor "squanders" his talents on the poor. Why pay that price? Couldn't these women, Teresa herself, and the doctor do something more productive in the world? Of course, we have the hindsight today to see how Teresa, as the first woman doctor of the Catholic Church, has made a difference in all sorts of ways. But the fact is that she did not set out to be "visible" in this sense. She rather responded in love to the wounded Christ in her midst. The hiddenness of this path can be seen in a number of ways. First, while Teresa vividly describes the visions she received (we will return to these in the following chapter), they nonetheless remain a profound mystery, the fullest meaning hidden even to her. Secondly, Teresa sought for herself and her order a deepening of humility. Such humility becomes the virtue by which one trusts in the grace and work of God even when it is hidden from plain view. Thirdly, for Teresa, as also for the monastic movement more broadly, the act of prayer becomes the key to living faithfully before God, the "effects" of which are often hidden from oneself, others, and the world.

Above all, however, the pilgrimage itself involves a willingness to travel into a divine mystery, where "mystery" is here understood not a simply a closed door, but as a grace so deep and so profound that travelers can never fully reach its depth. This is why the pilgrimage is always a providential one. To speak of God's providence is another way of describing how we learn to see God even as we recognize we are looking through a glass darkly (1 Cor 13). From this perspective, Teresa is saying to her sisters (and future readers), "You can not see this now, but as you keep journeying you will begin to see providential patterns at work in the

81. Farmer, *Mountain beyond Mountain*.

world—forming in your own lives patterns of faith, hope and love—even though the outcome of these patterns will be hidden."

HUMILITY, KNOWING, AND NOT KNOWING

In discussing "The Christian Way of Knowing," Jonathan R. Wilson states that the conception of "faith as a gift teaches much about the Christian way of knowing." Knowing is a gift that requires humility. "Humility, not enlightenment, is the first step toward the Christian way of knowing." This contrasts with the modern view that knowledge is achieved through human effort "in our quest to master the world." It also is an alternative to postmodern skepticism that knowledge is "interpretation (and therefore uncertain) and a disguised [bid] for power."[82] Such an emphasis on humility coincides with Teresa's exhortation that the pilgrim must constantly practice humility, which comes from dwelling in the room of self-knowledge. "However high a state the soul may have attained, self-knowledge is incumbent upon it, and this it will never be able to neglect even should it so desire. Humility must always be doing its work like a bee making its honey in the hive: without humility all will be lost."[83]

If mastery of knowledge and the world is the modern self's way towards enlightenment, then humility is the pilgrim's way to knowledge of self and world. Humility, rightly understood, has to do with expanding the capacity to receive what God desires to give us. Teresa depicts this expansion as a kind of wonder and discovery as we meander through the castle. What Josef Pieper says about the *philosophia negativa* applies to Teresa: "To wonder is not merely not to know; it means . . . that one understands oneself in not knowing. And yet, it is not the ignorance of resignation. On the contrary, to wonder is to be on the way, in via . . ."[84] Humility is a virtue that enables one to recognize that *not knowing* (in the sense of mastery or control or self-determination) becomes, in the journey through Teresa's castle, a kind of knowing that leads to a more profound gratitude before God.

---

82. Wilson, "Christian Way," 23. Wilson notes that for Christians knowing is a gift, not an achievement. It is not "a contest for power."

83. Teresa, *Interior Castle*, 13. This statement is especially vivid in Teresa's Spanish: ". . . que la humilidad siempre labra como la abega en la colmena de miel, que sin esto todo va perdida."

84. Cited in Hibbs, "Wisdom Transformed by Love," 40.

Being church together, in the midst of our present divisions and brokenness, is about trusting the providential ways—often hidden from our eyes now—that God works in the world. The truth is that we never fully know exactly what God is doing in any particular place and time. We do not have that kind of perspective on the grand scheme of things. Monasticism witnesses to this reality. It challenges the emphasis on "doing the important thing" or "making an obvious difference." The pilgrimage toward unity is the way of the cross, which involves a willingness to suffer. This willingness to suffer is not simply "playing the martyr," as is sometimes displayed in a parent who does everything for a child. Rather, it involves discerning together the path of faithfulness in any particular context and being willing to participate in the presence of Christ in the places where one is. To desire what Christ desires is to be willing to suffer, trusting patiently that God is at work, healing the church and bringing his kingdom to fruition.

CONCLUSION: A STORY

Isaac Singer tells the story of a traditional Jewish feast of the tabernacles:

> There the Rabbi sang the table prayer and preached. The Chassidim were enthusiastic because they had never heard such an interpretation of the Torah. The Rabbi had unveiled holy mysteries. In the evening, a festal cloth was finally spread over the table, and then they put a loaf of bread on it and placed a carafe filled with wine and a kaddish cup next to it. The participants had the impression that the tabernacle changed into one of the mansions in the house of God.[85]

Such a story, with its reference to one of the mansions of God, provides a suitable commentary of Teresa's use of mansions. The Feast of Tabernacles remembers the time when the Hebrew people lived in fragile dwellings during their forty years of wandering in the desert after their exodus from Egypt. The story is about the transformation of a humble and ordinary dwelling such as a tent into one of the mansions of the house of God. Such transformation is brought about through the Word—the teaching and preaching of the rabbi—and through the festal reception of the loaf of bread and kaddish cup of wine. Jesus participates in this divine tradition.

85. Told by Seewald in Ratzinger, *Salt of the Earth*, 174. Seewald adds, "What happens instead among us is that Christian celebrations turn into civil holidays with sausage and beer."

As a Jewish rabbi, he too teaches and "unveils mysteries." He too celebrates the Jewish feast with bread and wine. We see here an expression of "the great continuity of the history of faith," one that presents an authority that "does not come from the individual."[86] We see here, likewise, a manifestation of how God is providentially working in history through creating a people, delivering them from captivity, leading them toward the promised land, and sustaining them in the wilderness such that they are able to worship God.

For Teresa, too, humble dwellings (tents, poor convents, and spiritual poverty) are transformed through the Word and the Bread of Heaven. Christ becomes the manna, the One who sustains and gives life to the church, broken and fallen though it might be. The humble dwelling that we are becomes the very palace where Christ dwells, calling us through the Spirit to be pilgrims following God's providential patterns and paths.

86. Ibid., 176.

5

Teresa as a Saint for Unity

[The] synthesis of grace and intellect is lived, and finds its pinnacles in the Doctors of the Church.[1]

E ARLY ON, A SHORT forty years after her death, Teresa was canonized a saint in the Catholic Church, a testimony to her wide popularity. She was in many ways a product of her Spanish Catholic culture: a passionate Mediterranean, a woman committed to the Catholic Church, and a sister deeply formed by the sixteenth-century Catholic monastic tradition in its Carmelite key.

Yet, Teresa is not bound by her context. As we have seen, the space-time of the church, which is that of saints, is not chronological space-time. To confess the communion of saints is to confess the death and resurrection of Christ, and thus to acknowledge that our shared communion is not limited by the mere span of our lives. Our communion is, rather, dialogical as the church continually engages and rereads the lives of the saints.[2] Seen in this light, the saints are gifts to the *whole* church, not only one manifestation of the church.[3] As Hans Urs von Balthasar states, "the

1. Editors' Preface in de Lubac, *Corpus Mysticum*, xvii.

2. I am grateful to Jenny Howell for her emphasis on these points in her essay, "Reading History with the Saints." See also Carter, *Race*, for an example of such rich rereading.

3. If the saints are a gift to the church, then a question that comes easily to mind in the midst of a divided ecclesial identity is, "Who gets to determine and describe the saints?" Lutheran saints, for example, would not be regarded as such by Catholics, and vice versa. There are no abstract criteria to adjudicate these differing judgments. Are we, then, simply stuck with our differing accounts, accounts that easily reinforce

saints are tradition at its most living, tradition as the word is meant whenever Scripture speaks of the unfolding of the riches of Christ . . . [they are] like volcanoes pouring forth molten fire from the inmost depths of Revelation . . ."[4] Previous chapters have described how Teresa's teaching both relies upon and magnifies certain providential patterns in God's Word—dwellings, marriage, and pilgrimage—patterns that describe the life of the whole church. This present chapter turns to aspects of Teresa's own life to show how her biography is theology.[5] More specifically, I look at how Teresa's own life is an ecumenical window that can provide healing for wounds of ecclesial division.

A particularly significant gift that Teresa embodies is Christ through the Spirit desiring our friendship. A familiar story tells of Teresa caught in a torrential rainstorm in which her cart hit a pothole, throwing her head-first into the mud. In response, she is to have said to God, "If this is how you treat your friends, no wonder you have so few!" For Teresa, friendship with God is no sentimental ideal. Our dominant culture depicts friendship as determined by our personal choices, likes and dislikes. Teresa, however, shares with Augustine the conviction that we do not choose our friends; God does. This is but a way of acknowledging that friendship is first a gift made possible by God's grace. Friendship is thus a reality determined by Christ, who through the Spirit enables us to be friends with God and one another. As Jesus says to his disciples, "I do not call you servants any longer, because the servant does not know what the master is doing; but I have called your friends, because I have made known to you everything that I have heard from my Father" (John 15:15). That Jesus is speaking of the Father to his disciples indicates that friendship grounded in the Triune life of God makes possible a unity unknown to the world: ". . . I in *them* and you in me, that *they* may become completely *one*, so that the world may know you have sent me and have loved them even as you have loved me" (John 17:23; my emphasis). Such a passage indicates that friendship with the Triune God is inherently a communion of saints, where "saints"

---

ecclesial division? Seen in a fuller theological light, to confess the communion of saints is to acknowledge that we are in a shared communion, albeit one that is broken and divided. If this communion is truly a contemporaneous communion through the presence of the Spirit, then we are called continually to seek ways to live together faithfully as one body. This means that the saints may speak to us in ways that cast new light on past divisions. Such a conviction both frees and invites us to renarrate the lives of the saints in ways that might build up the unity of the church.

4. Balthasar, *Theology of History*, 105.

5. This phrase comes from McClendon's *Biography as Theology*.

is here understood as all disciples. In what follows, I explore how one particular saint's embodiment of such friendship enlarges our vision of what it means to be church in the midst of our present brokenness.

TERESA AND THE WOUNDED CHRIST

Teresa's lifetime (1515–82) spans the "great movements in European culture now know as Renaissance, Reformation and Counter-Reformation."[6] Two years after her birth, Martin Luther will nail his Ninety-Five Theses to the doors of Wittenberg. Some thirty years later, the Catholic Church will convene the Council of Trent (1545–63), in part to condemn Protestant "heresies." During this tumultuous period, increased division will settle permanently into the life of the Western church, making it more visibly divided in ways heretofore unknown.

Teresa herself appears to have little grasp of the doctrinal arguments that were pulling the church apart. She does know, however, that the "Lutherans" were opposing the Catholic Church and its teachings, and for her this appears to be a sufficient reason to oppose them. As Kavanaugh and Rodriguez note, "In Teresa's mind the Church and Christianity were identical. The attack of 'those Lutherans' was an attack against Christianity, she thought."[7] In fact, Teresa appears to confuse, or at least lump together, Lutherans and Huguenots. This highlights the fact that Teresa was not an academically trained theologian, a fact she readily admits. Her theological wisdom rather comes from her particular way of life. Although Teresa clearly opposed the Reformation, she did so not based on refined theological positions but because she perceived that it was harmful to the church. All this to say that Teresa's reaction to what became known as the Reformation need not obscure how her way of life provides rich resources for Christian unity.[8]

---

6. Bilinkoff, *Avila of Saint Teresa*, xi.

7. Kavanaugh and Rodriguez, "The Way of Perfection, Introduction," in Teresa, *Collected Works*, 2:20.

8. Some readers might see this approach as problematic. After all, if a person opposes a group (Protestants), how can that group turn to the person as a resource for unity? In response, it is important to see that many of the ways the lines today are drawn between Catholics and Protestants were not so firmly in place in the sixteenth century. For a development of this perspective, see Williams, "Scripture, Tradition and the Church." In addition to this historiographical point, however, is a theological one: learning to see "other" saints as gifts to the whole church can be a source of healing for all.

To look at Teresa and the wounded Christ, I wish first to turn to a significant encounter that Teresa describes in her autobiography. In *The Book of Her Life*, she tells of a crucial moment in her life, at age thirty-nine, when she comes upon a statue of "the much wounded Christ." This is an image of Christ as *ecce homo* ("behold the man"), a figure of Christ on the way to his crucifixion.[9] The suffering Christ, Teresa realizes in a profound moment of illumination, *needs* her. As Teresa describes this scene, she sees—in a way that she had not previously been able to see—how deeply Christ wants her company, even if only to wipe the sweat from his brow. Teresa confesses that she is drawn to Christ in his vulnerability, but at the same time feels inadequate to respond.

It is noteworthy that the Christ that appears to Teresa is suffering so intensely, given the divisions tearing the church apart at the time. As Teresa herself states, "The world is all is flames; they want to sentence Christ again . . . they want to ravage his Church."[10] The divisions will culminate after Teresa's death in the Thirty Years' War (1618–48), leaving tremendous death and destruction in its wake. Not only will this war intensify conflict in the supposedly one body of Christ, but it will also bring about the "birth pangs" of the nation-state,[11] an entity that will continue to divide the church and in some cases seek to eradicate it. Teresa's encounter with the suffering Christ resonates, then, with Christ still suffering "in every insult, rift, and war, where color, scorn, or wealth divide, he suffers still, yet loves the more, and lives, though ever crucified."[12]

In the face of the suffering of Christ, Teresa feels understandably inadequate. A possible rationale for this is that Teresa was a woman in a culture where women were less than men in many ways (i.e., they were not suitable for education, their identity was determined by their physical attractiveness, and so forth). At the same time, Teresa's sense of inadequacy can be seen as representative of a wider shared sense by others at the time: a feeling of helplessness before the divisions and violence tearing the church apart. What can anyone do to attend to the wounded body of Christ? There appears to be no fix that does not involve more violence, and thus more suffering.

9. Teresa of Avila, *The Book of Her Life*, 48. According to Kavanaugh and Rodriguez, the *ecce homo* ("Behold the Man") continues to be venerated in Avila's Monastery of the Incarnation, 321.

10. Teresa, *Way of Perfection*, in *Collected Works*, 2:43.

11. See chapter 4 for discussion of this idea. For a fuller development, see Cavanaugh, *Theopolitical Imagination*.

12. Wren, "Christ Is Alive."

Yet, as Teresa tells her story, the encounter with the suffering Christ enables her to see her own inadequacy and brokenness in a new light. Christ needs her *as she is* (not as someone more educated, more clever, more powerful, or more capable of fixing the church). This encounter will lead Teresa in later years to represent Christ to herself "in those scenes where I saw Him more alone. It seemed to me that being alone and afflicted, as a person in need, *He had to accept me*."[13] To the modern reader, this way of imagining Christ might seem like a psychological trick, where a partner at a dance has to choose you because everyone else is taken. For Teresa, however, this encounter with Christ is a revelation, or rather an assurance that Christ needs even her, and furthermore, needs her for the sake of the body, to attend to wounds on the body of Christ. This need in not dependent on her capacity—or lack thereof—but on Christ's presence to her. This way of inserting herself more fully in the Christian story enables Teresa to *reimagine her own identity and, at the same time, to reimagine the body of Christ*. She sees that Christ in his suffering needs her; by extension, she sees how the body of Christ needs her, even if she cannot fully articulate it at this point. "I strove to be His companion there. If I could, I thought of the sweat and agony He had undergone in that place. I desired to wipe away the sweat He so painfully experienced, but I recall that I never dared to actually do it [wipe away his sweat], since my sins appeared to me so serious."[14] Teresa thus hopes that a wounded, suffering Christ would be in such need that he would have to accept her. Teresa discovers that he does. As she puts it, "Clearly, it seems, He took pity on me and showed great mercy in admitting me before Him and bringing me into His *presence*, for I saw that if He himself had not accomplished this, I would not have come."[15] Teresa's own clouded vision and sense of inadequacy are no obstacles to her being with Christ, who, she discovers, is already with her.

She does not have to become more worthy. It is in light of this realization—this extension of friendship—that Teresa sees her own brokenness truthfully. Previously, for example, Teresa often put herself and all women down as unintelligent, a view as mentioned above that she would have absorbed in part from the dominant culture. Through friendship with Christ

13. Teresa, *Book of Her Life*, 49; my emphasis.

14. Ibid., 49. Teresa is here echoing a response by many who are invited to be God's friends. Moses, for example, argues with God: "Who am I that I should go to Pharaoh . . .?" (Exod 2:11); and "Oh, my Lord, I am not eloquent . . ." (Exod 4:10).

15. Teresa, *Book of Her Life*, 52.

and others, Teresa eventually comes to see such self-negation as sinful.[16] While she does not use the term "self-negation" (intended here to refer to a "diminished self" and a sinful refusal to see one's self as created for life with God), Teresa does come to see how her diminished sense of adequacy is no obstacle to Christ desiring her company.

Archbishop Rowan Williams states that "grace, for the Christian believer, is a transformation [of a form of life] that depends in large part on knowing yourself to be seen in a certain way: as significant, as wanted."[17] In this encounter, Teresa comes more fully to see herself as adequate and as *wanted* by Christ.[18] Teresa thus reimagines her own identity before the suffering figure of Christ. Such an encounter, seen through a modern lens, could be read as highly individualistic. Is this an earlier version of the familiar hymn "I Go to the Garden Alone," where Jesus "talks with me" and "walks with me"? We need to recall, however, the fuller context. Teresa notes that this encounter takes place when "one day entering the oratory I saw a statue they had borrowed for a certain feast to be celebrated in the house."[19] Teresa is thus in a communal place of prayer during a particular liturgical season, though we do not know which feast day it is. In other words, Teresa is already in a space-time landscape deeply shaped by the gospel. It is, however, the statue of a suffering Christ, a visual depiction of the gospel story, that enables Teresa more fully to think the scriptural story within her, to use Cézanne's language mentioned in the previous chapter. Far from a "me and God" experience, this encounter rather draws Teresa more fully into God's story with a people for the sake of the world.

Teresa's encounter and transformation before Christ suffering raises the question, what would it mean for the church itself to reimagine its identity before the suffering Christ on an ongoing basis? Any sense of

16. For further discussion of sin as a loss of identity, see Jones, *Embodying Forgiveness*. Jones gives a particularly vivid account of the nineteenth-century slave "Old Elizabeth," who receives from her encounter with Jesus "not a sense of unworthiness but rather 'somebodiness'" (169). Not only does she receive a new identity—from nobody to somebody—she also receives a mission to proclaim the gospel. Such healing, for Teresa as well, has a twofold dimension: personal healing is at the same time a healing in and within the church.

17. Cited in Rogers, *Theology and Sexuality*, 311.

18. Teresa's transformation, from feeling unworthy to receiving Christ's love, resonates with that of Martin Luther. Both are unable to earn God's love. Both hear or see a different way of being before Christ, a way in which Christ gives them what they cannot give themselves: forgiveness of sin (in Teresa's case the sin of self-negation) and the grace to participate in life with Christ.

19. Teresa, *Book of Her Life*, 48.

inadequacy or hopelessness is cast in a different light by Christ in his suffering. The church certainly appears inadequate in her agonistic divisions; the church has failed to be who she is. Too often, she has let sin, blindness, and apathy determine her visible shape. Time and again, when the church appears before the suffering Christ, she is inclined to withdraw. So unfaithful have we who are church been, so compromised, that we too can say, "Who is able to stand before the Lord, this holy God?" (1 Sam 6:20).[20] The church does, of course, reimagine its identity before the suffering Christ on an ongoing basis through the liturgy, the preached Word and the Lord's Supper. Here is Christ broken for us. Here is Christ needing us, in the sense of Christ desiring our reception, our communion, and our friendship. The inadequacy, failure, and brokenness of Christ's body as church can only be seen and confessed faithfully in the context of worship. Furthermore, when seen faithfully, these are not barriers. Christ becomes vulnerable to us precisely to heal our brokenness and sin, and to make communion with him possible. There are no obstacles, in any ultimate sense, to being before and in Christ both in his suffering and in his resurrection. Rather, Christ himself suffers our rejection and apathy. As Teresa discovers, Christ pursues his friends even when they draw back, even when they are unable simply to wipe the sweat from his brow.

A midrash story gives an account of why God chose the Hebrew people out of all the peoples on the earth. The story tells of how God went to many others nations and each turned him down. Finally, only the Hebrew people were left; God had to choose them. This narration seeks to deflect any assumption that the Jewish people were better than others, or that they somehow deserved God's election. It rather points to their peoplehood before God as a mysterious gift. Similarly, Teresa's story reminds us that God continues this mysterious election with the church, now grafted onto Israel. "It seems Christ had to accept me" is but a way of acknowledging the profound mystery of God's grace, God's gift of friendship in and through Christ on behalf of all nations.

If we turn more fully to the implications of the wounded Christ for Christian unity, Teresa's encounter with Christ shows us that "God's grace in this present history at least, is made visible only in human weakness."[21] Such a statement, from "The Princeton Proposal for Christian Unity,"

20. See also Ps 24:3: "Who shall ascend the hill of the Lord? And who shall stand in his holy place?"; and Rev 5:2: "I saw a mighty angel proclaiming with a loud voice, 'Who is worthy to open the scroll and break its seals?'"

21. Braaten and Wilken, *In One Body*, 15.

indicates that God's grace is present and visible in the human weakness we call division in the Body of Christ. This seems counterintuitive. Division is the result of human blindness and sin, a fact that prevents God's grace from coming to fruition in the life of the church. How is it that God's grace is made visible in this expression of human weakness? Such a position is not intended to condone sin, as if one needed to sin that grace may abound (see Rom 6:1–4). Rather, Teresa's encounter highlights the conviction that weakness and sin are no obstacles to Christ's love, but places through which God's grace enters our lives. Teresa's sense of inadequacy, the Apostle Paul's thorn in the flesh, or the brokenness that easily determines our lives in Christ's body can all be places where Christ unites our brokenness with his own. So understood, human weakness is a source of healing grace.

Given Teresa's encounter with the suffering figure of Christ, it is no surprise that she was also drawn to the figure of the Infant Jesus (a depiction of Jesus at three years old). When Teresa founded each of her seventeen convents, she carried a figure of the Infant Jesus with her. Legend has it that this figure made its way to Prague,[22] where it was housed in a church originally built by German Lutherans (1613). At the beginning of the Thirty Years' War, Catholic authorities gave the church to the Carmelites, who renamed it the Church of Our Lady Victorious. Bloody conflict, however, continued as both sides committed atrocities against the other.

The child Jesus, like the suffering Christ, is a *vulnerable* figure. In carrying this figure to the opening of each convent, would Teresa have intended her monasteries to be places of vulnerability to God—places, moreover, where the Child Jesus welcomes us as his children, and where we learn to see one another as sisters and brothers in Christ? Are not both the child Jesus and the suffering Jesus reminders that Christ is present as the vulnerable One, eager to heal all brokenness and division? Teresa's life witnesses to how such vulnerability is a source of grace through which Christ heals us and opens the door to friendship with God and others.

22. Whether or not this is the exact figure that Teresa used is unclear. Documented sources link the Infant Jesus of Prague to the duchess Maria Maxmiliana Manrique de Lara, who in 1556 married a Czech nobleman. In any case, the statue of Infant Jesus has been linked to the Carmelites in Prague, both in the seventeenth century and more recently, in the twenty-first, when the church was returned after communist rule to the Carmelite order.

TERESA AS *DOCTOR ECCLESIAE*

This understanding of Teresa before the wounded Christ provides some perspective on why it is fitting that she was declared, as mentioned in chapter 1, the first woman doctor of the church (*doctor ecclesiae*) in 1970. This title, as understood by the Roman Catholic Church, is not simply conferred from above by ecclesiastical authority. It is more properly understood as a kind of recognition. When Teresa was named *doctor ecclesiae*, Pope Paul VI stated in his homily, "We have conferred, or better, we have *recognized* the title doctor of the church for Saint Teresa of Jesus."[23] The conferral of this title is thus a process of acknowledgement. As Keith Egan states, "Just as saints are not created by the process of canonization but their holiness of life is thus recognized by the church, so too doctors of the church are not made by the church but the eminence of their doctrine and their holiness are acknowledged by the church."[24] The recognition involves a conviction that the doctor speaks for the whole church, not only one segment of it. Rightly understood, the whole church is not limited to a particular time or place. As Egan states, "What the saints were on earth, they continue to be in heaven, a revelation of God's love for His people." Thus, "the doctors of the church continue the mission they once carried out on earth, teaching their fellow members. The doctors of the church are in a very special way *the teachers of the Body of Christ*."[25] So understood, *doctor ecclesiae* is not simply a figure in the past, but a living member of the communion of all saints. As such, they can continue to teach the church today.

The title "doctor" in our context has become more associated with the medical profession than with ecclesial positions. Ecclesial doctors can easily seem a pale reflection of "real" doctors, who diagnose illnesses, prescribe medications, perform surgeries, and so forth. From the point of view of the church universal, however, ecclesial doctors are crucial to the

23. Cited by McGinn, *Doctors of the Church*, 3; my emphasis.

24. Egan, "Signficance for Theology," 161. Egan narrates in fascinating detail how the fact that Teresa was a woman presented an obstacle to her recognition as a doctor. For example, the three-hundredth anniversary of Teresa's canonization (1922) provoked the first request to the Holy See that Teresa be named a doctor of the church. Both the Bishop of Avila (publicly) and the Discalced Carmelites (confidentially) petitioned Pius XI on Teresa's behalf. The response relayed from Pius XI: "*Obstat sexus*," or, as Egan translates, "Her sex stands in the way of her being named a doctor of the church" (159). Egan continues by noting that the pope's response "left open some hope for the future: 'I leave the delicate question to be decided by my successor'" (159–60).

25 Ibid., 162.

health of the church. If the church is wounded by false belief and fragmentation, the doctors of the church can be resources for diagnosis and cure. Saint Isidore of Seville (seventh century) describes the similarity between a medical and ecclesial doctor when he writes, "Just as skilled physicians treat the body's varied illnesses with different medicine . . . so too a doctor of the church uses the fitting remedy of teaching for each and all, and will proclaim whatever is needed for each person, according to age, sex, and profession."[26] That the church has many doctors points to the realization and reception of the fact that God provides many ways of healing the wounds on Christ's ecclesial body.[27]

Thus, the doctors of the church, as members of an ongoing communion, can continue to provide healing for the whole church. Ecclesial doctors, like medical doctors, might focus on a particular area (such as prayer or Christology or grace, for example), but their medicine can affect the whole body. As a sixteenth-century Spanish Carmelite, Teresa might seem to have been focused on one particular place and time, i.e., reforming the Carmelite order of her day. Teresa's "medical practice," however, as we have seen, involves a figural diagnosis that applies to the whole church in its providential formation. Her diagnosis lies in seeing Christ present in the life of her members through key providential patterns, which are themselves extensions of Scripture. Though Teresa was on the "other side" of the Protestant Reformation in a superficial and anachronistic sense, she (oddly from a Reformation perspective) revivifies Scripture as a providential way of life. This is medicine for the whole church because the whole body is called to live into providential patterns as embodied in the Word of God.

26. Cited by McGinn, *Doctors of the Church*, 6.

27. In Roman Catholicism, the term *doctor ecclesiae* has been applied to thirty-three persons, eight of whom are Eastern and twenty-four of whom are Western. The term, however, is not limited to Catholic use. John Calvin, for example, used the term in ways similar to Catholic tradition: doctors are noted for their faithful and inspiring interpretation of Scripture. See Calvin, "Doctor and Ministers of the Church," in *Institutes*, 2:1053–68. While more loosely regarded, Protestants today rely upon certain theologians as "doctors" inasmuch as they consider particular theologians as faithful interpreters of God's Word. This team of doctors from different traditions points to the fact that the doctors can provide healing, but they can also prescribe different medicines. Exploration of this fact does not necessarily weaken the church; it could highlight more fully how we need each other. A particular doctor treats one condition, while another might be treating something else. To see this point is potentially to see a wide range of ways that God is healing the church.

Any healing that a *doctor ecclesiae* prescribes flows from the medicine that is in fact Christ. Teresa herself refers to Christ as a surgeon: "Humility is the ointment for our wounds because if we indeed have humility, even though there may be a time of delay, the surgeon, who is our Lord will come to heal us."[28] Augustine too employs the analogy of surgery to describe how Christ is our cure: "And just as surgeons, when they bind up wounds, do it not in a slovenly way, but carefully, that there may be a certain degree of neatness in the binding, in addition to its mere usefulness, so our medicine, Wisdom, was by His assumption of humanity adapted to our wounds . . ." Augustine continues that God who is "healer and medicine both in one" sometimes heals by using opposites; "We were ensnared by the *wisdom* of the serpent: we are set free by the *foolishness* of God." At other times, God cures our wounds by their likes: "He came as a *man* to save us who are *men*, as a *mortal* to save us who are *mortals*, by *death* to save us who were *dead*."[29] The doctors of the church are like Christ the Doctor, not in Christ's divinity but in their participation in Christ's healing of the church, humanity, and all creation.

Teresa's ability to heal as a *doctor ecclesiae* is a gift from Christ through the church. Teresa, of course, becomes a doctor in the initial context of life in monastic community: a community gathered in chapel for prayer, where the feast and fast time of the church was a lived reality, and where artistic depictions of a visible Christ played key roles in the theological imagination. As we saw, Teresa's encounter with Christ is no simple solitary experience but a further embodiment of a communal drama (a Divine drama) in which she was deeply embedded. It is her embodiment and living out of this drama that enables Teresa to become uniquely who she is before Christ. As have seen, Christ, in his divinity and humanity, heals her. In his humanity, Christ needs Teresa's assistance. At the same time, Christ as the Son of God heals her and brings her into Divine friendship. She can wipe the sweat from his brow. This is such a small gesture, but one that points proleptically to Teresa's own conclusion in *Interior Castle*: ". . . the Lord does not look so much at the magnitude of anything we do as at the love with which we do it."[30] Teresa is a doctor who teaches that the "true health" of the body lies in seemingly small gestures of unity and love.[31]

28. Teresa, *Interior Castle* (Kavanaugh and Rodriguez trans.), 311.

29. Augustine, *On Christian Doctrine*, 526; my emphasis.

30. Teresa, *Interior Castle*, 238.

31. As Augustine says, "His body, then, which has many members, and all performing different functions, He holds together in the bond of unity and love, which is its true health" (*On Christian Doctrine*, 526).

"AND YOUR YOUNG [WOMEN] SHALL SEE VISIONS" (ACTS 2:17)

Anyone who reads Teresa's autobiography will quickly realize that many of the stories she tells about herself are highly unusual, involving locutions, visions, and even levitations. We have already referred in chapter 1 to one of these well-known experiences, when Teresa describes an angel piercing her heart. "I saw in his hand a long spear of gold, and at the iron's point there seemed to be a little fire. He appeared to me to be thrusting it at times into my heart, and to pierce my very entrails; when he drew it out, he seemed to draw them out also, and to leave me all on fire with a great love of God."[32] As noted earlier, Bernini's statue *Ecstasy of Saint Teresa* has made this scene famous, especially by bringing out the not-so-subtle sexual undertones that modern readers easily hear and see. I do not wish to discount these undertones. Who can fully say how Teresa's own sexuality shaped her encounter? At the same time, I want to take seriously what Teresa herself says: that the Spirit is piercing her heart. Teresa believed that such kinds of spiritual experiences were not only about the recipient. She was convinced that God's provision in the form of visions, dreams, and locutions—and Teresa had all of these—was not for that person alone, but ultimately for the whole church.

For scriptural continuity, we can look at the example of Saul in the book of Acts. He hears the voice of Christ (a locution), he is blinded for three days (a kind of anti-vision), and his sight is restored through bizarre circumstances (a double vision to both Saul and Ananias). These encounters lead to Paul's conversion and transformation, and to his becoming one of the great evangelists and apostles in the early church. No less for Teresa as well did dreams, visions, and so forth transform her, such that she became eventually a saint and doctor of the church. Could she have done so without these odd sorts of experiences? The answer could be yes, but the deeper truth is that, as Teresa herself notes, God knows what each of us needs to live a life of faithfulness. The point is not the visions and locutions, but rather faithfulness to God in the places (dwellings) where we are. Teresa in fact warns her sisters against seeking after special experiences or equating these with being more holy or spiritual. Teresa, too, was hesitant to write about herself, but did so under obedience.

We are, of course, grateful that she did because the reader can see probably more fully than Teresa how her life follows a "this is that" pattern

32. Teresa, *Book of Her Life*, 200.

(as described by James McClendon). The reader will recall that McClendon uses this phrase to describe how our lives now participate in the same providential reality and pattern of lives narrated in Scripture. In this scene before Christ described earlier, for example, Teresa narrates a kind of Divine wounding not unlike that of Jacob as described in Genesis 32. For Teresa, the Holy Spirit in the presence of the angel is "other" as is the Divine stranger who wrestles with Jacob. Just as Jacob walks away wounded from an encounter with God, so too does Teresa. While Teresa does not receive a physical wound, there is nonetheless a kind of inner, "sweet" wound on her heart. "Heart" language can easily sound sentimental. Modern usage tends to equate it with fleeting emotions. Scripture, however, conveys a different sense. In Hebrew, the word for "heart," *lev*, refers to the whole personality, including thought, emotion, memory, desire, and courage. Relying upon this sense of wholeness, the psalmist cries out, "Create in me a clean heart, O God; and renew a right spirit within me" (Ps 51:10, KJV). In Acts, when the Israelites hear the Word of God, they are "cut to the heart" (2:37), and they see that a response of their whole selves is called for. In the Gospel of Luke, after the disciples walk with a mysterious companion, they say to one another, "Were not our hearts burning within us while he was talking to us on the road?" (24:32). In these instances, "heart" refers to the power of the Word transforming whole lives. Teresa's use is similar to this pattern. The piercing of her heart leads her to a heightened sense of God's love which is transforming.

What are we to make, however, of the sexually suggestive imagery? I would locate Teresa at this point (as we saw also in chapter 3) in the tradition of the Song of Songs. Here, for example, we read, "As an apple tree among the trees of the wood, so is my beloved among young men. With great delight, I sat in his shadow, and his fruit was sweet to my taste" (2:3–4). Some interpreters note that these poems were originally love songs, perhaps sung at a wedding feast. In a wider scriptural context, such passages can be read as descriptions of the relation between God and his people. It is in this light that Pope Benedict XVI emphasizes, "Yet *eros* and *agape*—ascending love and descending love—can never be completely separated . . . [Humans] cannot always give, [they] must also receive. Anyone who wishes to give love must also receive love as a gift." The wider theological context is that in order for us to become a source of love, "one must constantly drink anew from the original source, which is Jesus Christ, from whose *pierced heart* flows the love of God (cf. *Jn* 19:24)."[33]

33. Pope Benedict XVI, *Deus Caritas Est*, I.7; my emphasis. The fuller passages

In her account, Teresa stands within this tradition of describing the descending love of God and the ascending response of love from herself, a communion that Teresa describes as piercing her heart and, like the Song of Songs, as delightful and sweet.

The intimacy conveyed here is not intended to collapse the difference between the Creator and creature. Teresa's account thus differs from the ancient pagan myths in which the gods sleep with humans. Still, the challenge with Teresa's "ecstasy" appears to be that God is *too* close, perhaps even too much like humans in terms of intimacy. Yet Teresa's account supports the theological conviction that God is able to be intimate precisely because God *as Trinity* crosses the distance between Creator and creature while remaining God. As David B. Hart puts it, "God's power is manifest most profoundly in the Son's *kenosis* because God's power is the infinite peace of an eternal venture of love, the divine ecstasy whose fullness is the joy of an eternal self-outpouring."[34] The intimacy that Teresa describes in terms of ecstatic love is possible precisely because God's love is ecstatic, pouring forth his Son into creation through the Spirit so as to draw his creatures into loving communion with himself. Divine intimacy thus does not contradict Divine transcendence but fulfills it. Eugene Rogers makes a similar point when he writes, "The Spirit moves the heart *from the outside* and *most internally*, since it is a feature of God's transcendence of creatures to be more internal to them than they are to themselves."[35]

In another scriptural sense, Teresa's life points to and participates in the reality of Pentecost. At Pentecost, the Spirit unites believers across the

---

reads, "Yet *eros* and *agape*—ascending love and descending love—can never be completely separated. The more the two, in their different aspects, find a proper unity in the one reality of love, the more the true nature of love in general is realized. Even if *eros* is at first mainly covetous and ascending, a fascination for the great promise of happiness, in drawing near to the other, it is less and less concerned with itself, increasingly seeks the happiness of the other, is concerned more and more with the beloved, bestows itself and wants to 'be there for' the other. The element of *agape* thus enters into this love, for otherwise *eros* is impoverished and even loses its own nature. On the other hand, man cannot live by oblative, descending love alone. He cannot always give, he must also receive. Anyone who wishes to give love must also receive love as a gift. Certainly, as the Lord tells us, one can become a source from which rivers of living water flow (cf. *Jn* 7:37–38)."

34. Hart, *Beauty of the Infinite*, 323. Or again: "In Christ God brings about a return of the gift he has given in creation by himself giving it again, anew, according to that Trinitarian dynamism in which donation and restoration are one; Christ effects a recapitulation . . . that refashions the human after its ancient beauty and thus restores it to the Father."

35. Rogers, *After the Spirit*, 219.

national and linguistic barriers that divide them from one another. They speak in different tongues but they can understand one another as they tell of the mighty works of God (Acts 2:11). This fact, however, highlights a difference between Teresa and Pentecost: Teresa is often by herself with the Spirit, or at least there is at times no gathered community present as there is at Pentecost. This makes it more difficult to verify many of Teresa's visions, locutions, etc. It might be easier to be suspicious of Teresa in this regard, though suspicion is also present at Pentecost: outsiders regard the Jews as drunk. Teresa may have visions and dreams (Acts 2:17) and see "wonders in the heaven above and signs on the earth beneath . . ." (2:19, RSV), but could these not be the product of her overactive imagination?

Such questions cannot be answered in the abstract. Teresa herself would be the first to caution against too easily or readily accepting accounts of the Spirit working in unusual ways. She sometimes cautioned her sisters against over-imagining spiritual phenomena, and she maintained that unusual experiences of the Spirit should not be sought. Her advice was that God knows what we need, and God is present to us, above all, in ordinary ways: through the Word, the sacraments, friendship, and nature.

At the same time, she did provide some criteria for discerning whether a vision or locution was genuinely from God. Rightly discerned, visions, locutions, and so forth can be a means that God uses to accomplish his purposes in the world and to give souls fortitude to serve Christ. Thus Teresa describes various signs by which the church can read whether or not these particular gifts are from God. Above all, Teresa writes, "a locution bears the credential of being from God if it is in conformity with Sacred Scripture."[36] Teresa discusses three further signs by which to discern whether or not a locution is from the Spirit. First, she states that these will carry with them a "sense of power and authority." As an example, she describes a particular soul in a state of much aridity and darkness. A single word, such as "Be not troubled," will be "sufficient to calm it."[37] Or a fearful soul might hear, "It is I, do fear not," and will be "marvelously comforted."[38] The examples that Teresa gives are in fact words from Scripture (thus fulfilling her basic criteria), the words are not just heard and later forgotten. Rather, they come to form the person in a deep way. A second sign is that "great tranquility will dwell in the soul" so that it is ready to sing praises to

36. Teresa, *Book of Her Life*, 167.
37. Teresa, *Interior Castle*, 134.
38. Ibid., 135.

God. Finally, and most significantly in my view, the "words do not vanish from memory for a very long time: some, indeed, never vanish at all."[39] It is as if Teresa is describing words that are so vivid that they are imprinted on the body. She continues,

> For these last impress us by their complete certainty, in such a way that, although sometimes they seem quite impossible of fulfillment, and we cannot help wondering if they will come true or not, and although our understanding may hesitate about it, yet within the soul itself there is a certainty which cannot be overcome. It may seem to the soul that everything is moving in the contrary direction to what it had been led to expect, and yet, even if many years go by, it never loses its belief that, though God may use other means incomprehensible to men, in the end what He has said will come true; as in fact it does.[40]

Teresa's description of signs can be read as a kind of commentary on how God's word works in Scripture. It brings about a reality. It is a deed. From the very beginning, God speaks and in speaking creates. The certainty of God's word to Abraham can be seen, in part, in the fact that Abraham is willing to leave Ur of the Chaldeans. Even so, the words that Yahweh speaks to Abraham might seem "quite impossible of fulfillment"; thus Abraham asks, "how am I to know that I shall possess [the land]?" (Gen 15:8) Even more, how can Abraham and Sarah have descendents as numerous as the stars if Sarah is barren? As Teresa states, their understanding hesitates: "everything is moving in the contrary direction."

The key point that Teresa emphasizes, however, is that if a word is God's Word it does not fail: ". . . *in the end what He has said will come true; as in fact it does.*" As an example, Teresa writes that during a time of trial the Lord assures her, "I will fulfill what I have promised," to which Teresa adds, "And it was truly fulfilled later."[41] Teresa's reflections are more than advice for discerning a vision or locution. Inasmuch as she describes how God's word works—as promise and fulfillment—she is also describing how God's word forms a people.

Most significant for my purposes is Teresa's conviction that genuine words from God have a heuristic significance. Their truth will unfold over time. This means that discernment is inevitably a communal, ecclesial process because a single individual or community will not be able to discern

39. Ibid.
40. Ibid., 136.
41. Teresa, *Book of Her Life*, 172.

the full truth of particular lives or events. Reading the signs of the Spirit is an ecclesial process, the work of generations. After all, it took centuries for Teresa to be acknowledged as a doctor of the church. But the fact that she was recognized as such is an example of how God's word to a particular individual or community holds more truth than can be seen at the time.

TERESA AS A SCRIPTURAL FIGURE: ELIJAH AND MOUNT CARMEL

Across time, in fact, Teresa came to be seen within her Carmelite community as a kind of Elijah figure. Carmelite theologian James Boyce states that a memory of living in exile survives in the Carmelite communities; as they remember Mount Carmel, the birthplace of their community, they also recall their history of exile from their original home. The last friars at Mount Carmel were either killed or fled to Europe during the Turkish conquest of Mount Carmel and the surrounding land from 1229 onward.[42] For my purposes it will be helpful to review key themes in the Elijah story so as to see how Teresa's own story repeats these "non-identically."

The biblical prophet Elijah was and is central for Carmelite identity. Elijah is called by God to prophesy against false worship. In the well-known scene from Scripture, Elijah tells King Ahab to assemble the four hundred and fifty prophets of Baal and the people of Israel on Mount Carmel. Elijah challenges the people to see whose God or gods will send rain

42. Kavanaugh and Rodriguez note that the real circumstances that brought the Carmelites together near Mount Carmel may never be known: "Nonetheless, sometime around 1210, a definite community had formed there and decided to petition Albert, Patriarch of Jerusalem, who resided at Acre, to give them a formula of life" (in Teresa, *Collected Works*, 3:17). Andrew Jotischky states that the "Carmelite presence in the Holy Land did not end with the beginning of the westward migration in 1238/42 but only with the fall of Acre in 1291" (*Carmelites and Antiquity*, 36). Jotischky narrates how and why the Carmelites historically told the story of their order as having begun on Mount Carmel, under Elijah. Key reasons were to establish historical precedence and to identify with the Holy Land. While this unbroken continuity is "no longer accepted as objectively true by Carmelites themselves," Jotischky notes that "our judgement of its worth may rest as much on our own imaginative capacity to see the possibility of history as on our faithfulness to the idea of an objective truth" (339). I would add that this narrative identity with Elijah is also a powerful example of the Carmelite ability to see, as James McClendon states, that "this is that." Elijah's communion with God on Mount Carmel is continuous with the Carmelite communion with God across the centuries in its refusal to worship foreign gods and in its ability to prophesy. It is also important to note that the migration from the Holy Land to Europe led to the Carmelites moving from an eremitic to a mendicant order.

on the famished land, dry for three years. Though the prophets cry, rave, and even cut themselves, Baal is silent. When it is Elijah's turn, he tells the people, "Come closer to me" (1 Kgs 18:30). First, he repairs the altar that has been overturned with twelve stones, "according to the number of the tribes of the sons of Jacob" (18:31). Next, Elijah makes a deep trench. Then he places wood and cut bull pieces on the altar, and has the altar drenched with twelve jars of water. Finally, he prays fervently. Then "the fire of the Lord fell and consumed the burnt offering, the wood, the stones, and the dust, and even licked up the water that was in the trench" (18:38). When the people saw what happened, "they fell on their faces and said, 'The Lord indeed is God; the Lord indeed in God'" (18:39).

The story of Mount Carmel, Elijah, and the Israelites is a story of how God's Word, in the mouth of the prophet Elijah, heals the house of Israel. Elijah repairs the altar and in so doing repairs the unfaithfulness of the Israelites.[43] Peter Leithart notes that "Carmel is not only the place of Yahweh's victory, but Yahweh designates it as his '*house*,' where he is to be worshiped."[44] That Elijah's prayers bring down fire can be related to other events when Yahweh "initiates worship with fire from his presence,"[45] especially Pentecost. Even more, we can see that Elijah is a "prophet blown by the Spirit wherever he wills (18:12; John 3)."[46] He "obeys the word of the Lord, and as a result he not only eats but is able to feed others (17:9–16)."[47] While Israel's kings practice idolatry and bring down Yahweh's anger in the form of drought and famine, Elijah and Elisha are "eucharistic prophets, who provide bread and spread a table before the sons of the prophets." Israel suffers drought while Elijah provides food and water for the widow of Zarephath.[48]

---

43. Leithart, 1 & 2 *Kings*, 137. In the fullness of time, "when Israel has again turned from Yahweh to its own ways . . . God intervenes again prior to any turning from Israel. Carmel anticipates another mountain, a mountain outside Jerusalem, where the fire of God's judgment falls on a substitute Israel, when Jesus, the altar of God, is crucified to save his people." Leithart adds that just as God delivered Israel from drought in the third year, so also does God raise Jesus from the dead on the third day. The water and fire, too, parallel baptism and the Holy Spirit. Similar too is Yahweh's goal to show the nations that he is Lord.

44. Ibid.; my emphasis.

45. Ibid., 136. Leithart lists specifically Lev 9:22–24; 1 Chr 21:26–27; and 2 Chr 7:1.

46. Ibid., 122.

47. Ibid., 123.

48. Ibid.

Teresa's call, like that of Elijah, is also to repair and heal the house of God. Like Elijah, Teresa is a prophet of God's Word. Even more, she is a eucharistic prophet in that she offers God's word as food for others, as a way to strengthen and build up the ecclesial communities that she is addressing. Similar to Elijah as well is the fact that themes of exile and homelessness pervade both the story of Israel and Teresa's own context. Most broadly, Teresa assumes her readers are homeless in that they fail to see and thus live in their true dwelling. In her sixteenth century context, as noted, growing division in the Western church is making it more difficult to live together as Christ's one body. For Teresa, like Elijah, the key question is ultimately, "Which god(s) will we serve?" Or, as Teresa might put it, "How do we provide welcome to his Majesty?" This is not so much the question, "Where is the one true church?" Rather it is the question, "What does a faithful church look like?"[49] Or, we could also make this contrast: Teresa is not asking, "How can I prove myself theologically correct?"; she is more captivated by, "What is God doing in the church of which I am a part and how shall I serve it?"[50]

In the New Testament, Elijah appears along with Moses at the transfiguration, signaling God's gifts of prophecy (Elijah) and law (Moses). The Word itself is transfigured and fulfilled through Christ, as the Spirit falls mysteriously upon those present. That Elijah is present at the transfiguration, that he is not only a prophet in the distant past, shows how the figures that populate Scripture continue as living realities through the Spirit. Teresa herself embodies this pattern as the Spirit transfigures her, enabling her to speak God's word in her own context as well as ours.

In the Carmelite liturgy, the office of St. Elijah emphasizes his zeal for God, which characterizes the life of the prophet. Thus the first antiphon (typically a sung response) of the first Vespers states, "I have been most zealous for the Lord, the God of hosts" (from 1 Kgs 19:10, 14). Such zeal is also spoken of in the Psalms: "It is zeal for your house that has consumed me" (Ps 69:9), a verse that Jesus' disciples apply to him after the cleansing of the temple (John 2:17). A common thread is a passion to worship God and not see God's house destroyed. In the texts for St. Teresa's liturgy, we also

---

49. The key question that she addresses is thus not one that would come to dominate so many Protestants a century later: "Am I among God's elect?" Nor is her question, situated as she is at the beginning of the Reformation, "Where is the one true church?" See Radner, *Hope*, 199–214.

50. Ibid., 203. The emphasis on "what is God doing" captures Teresa's life and work; the phrase "the church of which I am a part" would have been perhaps more alien to her, since she would have understood the Catholic Church as the only church.

see an emphasis on zeal. Carmelite James Boyce observes that the opening antiphon—"With zeal I have been zealous for the honor of my spouse, Jesus Christ"—can be considered a "feminine counterpart to the text for the office of St. Elias."[51] Teresa is here portrayed as a prophet, leading others to a holy place so that God will be more fully worshipped. Repeatedly throughout *Interior Castle*, Teresa emphasizes not offending "His Majesty." When King Ahab and Jezebel worship false gods, Yahweh is offended, as is Jesus when the temple is desecrated by those seeking financial gain. False worship offends God. The challenge for the prophet, or for anyone in a situation of compromised worship, is the courage to speak truthfully. A consuming zeal for God's house provides Elijah as well as Teresa with the courage they need to prophesy. Teresa's life displays this zeal and courage in manifold ways: she establishes communities and seeks reforms often in the face of opposition, she writes "under obedience" when she would rather not, and above all as she seeks and struggles to be faithful to what God is calling her to do in the particular place where she it. The antidote to offending God, according to Teresa, is a people faithfully worshipping one God with their whole lives. In summary, we can say that Teresa, as an Elijah figure, is a Carmelite prophet speaking against the idols (political, economic, or otherwise) that separate humans from God in order that they may dwell more fully with him.

TERESA AS A REFORMER

The words "reformer" and "reformation" are, of course, deeply tied to the Protestant Reformation of the sixteenth century. Martin Luther is the great reformer who stood his ground over against the authorities of the Catholic Church—at least as one telling of this story goes.[52] From this perspective, the break in the church was necessary to sustain the reforms that Luther advocated, not the least of which was a deeper understanding and practice of "justification by faith alone." Much could be said about Luther and the direction he sought for the church universal, a church that he originally at least desired to strengthen. Most of us today—Catholics and Protestants alike—see the split as necessary. It has become typical for both sides to see division in the church in self-justifying ways. Theologian James Buckley, however, states that in attending to the wounds or divisions in the church

51. Boyce, *Praising God in Carmel*, 355. Teresa is also described as one who has "zeal for God and [a] thirst for wisdom."

52. For an alternative account, see Yeago, "Catholic Luther."

we need to preserve painful memories in a way that heals.[53] That is, we do not simply forget the past in order to move on. Nor do we remember the past in self-justifying ways. Rather we allow our memory now to be transformed by Christ such that we remember through the lens of forgiveness, repentance and love.

As already suggested, Teresa had little knowledge of Luther or of the kinds of reforms he was advocating. She does make occasional remarks about the Lutherans, but these represented for her people who had rebelled against the church. While "rebel" is probably too strong a word to describe Teresa, she too opposes certain church authorities at various points. While some provincials and bishops supported Teresa's efforts to reform the order more contemplatively in service to Christ, others were suspicious of her reforms and tried to undermine them. Teresa's typical strategy was to figure out ways to work around her opposition, and this she did quite successfully. Teresa's reforms, however, can be more fully illuminated if placed with the context of the church universal.

To see this different direction, it is helpful to turn to some contemporary comments from Pope Benedict XVI (at the time Joseph Cardinal Ratzinger). "Christianity," he states, "is always the mustard seed and the tree at the same time, always simultaneously Good Friday and Easter."[54] He means by this that the church is always in the position to receive a "new vitality . . . in Christianity there is always a new beginning."[55] When asked whether the church needs new reformers or saints, he responds, "every saint is a reformer in the sense that he revivifies the Church and also purifies her. But reformer is more frequently understood as referring to people who carry out structural measures . . . [but] what we really need are people who are inwardly seized by Christianity, who experience it as joy and hope, who have thus become lovers. And these we call saints." The pope specifically mentions Teresa of Avila as one who "lived [the faith] with originality in [her] own way, created forms of it, which then made possible necessary, healing reforms."[56] From this perspective, the healing reform that Teresa brings about comes not through specific structures (synods and so forth), though these are important, but through the healing way of life that Teresa lived in her own originality and inspiration in the life of the church. The purpose of any reform is not the "dilution of faith" but the presentation

---

53. Buckley, "The Wounded Body."

54. Ratzinger, *Salt of the Earth*, 268.

55. Ibid., 269.

56. Ibid.

of it "with its full impact."[57] It is from this perspective that we can under-stand Balthasar's statement, cited earlier, that "The saints are tradition at its most living, tradition as the word is meant whenever Scripture speaks of the unfolding of the riches of Christ . . ." This intensification of faith and tradition, of Christ's unfolding riches in the life of the church, provides a way to remember painful memories and divisions in a healing light. This is because the embodied truth of the gospel is *healing*. It does not erase a painful history but recasts it in the light of Christ.

One might wonder, however, exactly how Teresa as reformer can speak to the division in the church today. How, for example, can she heal disunity in the church between Catholics and Baptists? How does she speak/reform the church in its economic, national, or racial divisions? These seem insurmountable, especially when compared to the life of one saint. Teresa reminds her sisters, however, ". . . instead of setting our hand to the work which lies nearest to us, and thus serving Our Lord in ways within our power, we [try to] rest content with having desired the impossible."[58] As Teresa knew, faithfulness in a particular context, howev-er small and insignificant it might be, makes possible new ways of being in Christ. The shape of this faithfulness will be both cross and resurrection, the providential pattern par excellence. As Teresa states, "Do you know when people really become spiritual? It is when they become the slaves of God and are branded with His sign, which is the sign of the Cross, in token that they have given Him their freedom."[59] As Ratzinger notes, Christian-ity is always at the same time Good Friday and Easter. If it were only the cross, there would be no hope, no gift of the Spirit; if it were only Easter, we would fail to see the suffering and sin still present both in ourselves and the world. Living in unity with Christ in the places where we are, even or especially in small ways, calls for living as signs of both the cross and the resurrection. Seen in this light, unity in the church is both a gift (of the Spirit, already present) and a task (an ongoing effort to identify and name our sins). Teresa continues to reform by living into this providential pattern, and so illuminating and inspiring a way to continue our journey toward unity with Christ and one another.

As saint, doctor, and reformer, Teresa lives today as a figure for Chris-tian unity. As we have seen, for Teresa the Holy Spirit speaking through the Word (and the Sacrament, which is a visible Word) is the way that

57. Ibid., 75.

58. Teresa, *Interior Castle*, 237.

59. Ibid., 234.

pilgrims are drawn more fully into the love of Christ. But the journey also requires human watchfulness, hence Teresa's wide-ranging description of how to receive more fully what God desires to give—and is, in fact, already giving. In the final analysis, unity is a promise. As Teresa emphasizes in her writings, but especially witnesses to in her own life, one is free to respond to God's giving in either small or grand ways because the outcome rests in the promises of God.

The saints of the church, like the martyrs, illumine God's Word for the whole church, across time and place, across division and brokenness. "These brothers and sisters of ours, united in the selfless offering of their lives for the Kingdom of God, are the most powerful proof that every factor of division can be transcended and overcome in the total gift of self for the sake of the Gospel."[60] The lives of martyrs and saints like Teresa bear witness to the power of the gospel to be heard across ecclesial divisions. True, the church remains divided in a myriad of ways and doctrinal agreement can often seem to be at an impasse. Even so, the whole church can entertain Teresa as a guest, and in so doing receive a healing Word.

60. Pope John Paul II, *Ut Unum Sint*, §1. This statement is made specifically about the martyrs of the faith. I am applying it here to saints as well.

6

Ecclesial Practices as Dwelling Places

This work is fundamentally discernment, discernment of something that is possible and hidden, that is there and is not perceived.[1]

THE CHURCH'S HEALING TODAY continues to be, as it was in Teresa's time, learning more fully to receive Christ who desires that all may be one.[2] Is our path to unity today any different than it was in Teresa's time? Certainly, there are new challenges as contexts have shifted and as division has grown. Even so, Teresa directs our attention to the reality that God continues to heal through the Word, through providential patterns that display God's love for all creation.

In this chapter, I look at how one particular contemporary Christian community, Sant'Egidio, lives out similar gospel patterns. Tradition has it that Teresa loved to dance. A contemporary icon of Teresa portrays her holding a tambourine. Her dancing, like that of David before the ark of the covenant, is improvisational.[3] To improvise well is not simply to invent

1. Andrea Bartoli, one of the earliest members of Sant'Egidio. Cited by Johnston, "'To Be Holy in the World,'" 69.

2. The resurrection of Christ does not, as Mark McIntosh observes, "render him somehow more purely spiritual and less bodily but on the contrary he is more bodily than ever . . . he is more available than ever to all people, more explicitly and concretely the locus of a new communion among people" (*Mystical Theology*, 82).

3. After the ark was brought to Jerusalem, "David was dancing before the LORD with all *his* might . . ." (2 Sam 6:14, KJV). It is interesting that Saul's daughter sees in David's "wild" improvisational dancing a threat to the status quo (". . . she despised him in her heart," v. 16). She has something to lose in the new reality that David's dancing represents.

something new; it is rather to accept what is given (to always say yes in this sense) and carry it in creative directions.[4] The communities of Sant'Egidio improvise the gospel in ways both continuous and creative with Teresa. At the heart of their life together are three ecclesial practices: friendship, hearing the gospel, and worship and prayer. These practices roughly correspond, respectively, to Teresa's figures of marriage, pilgrimage, and dwelling. Before describing this community more fully, let me say that I am not suggesting that the church today needs to become exactly like Sant'Egidio. This would be to stifle improvisation. Rather, I see Sant'Egidio creatively embodying some of the "dance movements" in which Teresa took most delight. Rightly understood, Sant'Egidio can enliven our ecclesial imagination. Wherever one is in the church universal, the ancient but ever-new ecclesial practices of prayer, friendship, and hearing God's Word can enable the faithful to improvise the gospel more fully in the "dancing of the divine chorus."[5]

THE STORY OF SANT'EGIDIO

The Community of Sant'Egidio began in 1968, when a group of high school students, led by Andrea Riccardi, met with great zeal, desiring to change the world. In the revolutionary spirit of the 1960s, this was perhaps not uncommon. What was unusual, however, was that "instead of ideology, [the students] chose to change the world through Scripture."[6] They met every day for prayer and Gospel reading—"an act," one observer says, "which, despite the Second Vatican Council, was still regarded by many priests as suspiciously Protestant."[7] Their desire was to serve and hear the good news from and with the poor. Questions that haunted them included, "How can we spend our lives for others? How can we overcome the loneliness of the modern city?"[8] They eventually leased from the govern-

---

4. For a fuller discussion of improvisation, see Wells, *Improvisation*.

5. This phrase is from Gregory of Nyssa in his commentary on Psalm 50. The full quotation is: "Once there was a time when the whole rational creation formed a single dancing chorus looking upward to the one leader of this dance. And the harmony of motion that they learned from his law found its way into their dancing." While sin has made an end of the "sweet sounds of this chorus," that which was lost "will once more be [ours] to enjoy, and once again [we] will take part in the dancing of the divine chorus" (quoted in Mannion, "Rejoice, Heavenly Powers!" 49).

6. Ivereigh, "Changing the World."

7. Ibid.

8. Quoted in ibid.

ment a building that had once been a Discalced Carmelite convent in the Piazza de Sant'Egidio, located in the Trastevere neighborhood in Rome. This convent will be the only "direct" connection to Teresa, though; as we will see, the community shares a gospel vision of life together.

The community eventually took the name of the piazza as their own. Sant'Egidio is, in English, "Saint Giles," a sixth-century saint known for protecting the weak from the strong. A portrait of the saint in the church in the square depicts him in a familiar scene: protecting a doe (a symbol of his defense of the poor) being hunted by the Visigoth King Wamba. Saint Giles is also an ecumenical figure; he came from the East (Thessalonika) and died in France.[9] While Sant'Egidio was begun by Catholic lay people, and was recognized in 1986 by the Holy See as a public lay association of the Church, it is also ecumenical. This is powerfully symbolized by another location where one of the Sant'Egidio communities worships every evening: the Basilica of Saint Bartholomew. Here one finds tributes to martyrs from across the Christian tradition.[10] The martyrs, says Claudio Betti, Vice President of and one of the founders of Sant'Egidio, were the first ecumenists.[11] Today Sant'Egidio has more than sixty thousand members in seventy countries. Many of these communities include Catholics worshiping alongside Protestants as well as Orthodox.

Austen Ivereigh draws a comparison between Sant'Egidio and some forms of ancient monasticism: "The contemporary city for the Community of Sant'Egidio is what the desert was for St Antony of Egypt: on the surface a vast, unfriendly place, where the individual is isolated, and must face his or her devils. But it is also the place out of which Christian community, a glimpse of the Kingdom, can be born, through prayer and friendship with the poor."[12] The image of the city as desert provides keen insight into the Community of Sant'Egidio. The community sees the homeless, the migrants, the deserted elderly, broken homes, and so forth as the desert, in the monastic sense that this is the place where the kingdom of God can be received and given. This vision continues to expand as the community has

9. Ibid.

10. For example, there is a letter by the evangelical pastor Paul Schneider to his family, written in the Nazi concentration camp of Buchenwald, where he died on July 18, 1939. From the Orthodox Church, there is a Paraman (scapular) of Sofián Boghiu, Archimandrite of the Orthodox Church of Rumania, Staretz of the monastery of Antim, Bucharest, sentenced to sixteen years of hard labor under the accusation of anticommunist activity.

11. Claudio Betti in an interview by the author, Rome, June 14, 2009.

12. Ibid., 3.

grown around the world. The "desert" now includes those suffering from AIDS, those in war-torn countries, those on death row,[13] and many more. Sant'Egidio thus sees the desert or wilderness where one goes to become holy as instead the places where we already are. Sant'Egidio, however, does not seek to fix the world's problems. Rather, their desire is to participate or dwell, as Teresa would say, in God's love in the places where they are, attending especially to the poor and weak in their midst. One sees this most fully in their emphasis on the practice on friendship.

Friendship as Participation in Divine Love

Many of the members of Sant'Egidio choose less demanding work in order to be more available for prayer and friendship. The vision of Sant'Egidio is not simply to serve the poor, the sick, or the prisoner. It is rather to become friends with the poor and others. "What springs from the friendship in terms of practical assistance depends, like all friendships, on what people need, and what can be given."[14] Sant'Egidio understands friendship in a theological sense. Friends, no matter their economical status, are first of all gifts from God who have something to give. Such a perspective echoes Teresa: "What friendship there would be among all if there were no self-interest about honor and money."[15] Teresa saw that when friendship is not determined by distorted concerns it frees friends truly to receive each

13. For a description of Sant'Egidio and its involvement in the life of one man on death row, see Cahill, *Saint on Death Row*.

14. Ivereigh, "Changing the World."

15. Teresa, *Book of Her Life*, 132. Teresa does write, in the *Constitutions*, that the "Sisters should not have particular friendships but should include all in their love for one another, as Christ often commanded His disciples. Since they are so few, this will be easy to do" (*Collected Works*, 3:328). Teresa is here following a monastic tradition against "particular friendship," believing these would lead to disruption in the community, possibly making such friendships idolatrous substitutes for love rightly ordered toward God. One hears Augustine's wisdom in the background at this point, particularly in his distinction between "use" and "enjoy." Augustine argues that God alone is to be enjoyed. He meant by this that true love and joy derive from the Triune God. Thus, Augustine states, "For if a thing [a neighbor or friend] is to be loved for its own sake, then in the enjoyment of it consists a happy life, the hope of which at least, if not yet the reality, is our comfort in the present time. But a curse is pronounced on him who places his hope in man." "Particular friendships," so understood, are closed off in that they fail to be a "channel of the love of God, which suffers no stream to be drawn off from itself by whose diversion its own volume would be diminished" (*On Christian Doctrine*, 528). Friendship, however, practiced within the stream of God's wide love, is central in Teresa's life and work.

other as extensions of God's love. In a similar way, Riccardi states, *"The community's friendship with the poor teaches us that each one of us always has something to give—there is always some way to help."*[16]

This understanding of friendship is grounded in at least two theological convictions. First, no problem, sin, or human insufficiency can keep Jesus away. "Jesus approaches everyone."[17] This is a simple, if not obvious, Christian conviction. But Sant'Egidio carries it into their way of life together by welcoming others, especially the poor, because the "Lord goes so far as to identify himself with the poor."[18] A second theological conviction that shapes Sant'Egidio's practice of friendship is the realization that God desires to be in communion not simply with individuals but with a people. Riccardi goes so far as to say that *"to convert means, for a man and a woman, to become part of this family, with one accord devoted to prayer, gathered around the apostles, their witness and their preaching."*[19] To convert is to become a member of Christ's body. There is no individual conversion, no private transformation. Sant'Egidio thus witnesses to the inherently ecclesial nature of the gospel. To convert is to discover friends you did not know that you had: friends from different economic backgrounds, friends from different nationalities, and friends across time and space who worship together even when separated by the designations "heaven" and "earth." In the worship space of the Sant'Egidio communities, one often sees not only people from a range of economic and geographical places, but also icons and other images of saints and apostles, as well as relics of martyrs from across the Christian tradition. All of these friends, in Sant'Egidio's understanding, share a communion in Christ even in the midst of ecclesial division. From this perspective, Riccardi can emphasize that "the communication of the Gospel is the foundation of a life of friendship open to people of different nations and cultures [and times]."[20]

This account of friendship does not mean that the poor or other interreligious friends (such as Jews or Muslims) will necessarily recognize Christ, or be friends with Christ. When I visited Sant'Egidio at the

16. Riccardi, *Sant'Egidio Book of Prayer*, 68; emphasis in original.

17. Ibid., 22.

18. Ibid., 67. The well-known Parable of the Great Judgment reflects this conviction: ". . . for I was hungry and you gave me food, I was thirsty and you gave me something to drink, I was a stranger and you welcomed me" (Matt 25:35).

19. Ibid., 44; emphasis in original.

20. Ibid., 5.

Church of Santa Maria in Trastevere, on several occasions I saw one of the gypsy women whom the church had befriended standing outside, begging as people entered the doors.[21] Sant'Egidio accepts her presence (some of the members gave her money) because friendship does not have ulterior motives, i.e., getting people to change, to become more acceptable or "normal," or even to live differently. Rather, they seek to be with the "other" in the way that Christ is, regardless of whether the person meets society's expectations. In other words, the primary purpose of friendship is not to change the other, but to share in the love of Christ.

One might wonder, though, if friendship ought not to be transformative. Do we not hope, for example, that friendship with Christ will transform us to become more visibly his body for the world? This conviction certainly lies at the heart of Sant'Egidio's practice of friendship with Christ and others in the context of daily worship. Worship is a gift given in response to Christ as gift. Hope for transformation, however, is not the final purpose of worship but its byproduct. The purpose of worship is participating, through the Spirit, in the Triune love of God. Such a conviction is true of Sant'Egidio's friendship with the poor and others as well; it is a sharing in God's love. The hope is that the byproduct of such friendship, like that of worship, will be transformative for all involved. What this will look like, however, is unpredictable, and thus open to delight and surprise.

Such friendship has played itself out in a range of ways within Sant'Egidio over the years. Perhaps one of the most surprising, or unexpected, ways was how friendship with some of the people of Mozambique unfolded. Sant'Egidio had taken root in Mozambique and had established communities in the country. The civil war, however, was killing some of their members. As Ivereigh states about this situation, "When your friends are dying in a war, you try to end it; if wars persist, it is because you have too few friends caught up in them."[22] Consequently, the wider Community of Sant'Egidio became involved "behind the scenes," eventually helping to arrange a peace agreement between the guerrillas and the government in 1992 (after sixteen years of war and one million casualties). The peace has held and Sant'Egidio, believing that war is the greatest poverty of all,[23]

21. Friendship with some of the gypsy population in Rome has made possible a lively exchange and ministry. I visited one gathering where gifts of food were given to their gypsy neighbors, and where it was clear that members of Sant'Egidio had become friends with those gathered. Those present knew one another's names, asked after relatives, enjoyed each other's humor and so forth.

22. Ivereigh, "Changing the World."

23. As Riccardi says, "War is something like the mother of all forms of poverty. War makes everyone poor, even the rich" (*Sant'Egidio, Rome*, 80).

has continued to work toward peace through friendship in such places as Algeria, Guatemala, and Liberia.

This work for peace has extended to building friendships both inside and outside of the church. Claudio Betti describes friendship as an *alternative* to ecclesial division.[24] Such a perspective does not deny the very real convictions that separate members in the body of Christ from one another. Nonetheless, the practice of friendship can be a means of healing the wounds of disunity. Like friendship with the poor, so also friendship within the body of Christ is the way the church discovers both the gifts and the needs of the whole body. Both Protestants and Orthodox, as noted, participate in the prayers and preaching in the communities of Sant'Egidio. The Waldensian pastor Valdo Vinay (a disciple of Karl Barth), for example, preached every Thursday evening for ten years in the Santa Maria community.[25] Such ecumenical friendship can restore a "vital communication and a circulation of gifts."[26] While not intended to replace a "dialogue of documents," says Riccardi, an authentic dialogue of life and friendship can fill some of the gaps that the document approach is not able to heal.[27]

In a similar vein, Sant'Egidio has organized, for the past twenty-five years, a gathering of prayer for peace called the "International Meetings of Prayer for Peace." This gathering has taken place in cities around the world, such as Assisi, Barcelona, and Krakow. The meetings include international religious leaders: bishops, cardinals, patriarchs, metropolitans, pastors, rabbis, imams, sheiks, monks and nuns. Others attending also include public intellectuals, activists, heads of state, and journalists. The purpose of this gathering goes beyond mere tolerance. As Katherine Marshall notes, "The different religious groups pray separately, thus symbolizing the understanding that dialogue means deepening, not watering down or combining different religious traditions."[28] To carry out this pilgrimage of peace means to go to the roots of each religious belief and find there a message of peace. The resulting dialogue does not mean a loss of identity, but rather its enhancement. "Dialogue is an art of living in our fragmented and careless world. The friendship between believers must stand up to obvious difficulties and differences, in the awareness that there

24. Betti, in interview by the author, Rome, June 12, 2009.

25. Ricarrdi, *Sant'Egidio, Rome*, 52.

26. Ibid., 117.

27. Ibid., 109.

28. Marshall, "Creating Peace in War Zones."

is no alternative to dialogue . . ."[29] So understood, dialogue is an invitation to strengthen friendship and to acknowledge "our common state as pilgrims bound for a new heaven and a new earth."[30] One sees in this Prayer for Peace, as well as other initiatives Sant'Egidio that is involved with, an extension of friendship across lines of division. The purpose is not to ignore differences and thus fail to take the other seriously. It is rather to embody, as John Paul II said to the Community of Sant'Egidio, the fact that "Your small Community from the beginning has not given itself any other boundary than that of charity."[31]

Dwelling in the Word

Sant'Egidio's practice of friendship—to the poor, across Christian divisions, to those in other religions, to those in war-torn countries—has been an extension above all of seeking to live the Word. As Riccardi states, "This is the revelation of the Gospel: being brothers and sisters, having a common destiny notwithstanding difference, and feeling solidarity with one another. This is the experience of the Community of Sant'Egidio. A Christian community is a tree that grows in many different soils, because it is founded on the word of God and rooted in charity."[32] Since 1973, Sant'Egidio has gathered every evening for worship, sustained by the conviction that Christians are "people of the word; we don't have any other weapons, but it *is* a force."[33] In Riccardi's description of Sant'Egidio, the providential figure of dwelling, so central in Teresa's work, is key: the Word of God makes possible a new way of life because God himself dwells with us through the Word. Thus, "the word of God is able to give birth to and nurture a life that is able to open hearts, defeat violence, produce generosity and love."[34] As Riccardi notes, this theme is present, for example, in the prologue to John's Gospel, and in the book of Revelation: "I am stand-

---

29. Community of Sant'Egidio, "Peace and Dialogue between Religions."

30. Ibid., This is a citation from Pope John Paul II's address to the International Meeting of Prayer for Peace in Lisbon, September 2000.

31. Cited in Riccardi, *Sant'Egidio Book of Prayer*, 3.

32. Ibid., 73. Riccardi, a self-described autodidact, is deeply influenced by Saints Francis's and Benedict's living of the gospel, as well as by Orthodox theologians (Paul Evdokimov, for example) and Protestant theologians (Karl Barth and Dietrich Bonhoeffer, for example).

33. Riccardi, *Sant'Egidio, Rome*, 100.

34. Riccardi, *Sant'Egidio Book of Prayer*, 91.

ing at the door knocking; if you hear my voice and open the door, I will come in to you and eat with you, and you with me" (Rev 3:20). Reflecting on the Revelation passage, Riccardi comments that "when the community listens to the word of God, he comes in its midst and has supper with it." He adds, "The community of the poor disciples in the world becomes the *dwelling* of God."[35] The poor includes those who are the "least of these" in society as well as disciples who are called to live by "weak strength." That is, one lives not by the pursuit of material wealth, arrogance, overbearing manners, riches, or power, but by "love, prayer, fraternity, friendship, meekness and compassion."[36] Every community, no matter how large or small, says Riccardi, can live by these "evangelical instruments," and then it will be a gift wherever it is, even if it is small and fragile. Just as Teresa's life is produced by the Word, so also does Sant'Egidio see the Word as an ecclesial dwelling place where a given community, no matter how small or seemingly insignificant, can nonetheless be an embodiment of the gospel.

Prayer as Pilgrimage

Riccardi states that naming Sant'Egidio "after the church where they prayed was not simply a designation of place. It was meant to highlight the importance prayer had in the community and its members' lives."[37] The daily gathering for prayer indicates that the journey of friendship in Christ is a pilgrimage. Like the church universal, Sant'Egidio is a people on the way. Like Israel, the church too wanders even as it receives manna from God. The pilgrimage might involve geographical travel for some (especially in their work for peace) but for all it involves journeying into a different time, namely, the "eschatological sense of daily life."[38] This eschatological sense becomes most visible at the liturgy of the great Sabbath, "the day on which God [invades] daily life," enabling those gathered to see all time and space in a new light, a light that does not deny the world but illuminates it.[39] Prayer and worship, then, become the way of entering into God's time, the time of God's kingdom, now present. There is no break or leap in continuity, therefore, between the liturgy and service to the poor, just as there is no leap in Luke's Gospel between the parable of the Good

35. Ibid., 205; my emphasis.
36. Ibid., 87.
37. Ibid., 4.
38. Riccardi, *Sant'Egidio, Rome*, 185.
39. Ibid.

Samaritan (10:29–37, service to others) and the story of Mary and Martha (10:38–42, service to Christ).[40] As did Teresa, Sant'Egidio sees service, or better, friendship with the poor as an extension of worship. It is, as the Orthodox say, the "liturgy after the liturgy."

While to be on pilgrimage is to enter into an eschatological sense of time, it is also true that the communities of Sant'Egidio and the church universal do not yet fully live in God's time. One of the signs of the not-yet status of the journey in Sant'Egidio is that, while the Word unites those gathered, the Table does not (or at least not fully). Riccardi does state, "The bread is his body, and the wine is his blood; and in this unity nothing separates us any longer from anything or anyone."[41] Full participation at the Table, however, would require a change at the level of the Magisterium (for Catholics) and in different authoritative bodies in other traditions. While such dialogue at this level is crucial, part of the wisdom of Sant'Egidio's shared worship and liturgy is that partial or limited acts of reconciliation are still powerful "healing practices." As Douglas M. Koskela notes, "It would not be inappropriate to consider the recovery of some *degree* of visible communion—at the global, congregational, and/or social levels—to be representative of ecclesial reconciliation."[42] Degrees of ecclesial healing can take place in a wide variety of ways—even, perhaps especially, in seemingly small ways—as Christians journey together toward life with God.

So understood, daily prayer and worship are healing practices in the life of Sant'Egidio. The healing is not only for Sant'Egidio, but also for the whole church in as much as the Spirit heals painful memories as Christians across traditions worship together. In this sense, Sant'Egidio lives out these words of Pope Benedict XVI: "the commitment to ecumenism must be based upon the conversion of hearts and upon prayer, which will also lead to the *necessary purification of past memories*."[43] The context of ecumenical prayer and worship that we see in Sant'Egidio makes possible the healing of wounds and thus a fuller reformation for the church universal in her pilgrimage toward God. Sant'Egidio thus contributes to the

---

40. Ibid.

41. Ibid., citing O. Clement, *Atenagora: Chiese ortodossa e futuro ecumenico.*

42. Koskela, "Healing Practice," 112. Even though such gestures might be limited in scope, Koskela states, they nonetheless "serve as visible indicators of the power of God's reconciling grace and thus are indeed healing practices" (120).

43. Pope John Paul II, *Ut Unum Sint*, §2; my emphasis.

"continual reformation"[44] that is constitutive of the church's being in this time between the now and not-yet of the kingdom of God.

Thus, like Teresa, Sant'Egidio participates in a reforming process in the life of the church universal. Twenty years ago, leaders from the Jesuits, Franciscans, Dominicans, White Fathers, Sisters of the Sacred Heart, and Benedictines sent a letter of friendship to Sant'Egidio, writing, "Your existence is for us a source of joy. We believe that you are one of the contemporary forms of the gospel dream that guided Dominic, Francis, and Ignatius." The authors continue, "It's important for the Church to have people who have the courage to run risks, throwing themselves into new initiatives, even if these can sometimes be judged controversial. Perhaps you suffer sometimes from the feeling that your efforts have not been understood. Don't lose heart. You are a marvelous example of the diversity and richness of the charisms in the Church."[45] These leaders of the various religious communities describe how the community of Sant'Egidio embodies in a new key the gospel vision of Dominic, Francis, Ignatius, and so forth. I would add Teresa to this list as well. There is a deep continuity amongst these various communities even as they represent different charisms. For Sant'Egidio, the charism is friendship made possible by the Word, a charism not unlike Teresa's emphasis on dwelling through the Word with Christ who already dwells with us.

Just as Teresa improvises the gospel in the context of the Carmelite communities in sixteenth-century Spain, so also does the Community of Sant'Egidio improvise the gospel in the international context of the twenty-first century. It is important to note that improvisation is not perfection. To read Teresa's description of her foundations and of her own life in community is to discover very human flaws: envy, pride, greed, and so forth. The same is true of the Community of Sant'Egidio. But both Teresa and Sant'Egidio witness to the fact that God desires not perfection (understood on human terms) but faithfulness to the gospel in the context of friendship. Both the Community of Sant'Egidio and Teresa's Carmelite communities serve the church universal by being parables of friendship in Christ.[46]

44. The language of "continual reformation" is from ibid., §16.

45. Riccardi, Sant'Egidio, Rome, 31–32.

46. The language of "parable of friendship" or "communion" has been applied as well to the Community of Taizé, an ecumenical monastic community located in France.

IMPROVISING UNITY

God gives the body of Christ a unity made possible in Christ through the gift of the Holy Spirit. At the same time, as we have noted, unity is an ongoing task in the life of the church. As such, the church must continually seek Christ and the unity that Christ gives. "Improvising unity" describes the challenge of creating new possibilities for reconciliation and friendship. To improvise, as I noted earlier, is not to invent or to create something completely new. Rather, to improvise unity is always to seek to receive and respond to God's Word in our midst. It is the nature of God's Word to be endlessly creative, bringing forth heretofore-unseen possibilities. God's Word, when received and embodied, makes new worlds appear.

Keith J. Egan captures this sense of improvisation when he describes Teresa's reform as a paradigm of the wisdom that was given to contemporary religious communities in Vatican II in *Perfectae caritatis*.[47] In this document we read, "The appropriate renewal of religious life involves two simultaneous processes: (1) a continuous return to the sources of all Christian life and to the original inspiration behind a given community and (2) an adjustment of the community to the changed conditions of the times."[48] Rightly understood, improvisation involves a continuous return to the sources of all Christian life and, at the same time, a response to the context in which one finds oneself. In this sense, improvisation is like contrapuntal music, in which two independent but harmonically related melodic parts sound together. Since context varies, good improvisation will too, though the general patterns (such as pilgrimage, dwelling, marriage) and themes (unity in Christ) will be present in rich and inspiring ways.

Riccardi reflects this sense of improvisation when he observes, "Francis of Assisi and his story vividly teach us how the Gospel can be the source of renewal for Christian life. But the reforms of St Francis came out of the Middle Ages, from a society that was completely Christian, under a Christian regime. In our secularized and post-Christian world things are different . . . We have to continue and at the same time reinvent."[49] Riccardi thus speaks of the need not only to return to the sources of Christian life, but also to attend to the changed conditions in which one finds oneself.

47. See Egan, "Ecclesiology of Teresa of Avila."

48. Cited in ibid.

49. Riccardi, *Sant'Egidio, Rome,* 12.

A significant changed condition for the church today has to do with how it understands itself vis-à-vis the "public order." As Riccardi notes, St. Francis came out of a Christian society. Teresa, too, lived in a time when politics was inconceivable apart from Catholicism. The church today, however, lives in a time when various secularities have come to dominate public life, relegating religious faith to a private domain.[50] As Talad Asad puts it, "If secularism as a doctrine requires the distinction between private reason and public principle, it also demands the placing of the 'religious' in the former by the 'the secular.'"[51] Where the church has become a kind of private outpost, it loses its visibility in the world, becoming instead a gnostic phenomenon, a spiritual expression disconnected from a material way of life. Riccardi, citing Pietro Rossano, describes a gnosticized faith when he writes, "A faith that would accept being closed up in private and concealed in the secret places of the heart without becoming socialized, without acting on the external expressions of human beings . . . would no longer be responding to the vital implications of the Christian message . . ."[52]

Yet, some privatization of religious belief seems to be necessary today in the face of various sorts of religious violence.[53] There seems to be something right about keeping religion out of the public sphere. Many of us do not want our government to be Christian, not only because it might not be our "brand" of Christianity but also because we see this as unfair to Jews, Muslims, and others. The separation of church and state, and of the private and public sectors, seems to assure the freedom that all should have.[54] Even more, in light of "improvising unity," a public sphere separate

50. Kettle, following Martin Marty, distinguishes at least three kinds of modern secularity. First, "utter secularity" in continental Europe, originating in earlier European Enlightenment thinking, involves an unrelenting attack on churches and gods, striving to replace them. Secondly, "controlled secularity," as in the United States, uses a contractual, controlled approach to the relation between church and state. Finally, in Britain there is a "mere secularity," in which the path to secularization has involved more of a "practical tendency simply to *ignore* Christian religion" (*Western Culture*, 330). I would add to the second secularity above the underlying conviction, from both the right and left, that Christianity needs democracy in order to survive. Such a conviction is revealed in the familiar statement that democracy protects and makes possible freedom to worship.

51. Asad, *Formations*, 8.

52. Riccardi, *Sant'Egidio, Rome*, 118.

53. For a thoughtful analysis and critique of how religious violence is typically regarded today, see Cavanaugh, *Myth of Religious Violence*.

54. As Thomas Jefferson famously said, "It does me no injury for my neighbor to

from religion seems to make unity more likely. This is because it provides space for all people to get along despite their personal religious or non-religious beliefs.

It is also true, however, that Christianity is not a private religion in the sense—as I have argued in previous chapters—that it can be separated from politics, economics, education, and so forth. As is well-known, early Christians in the face of imperial threat refused to designate their faith as a private cult, an act that would have prevented severe persecution and martyrdom. Instead of identifying itself as a private religious association, the early church adopted the language of *ekklesia* to describe itself, a political term referring to public gatherings. Such usage underscored the inherently public and political nature of the body of Christ. There is no church apart from a public, that is, apart from a people. There have, of course, been times in the course of history when Christians have been unable to gather as a people due to severe persecution. Even in these times, however, Christians have risked their lives to meet and worship together, a fact that underscores how the church can be a public, political threat to the powers that be. At the same time, the people called church can never be fully scattered because it includes the communion of saints on earth and in heaven.

In our context, however, the increasing privatization of religious belief (along with its public, political trivialization) easily turns membership in any religious community into a kind of harmless hobby. As Manfred Vogel classically stated in 1974, "While America has been good for Jews, it has been bad for Judaism."[55] Vogel believed that Jews had been easily assimilated into the dominant politics, threatening to make "Jews *qua* Jews an ethically, socially, and theologically irrelevant category."[56] In other words, it threatened the very heart of what it means to be a Jewish people. To the extent this is true, the reforming challenge in the church today is not only to purify the church (rid it of corruption and so forth). It is also to speak and live in such a way that the church is seen as necessary for salvation. I mean by this not simply that a particular individual is damned if she does not join the church. Rather, in the face of a privatized "harmless hobby" approach to being church, reform must recover being church as God's way of healing both the world and ourselves.

---

say there are twenty gods or no God. It neither picks my pocket nor breaks my leg." This is because, as Jefferson held, religion is separate from the public world of politics.

55. Cited by Black, *Kingdom of Priests*, 28.

56. Ibid.

Sant'Egidio helps us see friendship in Christ as a political reality in that a shared communion comes into being with and through Christ. This reality is more public than any regional or national politics; it is universal. It does not acknowledge geographical or racial lines of division or, as noted above, lines of division between heaven and earth. Christ desires friendship with all; Christ invites all into the unity the Father shares with the Son through the Spirit. As Karl Barth famously emphasizes, covenant is internal to creation, meaning that creation names a relation between God and all that is not God. As God's invitation into communion is received, friendship becomes a reality. This practice of friendship becomes an ecclesial dwelling place, crucial for healing wounds of division in Christ's body. Such friendship enables a church divided to improvise unity: to discover creative ways to be Christ's body, even if these are in the present time not fully complete. Rightly understood, then, friendship in Christ is not a sentimental expression, but a form of discipleship. As we have seen, such friendship flows out of a common friendship with Christ, who gathers the community to worship and who prays in, with, and for us. While a particular community might not be able to improvise friendship exactly like Sant'Egidio, or Teresa, it can nonetheless practice a friendship of humble gestures: praying together, seeking friendship across lines of division (whether economic, ecclesial, by age and so forth), befriending those who are needy (versus only helping them) and seeking to live a discipleship of charity.

For both Teresa and Sant'Egidio, the lines of division in the time that God would have us dwell are not "inner" (or private time) in contrast to "outer" (or public time). The division between inner and outer time makes possible the invention of the "timeless" individual who mistakenly assumes the self can withdraw from any wider story that defines it. Rightly understood, the storied time and space of the church takes its space from God's inbreaking kingdom. Sunday is the day of resurrection (analogous to Heschel's "palace in time," discussed in chapter 3), the day Christians live into and celebrate the fullness of time. Death is defeated; sin no longer determines one's life. This is not an otherworldly or private time. It is rather creation renewed, where God gives us the time and space to live together in Christ.

FRIENDSHIP AND CREATION RENEWED

During the writing of this book, I had the opportunity to visit the church of San Clemente in Rome, not far from the home community of Sant'Egidio in Trastevere. Upon entering San Clemente, one sees a spectacular mosaic covering the entire front apse (dated to the twelfth or thirteenth century). At the center of the mosaic is a crucified Christ, his blood watering a vine, a tree of life whose branches reach in all directions. They encircle a woman feeding her chickens, birds caring for their young, a man tending his flock, demons, such as a sea god depicted on a dolphin (believed to be Roman Jupiter), and much more. The beauty of the mosaic lies in the fact that Christ touches every living thing, embracing and nourishing all of creation. As the encircling inscription at the top of the mosaic reads, the cross is the throne from which Christ reigns. Above the cross, a hand reaches down holding a wreath, signaling divine victory over death and sin. G. K. Chesterton, writing about this mosaic, offers this description: God's hand, he writes,

> seems to take the cross as if by the cross-hilt and thrust it like a sword into the earth below. Yet in one sense it is the very reverse of a sword, since its touch is not death but life; life springing and sprouting and shooting into the air, that the world may have life, and that it may have it more abundantly. It is impossible to say too much of the fruitful violence of this effect. It is not the normal groping of roots or branches. It is more like the blood of the earth spurting instantly from its arteries at the first wound ... No one but a mad man could stand before it and say that our faith is anti-vital or a creed of death.[57]

I turn to this description of a Roman mosaic because it depicts the cruciform grasp of reality that lies at the heart of Teresa's life as well. In Teresa's literary work, a radiant, luminous Christ stands at the center of all dwellings, his rays stretching in all directions, casting light upon all of creation. So all-encompassing is the light of Christ that no place, time, or creature is left untouched. If the San Clemente mosaic is a brilliant depiction of Christ's words, "I am the vine, you are the branches" (John 15:5), then Teresa's work and life are a splendid interpretation of Christ's words, "I am the light of the world; whoever follows me will never walk in darkness ..." (John 8:12). The indicative denotes that Christ as light and vine is not

---

57. Chesterton, *Resurrection of Rome*, 341–42.

dependent upon human grasp or response: Christ is, Christ dwells, Christ shines. Creation itself is ordered through Christ and toward Christ.

The organic image of growth, so vivid in the San Clemente mosaic, is present in Teresa's work as well. She turns, for example, to the language of "garden" when describing how God nourishes creation, specifically the new creation that is Christ's body, the church. God "grants us a great favor," Teresa writes, "in wanting us to desire to dig in His garden and be in the presence of its Lord who certainly is present with us."[58] As Teresa indicates, God is the source of our desire to be in his garden, to be with him. Teresa thus understands that the "human thirst for God becomes God's thirst for our love."[59] She continues with her garden metaphor: "Should He desire that for some these plants and flowers grow by the water they draw, which He gives from this well, and for others without it, what difference does that make to me? Do, Lord, what You desire."[60] In the creative variety of the garden, there is a reflection, not merely of individual refractions, but of a "corporate one."[61] The Spirit provides in different ways and disperses gifts for the good of the whole body, the entire garden. As in the San Clemente mosaic, Teresa too sees Christians not as individuals in "their

58. Teresa, *Book of Her Life*, 64. Sant'Egidio, too, refers to imagery from nature to describe both communion and growth. "A Christian community is a tree that grows in many different soils, because it is founded on the word of God and rooted in charity" (Riccardi, *Sant'Egidio Book of Prayer*, 73).

59. Barron, *Priority of Christ*, 334. Barron is discussing how the image of thirst became so central for Mother Teresa of Calcutta and for the order she would establish. She interpreted Jesus' words, "Give me a drink," to the Samaritan woman as "God's thirst for our faith and friendship." In Teresa's congregations, the words "I thirst" are next to the image of the crucified Jesus. For a reflection of how the Samaritan woman at the well is a key figure for Teresa of Avila across the course of her life, see her *Book of Her Life*, 211.

60. Teresa, *Book of Her Life*, 64.

61. Cyril of Jerusalem describes the great variety of the corporate body as follows: "For consider, I pray, with mind enlightened by Him, how many Christians there are in all this diocese, and how many in the whole province of Palestine, and carry forward thy mind from this province, to the whole Roman Empire; and after this, consider the whole world; races of Persians, and nations of Indians, Goths and Sarmatians, Gauls and Spaniards, and Moors, Libyans and Ethiopians, and the rest for whom we have no names. . . . Consider, I pray, of each nation, Bishops, Presbyters, Deacons, Solitaries, Virgins, and laity besides; and then throughout the world He gives to one chastity, to another perpetual virginity, to another almsgiving, to another voluntary poverty, to another power of repelling hostile spirits. And as the light, with one touch of its radiance, shines on all things; so also the Holy Ghost . . ." (cited in Rogers, *After the Spirit*, 159). The challenge, of course, is how to discern when diversity reflects the "corporate one" and when it tears it down.

apartness from each other." Rather they are defined "by their place in the whole world being made one, in their service to the whole human nature being made new."[62] Teresa thus assures her readers that we can have great confidence in what God is doing, because God provides for the garden as a whole.

While the light of Christ is reflected in manifold ways throughout creation, it is also true for Teresa that Christ renews creation through the church. In the San Clemente mosaic, the blood of Christ waters a vine at the foot of the cross, which symbolizes the church.[63] For Teresa, as we have seen, one cannot dwell in Christ apart from dwelling in the body of Christ. This is because the church is not simply a place one goes for service or Mass, nor is it only a voluntary gathering of individuals. For Teresa, being church means being friends with God in and through the body of Christ. Remembering John 17, Teresa writes, "Thus, one day, when Jesus Christ was praying for His Apostles . . . He asked that they might become one with the Father and with Him, even as Jesus Christ our Lord is in the Father and the Father is in Him. I do not know what greater love there can be than this."[64] This abiding can be frightening since it requires giving up the conviction that one's life is one's own to determine and control. But the figure of dwellings suggests that one's life is never one's own. "You did not choose me but I chose you" (John 15:16). The "you" here is plural: Christ chooses disciples to be one body.

Does this mean there is no place for human choice? No, but "choice" ceases to be the primary lens through which one understands him or herself as members one of another. Teresa, we can recall, is Augustinian on this point, in that Augustine emphasizes that we do not choose our friends; God does. Such a conviction is not a denial of free will, but rather a reinterpretation of it. One is free to the extent that one abides in Christ, who is present in and through his body. Rightly understood, friends (including friendship with Christ) are not choices but gifts. If "church" is another word for friendship in and through Christ, then "church" names not a human choice or a Divine imposition, but rather a gift given and received through the grace of God manifest in creation.

Friendships with those outside the church are also gifts to be celebrated, though these would be of a different kind of friendship, no less

62. Ibid.

63. "Here, [the Vine] takes on the character of the Tree of Life of the Paradise, hitherto lost, but now restored by Christ" ("Mosaico Di S. Clemente").

64. Teresa, *Interior Castle*, 218.

a gift, however. Ecclesial friendships are unique in that such friendships explicitly participate in and make visibly present the body of Christ, which can be said to take three forms: the historical Christ, now glorified; the broken body of Christ in the Eucharist or Lord's Supper; and the body of Christ that is the church.[65] These forms of Christ's body illumine how friendship, as Teresa would have understood it, is not a spiritualized or gnostic phenomenon. The soul does not "access" the Divine Spirit alone. Friendship is rather a form of being church, a grace in and through creation renewed in Christ.

This understanding of friendship in no way denies the sinfulness of the church. Friendship with Christ has been and continues to be compromised in all sorts of ways: distorted politics, compromised economics, and crippling divisions, to name a few. These and other failures darken the visibility of the church. Teresa does not ignore these failures. Indeed, her reforms revolved around building up the body of Christ in the context of communities of prayer and friendship.

To dwell in such ecclesial friendship, moreover, is not to isolate oneself from the wider world. As in the San Clemente mosaic, the depiction of Christ in Teresa's dwellings *leaves nothing untouched.* In the mosaic, the branches of the vine touch humble folks doing the ordinary chores of daily life. So also does Teresa understand the presence of God in the humble tasks of a small band of women living in a seemingly obscure time and place, cooking, cleaning, and praying together in a seamless routine. The modern person might be tempted to see these women as quaint and charming relics from an era long past. The deeper truth, however, is that the artists who created the San Clemente mosaic and the communities that sustained Teresa are embedded in a similar logic: an incarnational logic that, as we have seen, is unable to divorce Christ from the politics and economics of everyday life.

Balthasar describes this alternative logic well when he writes, "the law of the Incarnation is not abrogated by the Resurrection: it operates in the witness to faith offered by specific human beings, in their life in common as a loving community, to which Scripture, sacraments and ecclesial law belong."[66] The key point, for my purposes, is that the resurrection does not abrogate or overcome the incarnation. The resurrection is not a departure from creation (leaving the world as it is), but rather its fulfillment, thus

65. For a development of how the body of Christ is at one and the same time three-fold, see de Lubac, *Corpus Mysticum.*

66. As cited by Schindler, *Heart of the World,* iv.

making possible a different way of life. So much of the world, however, seems devoid of any resurrection light or hope. Is this a case of looking at the world through rosy glasses?

Teresa herself was certainly aware of the world's fallen nature and of the blindness and sin that touches all of our lives. She even claims that her own sin is greater than that of others.[67] Even so, Teresa's incarnational logic enables her to see that God transforms the world not in spite of creation but through it, specifically through Christ and his body. Seen in this light, friendship becomes part of the logic of re-creation. Friendship itself becomes the alternative "politics of concreteness"[68] to all political distortions. To see friendship as an alternative politics, an alternative way of ordering life together, makes the church more, rather than less, vulnerable to both Christ and the world. To cite Balthasar again, "the less Church is identical with world and the more it is itself, the more open and vulnerable it is to the world and the less is can be marked off from it."[69] "World" in this usage refers to fallen creation; it is that which is not as God intended it to be. It is thus not so much a fixed place as it is a way of being that is not in harmony with God's desires. The more the church, according to Balthasar, is fulfilling God's purpose for it, the more it is living in unity with Christ, the more will it become *vulnerable* to the world thereby participating in God's renewal of all creation. Friendship is a way of naming how the church becomes vulnerable to the world.

ECCLESIAL PRACTICES AND UNITY

Teresa of Avila, and communities like Sant'Egidio, raise the question of *how* the church will live in the midst of its brokenness, alienation, and division. One could try to make things better by persuading, say, Baptists to be more Catholic, or vice versa. Conversely, one could reject the brokenness within one's own tradition and move to a better church. These could all

67. One of many examples would be the following: "What I've understood is that the Lord desires and permits this and gives the devil license to tempt us as He did when the devil tempted Job, although in my case—since I'm so wretched—not so severely" (Teresa, *Book of Her Life*, 206). Why does Teresa refer to herself as "so wretched"? Did she have some secret sin that we do not know about? Was she simply caught up in the exaggerations of a female Spanish mystic? In my view, her sense of sinfulness is best understood as a byproduct of her profound awareness of being in the presence of Christ.

68. Betti, interview by author, Rome, June 14, 2009.

69. Quoted in Schindler, *Heart of the World*, 1.

be positive moves. The language of poverty or "weak strength," however, points to staying in those places that might *seem* weak, powerless, and ineffective because, in the reality of how God works, they are not ultimately so. As Teresa's reforms suggest, the providential patterns through which God works in the world are not always highly visible. Such a reality reflects the parable of the mustard seed: "the smallest of all seeds on earth . . . yet . . . becomes the greatest of all shrubs, and puts forth large branches, so that the birds of the air can make nests in its shade" (Mark 4:31–32). Pope Benedict XVI relates this verse to our contemporary context, "Maybe we are facing a new and different kind of epoch in the Church's history, where Christianity will again be characterized more by the mustard seed, where it will exist in small, seemingly insignificant groups that nonetheless live an intensive struggle against evil and bring the good into the world—that let God in."[70]

Teresa's approach is that of the mustard seed in that she embraces small, seemingly insignificant communities of women, and gathers with them around the Word, Table, and prayer. Her communities sought to be faithful in their daily lives, attentive to Christ's presence and love in their midst. Their lives, on the face of it, did not seem to make much difference in the grand scheme of things. Their way of life could appear to offer little in the way of reform for the whole church. The church continued to suffer the deep wounds of violence and division within its own body. Was Teresa, cloistered in her community, really making any difference? In a similar vein, do the prayers and Gospel readings of the Community of Sant'Egidio have any real, lasting impact? It is perhaps easier to see how their friendship with the poor and their work on behalf of peace make a difference. But even here, these are not always "accomplishments." There continue to be poor and suffering people living is desperate conditions; conflicts and wars continue around the globe. The measuring stick, however, is not that of accomplishments. Riccardi, in discussing Sant'Egidio's friendship with old people, describes this as a kind of counter response to the idea that life is a "form of production."[71] A wholly "production-oriented vision," says Riccardi, "has disturbed the ecosystem . . . it's the way a barbarous future is being readied for everyone, a future in which life will no longer be a value or a gift."[72] As the Community of Sant'Egidio professes, the boundary of their life together is love. This means that love—the love of Christ—

70. Ratzinger, *Salt of the Earth*, 16.

71. Riccardi, *Sant'Egidio, Rome*, 196.

72. Ibid.

becomes the mustard seed that will blossom into a tree, perhaps in some future way and time not yet visible.

Mother Benedict Duss, OSB, relies upon a similar wisdom when, reflecting on her leadership in the Benedictine community, she writes, "I lean on one of Saint John of the Cross' basic principles. He said, in a situation where there is no love, you put in love and love will be there."[73] Teresa, friend and teacher of St. John of the Cross, likewise states, "the important thing is not to think much, but to love much; do, then, whatever most arouses you to love."[74] Such a passage could be interpreted as a form of anti-intellectualism ("do not use your mind") or license ("do whatever you want"). Teresa continues, however: "Perhaps we do not know what love is: it would not surprise me a great deal to learn this, for love consists, not in the extent of our happiness, but in the firmness of our determination to try to please God in everything, and to endeavour, in all possible ways, not to offend Him, and to pray Him ever to advance the honour and glory of His Son and the growth of the Catholic Church."[75] Love, according to Teresa, grows in the context of desiring what God desires (which includes love of the church, thus Teresa's emphasis on the "growth of the Catholic Church"). When Saint John of the Cross believes that where "there is no love, you put in love and love will be there," he, like Teresa, is describing a way of receiving and becoming the body of Christ for the world.

The practices that are so central to Teresa—hearing the gospel, prayer, worship, and friendship—are, from the perspective of the world, small and humble. They are, however, the way toward unity in and through Christ. Scriptural figures such as dwelling, pilgrimage, and marriage—so vivid, as we have seen, in Teresa's life and imagination—continue to be God's providential pattern for creating a people.

At the same time, both Teresa and Sant'Egidio are signs that the journey toward unity is always a penitential one.[76] Early on in Teresa' life, before she began founding monasteries, she used to gather with a group of sisters and lay friends at the Monastery of the Incarnation. Their meetings, in Teresa's cell, are described by Sister María de San José: "One day the Saint [Teresa] together with María de Ocampo and other nuns from the Incarnation began to discuss the saints of the desert. At this time some of them said that since they couldn't go to the desert, they should found

---

73. Bosco, *Mother Benedict*, 370.

74. *Interior Castle*, 57.

75. Ibid. For Teresa, the Catholic Church was the only ecclesial reality.

76. Prayers of repentance are part of the daily liturgy of Sant'Egidio.

a little monastery with a few nuns and that there they could join together to do penance."[77] Teresa and her friends, in their emphasis on penance, were embracing an ancient Carmelite practice. A 1281 statement from the Carmelite Chapter of London states: "We declare, bearing testimony to the truth, that from the time when the prophets Elijah and Elisha dwelt devoutly on Mount Carmel, holy Fathers both of the Old and New Testament, whom the contemplation of heavenly things drew to the solitude of the same mountain, have without doubt led praiseworthy lives there by the fountain of Elijah in holy *penitence* unceasingly and successfully maintained . . ."[78] Since Teresa and her sisters cannot go to the desert or to a mountain, they generate the idea of beginning where they are (as Sant'Egidio will also do centuries later). They are not seeking to create something entirely new, but are renewing an ecclesial practice. This practice, especially in the Carmelite tradition, recalls and in a sense repeats the prophets Elijah and Elisha, who, by God's grace and acts, help mold Israel into a repentant people.

Such an emphasis on penance is significant because it involves what Ephraim Radner calls a shared "penitential history." The contours of such a history, Radner notes, can neither be defined in advance nor precisely articulated. Rather, the "condescension of the Word" and "direction by the Spirit" ultimately "determine both the progress and the object of the history's practice."[79] The practice of penance, Radner emphasizes, is crucial for a more fully realized unity in the body of Christ. "Almost five hundred years after the sixteenth-century debates and division, we can no longer ask ourselves the same questions that John Dunne asked (where is the true church and does it matter?). By contrast, I believe that the Scripture teaches us today the following: God has allowed us to come to faith and to practice our faith within divided Christian communities so that, forced to follow Jesus where we have been placed, we might learn repentance."[80] Israel emerges from the desert a repentant people. Jesus, in the desert, reveals himself to be the "perfect penitent"[81] as he allows the Holy Spirit

77. Cited in Teresa, *Book of Her Life*, 333.

78. Boyce, *Praising God*, 33.

79. Radner's full definition of penitential history is as follows: "an experienced discipline, whose exact contours are neither defined in advance nor precise in their articulation, because they are granted by the grace of God whose condescension of the Word and (sometimes paradoxical) direction by the Spirit determine both the progress and the object of the history's practice" (*End of the Church*, 8).

80. Radner, *Hope*, 206.

81. As Radner notes, this phrase is from C. S. Lewis, who applies it particularly to Jesus on the cross. Christ is penitent not in the sense that he must repent of his own

to work fully in him. Teresa and her sisters and friends likewise desire to join together "to do penance." Teresa herself well understood that the path to renewed life together was, at its heart, cruciform. By this she meant that our lives as Christians should take the form of the life of Christ: the dwelling of God, the One who journeys to where we are, and the faithful Spouse who enables us to live in covenant with each other in Christ.

To live the form of Christ, through the Spirit, is above all to be willing to be humble, small, even apparently insignificant. As Teresa writes, "Being at this juncture, always having the help of many prayers, and having already bought the house in a good section, I didn't worry about it being small. The Lord had told me to get started as best I could, that afterward I would see what His Majesty would do. And how well I have seen it!"[82] Teresa herself could not have imagined that centuries later the church would say of her, "How well we see Christ's presence!" That such is the case witnesses both to God's extravagant abundance and to the words that Teresa herself famously penned, "Those who seek God shall never go wanting."[83]

---

sins (which would deny his divinity), but in the sense that he shares in the temptations and death of the world so as to overcome these. The temptations of scarcity, idolatry, and faithlessness are all present in the temptation narrative that Jesus engages and defeats through the Word and, most fully, through the cross. This suggests that the way of penance for the church divided is the way of the cross, whereby the church shares in the suffering and brokenness of both the church and the world.

82. Teresa, *Book of Her Life*, 232.

83. These words are from Teresa's well-known poem, *"Nada te turbe"* ("Nothing can trouble").

Bibliography

Anderson, Benedict. *Imagined Communities: Reflections on the Origin and Spread of Nationalism*. New York: Verso, 1983.

Asad, Talal. *Formations of the Secular: Christianity, Islam, Modernity*. Stanford, CA: Stanford University Press, 2003.

———. *Genealogies of Religion: Discipline and Reasons of Power in Christianity and Islam*. Baltimore: Johns Hopkins University Press, 1993.

Athanasius. *On the Incarnation: De Incarnatione Verbi Dei*. Translated by a religious of C.S.M.V. Crestwood, NY: St. Vladimir's Seminary Press, 1944.

Augustine. *The Confessions*. Translated by Maria Boulding. Hyde Park: New York City Press, 1997.

———. *On Christian Doctrine*. In *Nicene and Post-Nicene Fathers*, ser. 1, vol. 2. Edited by Philip Schaff. Grand Rapids: Eerdmans, 1977.

Bader-Saye, Scott. *Church and Israel after Christendom: The Politics of Election*. Boulder, CO: Westview, 1999.

Balthasar, Hans Urs von. *The Theology of Henri de Lubac*. San Francisco: Ignatius, 1983.

———. *A Theology of History*. New York: Sheed and Ward, 1963.

Baptist World Alliance. "Are Baptist Churches Autonomous?" Concluding statement at the BWA Symposium on Baptist Identity and Ecclesiology, Elstal, Germany, March 21–24, 2007.

Barron, Robert. *The Priority of Christ: Toward a Postliberal Catholicism*. Grand Rapids: Brazos, 2007.

———. *Thomas Aquinas: Spiritual Master*. New York: Crossroad, 1996.

Barth, Karl. *The Doctrine of Reconciliation*. Vol. 4 of *Church Dogmatics*. Edited by G. W. Bromiley and T .F. Torrance. New York: T. & T. Clark, 1956.

Bauerschmidt, F. C. "The Abrahamic Voyage: Michel de Certeau and Theology." *Modern Theology* 12/1 (January 1996) 1–26.

———. "The Politics of the Little Way: Dorothy Day Reads Therese of Lisieux." In *American Catholic Traditions: Resources for Renewal, College Theology Society, Annual Volume 42*, edited by Sandra Yocum Mize and William Portier, 77–95. Maryknoll, NY: Orbis, 1997.

Baxter, Michael J. "Notes on Catholic Americanism and Catholic Radicalism: Toward a Counter-Tradition of Catholic Social Ethics." In *American Catholic Traditions, Resources for Revival, College Theology Society*, edited by Sandra Yocum Mize and William Portier, 53–71. Annual Publication of the College Theology Society 42. Maryknoll, NY: Orbis, 1997.

Benedict XVI, Pope. *Deus Caritas Est*. Libreria Editrice Vaticana, 2005. Online: http://www.vatican.va/holy_father/benedict_xvi/encyclicals/documents/hf_ben-xvi_enc_20051225_deus-caritas-est_en.html.

Bibliography

Berger, Peter. "On the Obsolescence of the Concept of Honor." In *Liberalism and Its Critics*, edited by Michael Sandel, 149–58. New York: New York University Press, 1984.

Bilinkoff, Jodi. *The Ávila of Saint Teresa: Religious Reform in the Sixteenth-Century City.* Ithaca, NY: Cornell University Press, 1989.

Black, Andrew. "Kingdom of Priests or Democracy of Competent Souls?: The 'Baptist Manifesto,' John Howard Yoder, and the Question of Baptist Identity." Masters thesis, Baylor University, 2006.

Bonhoeffer, Dietrich. *Life Together; Prayerbook of the Bible.* Dietrich Bonhoeffer Works 5. Minneapolis: Fortress, 2005.

Bosco, Antoinette. *Mother Benedict: Foundress of Regina Laudis Abbey: Memoir.* San Francisco: Ignatius, 2007.

Boyce, James O. *Praising God in Carmel: Studies in Carmelite Liturgy.* Washington, DC: Carmelite Institute, 1999.

Boyle, Nicholas. *Who Are We Now?: Christian Humanism and the Global Market from Hegel to Heaney.* Notre Dame, IN: University of Notre Dame Press, 1998.

Braaten, Carl E., and Robert W. Jenson, editors. *In One Body Through the Cross: The Princeton Proposal for Christian Unity.* Grand Rapids: Eerdmans, 2003.

Branch, Lori. *Rituals of Spontaneity: Sentiment and Secularism from Free Prayer to Wordsworth.* Waco, TX: Baylor University Press, 2006.

Brown, Dan. *Angels and Demons.* New York: Pocket Books, 2000.

Buckley, James J. "The Wounded Body." In *Knowing the Triune God: The Work of the Spirit in the Practices of the Church*, edited by James J. Buckley and David S. Yeago, 205–30. Grand Rapids: Eerdmans, 2001.

Cahill, Thomas. *A Saint on Death Row: How a Forgotten Child Became a Man and Changed a World.* New York: Anchor, 2009.

Calvin, John. *Institutes of the Christian Religion.* Edited by John T. McNeil, translated by Ford Lewis Battles. 2 vols. Philadelphia: Westminster, 1960.

Cantoni, Davide. "The Economic Effects of the Protestant Reformation: Testing the Weber Hypothesis in the German Lands." November 10, 2009. Online: http://www.people.fas. harvard.edu/~cantoni/papers.html.

Carroll, Eamon R. "The Saving Role of the Human Christ for St. Teresa," *Centenary of St. Teresa: Catholic University Symposium, October 15–17, 1982*, edited by John Sullivan, 135–52. Carmelite Studies 3. Washington, DC: ISC Publications, 1984.

Carter, J. Kameron. *Race: A Theological Account.* New York: Oxford University Press, 2008.

Cavanaugh, William T. *Being Consumed: Economics and Christian Desire.* Grand Rapids: Eerdmans, 2008.

———. *The Myth of Religious Violence: Secular Ideology and the Roots of Modern Conflict.* New York: Oxford University Press, 2009.

———. *Theopolitical Imagination: Christian Practices of Space and Time.* New York: T. & T. Clark, 2002.

———. *Torture and Eucharist: Theology, Politics, and the Body of Christ.* Malden, MA: Wiley-Blackwell, 1998.

Certeau, Michel de. *The Mystic Fable.* Translated by Michael B. Smith. Chicago: University of Chicago Press, 1992.

Chesterton, G. K. *The Resurrection of Rome.* London: Hodder & Stoughton, 1930.

Clapp, Rodney. *The Consuming Passion: Christianity and the Consumer Culture.* Downers Grove, IL: InterVarsity, 1998.

Conyers, A. J. *The Long Truce: How Toleration Made the World Safe for Power and Profit.* Dallas: Spence, 2001.

Cunningham, Larry. *The Catholic Faith: An Introduction.* New York: Paulist, 1986.

Daley, Brian E. "Rebuilding the Structure of Love: The Quest for Visible Unity among the Churches." In *The Ecumenical Future: Background Papers for "In One Body Through the Cross: The Princeton Proposal for Christian Unity"*, edited by Carl E. Braaten and Robert W. Jenson, 73–105. Grand Rapids: Eerdmans, 2004.

Dawson, Christopher. *Christianity and European Culture: Selections from the Work of Christopher Dawson.* Edited by Gerald J. Russello. Washington, DC: Catholic University of America Press, 1998

Du Boulay, Shirley. *Teresa of Avila: An Extraordinary Life.* New York: BlueBridge, 2004.

Duffy, Eamon. *The Stripping of the Altars: Tradition Religion in England, 1400–1580.* New Haven, CT: Yale University Press, 1992.

Egan, Keith J. "The Ecclesiology of Teresa of Avila: Women as Church Especially in *The Book of Her Foundations*." In *Theology: Expanding the Borders*, edited by Maria Pilar Aquino and Robert S. Goizueta, 145–61. Annual Publication of the College Theology Society 43 (1997). Mystic, CT: Twenty-Third Publications, 1998.

———. "The Significance for Theology of the Doctor of the Church: Teresa of Avila." In *The Pedagogy of God's Image: Essays on Symbol and the Religious Imagination*, edited by Robert Masson, 153–70. Annual Publication of the College Theology Society 26. Chico, CA: Scholars, 1981.

———. "St. Teresa of Ávila: First Woman Doctor of the Church." Delivered at the "Saturdays with the Saints" series at the Institute for Church Life, University of Notre Dame, October, 2011.

———. "Teresa of Jesus: Daughter of the Church and Woman of the Reformation." In *Centenary of St. Teresa: Catholic University Symposium, October 15–17, 1982*, edited by John Sullivan, 69–91. Carmelite Studies 3. Washington, DC: ISC Publications, 1984.

Fassler, Margot Elsbeth, et al. *Joyful Noise: Psalms in Community.* DVD. New Haven, CT: Yale University, Institute of Sacred Music, 2006.

Fiddes, Paul S. *Tracks and Traces: Baptist Identity in Church and Theology.* Studies in Baptist History and Thought. Eugene, OR: Wipf & Stock, 2007.

Fowl, Stephen. "Theological and Ideological Strategies of Biblical Interpretation." In *Scripture: An Ecumenical Introduction to the Bible and Its Interpretation*, edited by Michael J. Gorman, 163–75. Peabody, MA: Hendrickson, 2005.

Gallegher, Michael Paul. "The Tone of Culture: From Prometheus to Narcissus." Online: http://www.gospel-culture.org.uk/Gallagher.htm.

George, Timothy. "An Evangelical Reflection on Scripture and Tradition." *ProEcclesia* 11/2 (Spring 2000) 184–207.

Gillespie, Michael Allen. *The Theological Origins of Modernity.* Chicago: University of Chicago Press, 2008.

Ginhoven, Christopher van. "The Theurgic Image: Ignatius of Loyola, Teresa of Ávila, and the Institutional Praxis of the Counter-Reformation." PhD diss., New York University, May 2010.

Gomes, Peter J. "Introduction" in *The Courage to Be*, by Paul Tillich. 2nd ed. New Haven, CT: Yale Unviersity, 2000.

Goodchild, Philip. *Theology of Money*. Durham, NC: Duke University Press, 2009.

Goodson, Jacob Lynn. "The Adoption of American Pragmatism in the Baptist Theology of Martin Luther King, Jr." Presented at "Faithful Historians, Faithful History, & the History of the Faithful," Conference on Faith and History Biennial Meeting, Oklahoma Baptist University, Shawnee, OK, September 21–23, 2006.

———. "A Baptist Theology of Mary?: Reading Paul, Remembering Mary." Annual Meeting of the College Theology Society and National Association of Baptist Professors of Religion Meeting, New Port, Rhode Island, May 29 – June 1, 2008.

Grief, A. Katherine. "Teresa of Ávila: *The Interior Castle*." *Theology Today* 62 (July 2005), 230–34.

Griffiths, Paul J. "Deranged Desire: A Theological Requiem for the Natural." Inaugural Lecture as Warren Chair of Catholic Theology, Duke Divinity School, Durham, NC, October 10, 2008. Audio recording. Online: http://itunes.apple.com/us/itunes-u/desire-deranged-theological/id420546728.

———. *Intellectual Appetites: A Theological Grammar*. Washington, DC: Catholic University of America Press, 2009.

Gulker, Michael. "*Schola Caritatis*: Why the Church and the Academy Should Reunite as a 'School of Charity.'" Unpublished paper, 2008.

Hanby, Michael. *Augustine and Modernity*. New York: Routledge, 2003.

Harink, Douglas. *Paul among the Postliberals: Pauline Theology beyond Christendom and Modernity*. Grand Rapids: Brazos, 2003.

Harmon, Stephen. *Toward Baptist Catholicity: Essays on Tradition and the Baptist Vision*. Studies in Baptist History and Thought. Eugene, OR: Wipf & Stock, 2006.

Hart, David Bentley. *The Beauty of the Infinite: The Aesthetics of Christian Truth*. Grand Rapids Eerdmans, 2003.

Harvey, Barry. *Another City: An Ecclesiological Primer for a Post-Christian World*. Harrisburg, PA: Trinity, 1999.

———. *Can These Bones Live?: A Catholic Baptist Engagement with Ecclesiology, Hermeneutics, and Social Theory*. Grand Rapids: Brazos, 2008.

Hauerwas, Stanley. *A Better Hope: Resources for a Church Confronting Capitalism, Democracy, and Postmodernity*. Grand Rapids: Brazos, 2000.

———. "America's God." *The Living Church*. Online: http://www.livingchurch.org/news/news-updates/2010/3/9/americas-god.

———. *In Good Company: The Church as Polis*. Notre Dame, IN: Notre Dame University Press, 1995.

———. *Unleashing the Scripture: Freeing the Bible from Captivity to America*. Nashville: Abingdon, 1993.

———. *With the Grain of the Universe: The Church's Witness and Natural Theology*. Grand Rapids: Brazos, 2001.

Hauerwas, Stanley, and Michael Baxter. "The Kingship of Christ: Why Freedom of 'Belief' Is Not Enough." In *In Good Company: The Church as Polis*, edited by Stanley Hauerwas, 199–216. Notre Dame, IN: University of Notre Dame, 1997.

Hauerwas, Stanley, and Samuel Wells, editors, *The Blackwell Companion to Christian Ethics*. Malden, MA: Blackwell, 2006.

Henry, Douglas V. "The End(s) of Baptist Dissert." Delivered at "The Life of the Church and the Baptist Academy," the annual meeting of the Young Scholars in the Baptist Academy, Honolulu, HI, July 27, 2010.

Heschel, Abraham Joshua. *The Sabbath: Its Meaning for Modern Man*. With wood engravings by Ilya Schor. New York: Farrar, Straus, and Young, 1951.

Hibbs, Thomas S. "Wisdom Transformed by Love." In *Christian Reflection: A Series in Faith and Ethics*, edited by Robert B. Kruschwitz, 38–45. Waco, TX: Center for Christian Ethics, Baylor University, 2009.

Hollon, Bryan. "Knowledge of God as Assimilation and Anticipation: An Essay on Theological Pedagogy in the Light of Biblical Epistemology." *Perspectives in Religious Studies* 38/1 (Spring 2011) 85–106.

Howell, Jenny. "Reading History with the Saints: An Examination of McClendon's 'Biography as Theology.'" Delivered at "Baptists and History," the annual meeting of the Young Scholars in the Baptist Academy, Prague, July 24, 2011.

Hütter, Reinhard. "Ecclesial Ethics, The Church's Vocation, and Paraclesis." *Pro Ecclesia* 2/4 (1993) 433–50.

Inge, John. *A Christian Theology of Place: Explorations in Practical, Pastoral, and Empirical Theology*. Burlington, VT: Ashgate, 2003.

Irenaeus of Lyons, *Against Heresies*. Translated by Alexander Roberts and William Rambaut. In *Ante-Nicene Fathers*, vol. 1, edited by Alexander Roberts, James Donaldson, and A. Cleveland Coxe. Buffalo, NY: Christian Literature, 1885. Online: http://www.ccel.org/ccel/schaff/anf01.ix.vii.i.html.

Ivereigh, Austen. "Changing the World Via the Crucified: The Community of Sant'Egidio." *GodSpy: Faith at the Edge*, March 2008. Online: http://oldarchive. godspy.com/reviews/Changing-the-World-Via-the-Crucified-The-Community-of-Sant-Egidio-by-Austen-Ivereigh.cfm.html.

Jardine, Murray. *The Making and Unmaking of Technological Society: How Christianity Can Save Modernity from Itself*. Grand Rapids: Brazos, 2004.

Jaspers, Karl. *Kant*. New York: Harcourt, Brace, Jovanovich, 1957.

Jenson, Robert W. *Systematic Theology*, vol. 1, *The Triune God*. New York: Oxford University Press, 1997.

Jenson, Robert W. "Scripture's Authority in the Church." In *The Art of Reading Scripture*, edited by Ellen F. Davis and Richard B. Hays, 27–37. Grand Rapids: Eerdmans, 2003.

John Paul II, Pope. *Dives in Misericordia*. November 30, 1980. Libreria Editrice Vaticana. Online: http://www.vatican.va/holy_father/john_paul_ii/encyclicals/documents/hf_jp-ii_enc_30111980_dives-in-misericordia_en.html.

———. *Ut Unum Sint*. May 25, 1995. Libreria Editrice Vaticana. Online: http://www.vatican.va/holy_father/john_paul_ii/encyclicals/documents/hf_jp-ii_enc_25051995_ut-unum-sint_en.html.

Johnston, Laurie. "'To Be Holy in the World': The Influence of Yves Congar on the Spirituality and Practice of the Community of Sant'Egidio." In *Catholic Identity and the Laity*, edited by Tim Muldoon, 59–74. Annual Publication of the College Theology Society 54. Maryknoll, NY: Orbis, 2009.

Lutheran World Federation and the Catholic Church. "Joint Declaration on the Doctrine of Justification by Faith." Signed October 31, 1999. Online: http://www.vatican.va/roman_curia/pontifical_councils/chrstuni/documents/rc_pc_chrstuni_doc_31101999_cath-luth-joint-declaration_en.html.

Jones, L. Gregory. *Embodying Forgiveness: A Theological Analysis*. Grand Rapids: Eerdmans, 1995.

Bibliography

Jotischky, Andrew. *The Carmelites and Antiquity: Mendicants and Their Pasts in the Middle Ages*. Oxford: Oxford University, 2002.

Kant, Immanuel. *Critique of Pure Reason*. In *The Critique of Pure Reason; The Critique of Practical Reason, and Other Ethical Treatises; The Critique of Judgment*, translated by J. M. D. Meiklejohn et al. 2nd ed. Chicago: Encyclopedia Britannica, 1990.

———. *Foundations for the Metaphysics of Morals, and What Is Enlightenment?* Translated by Lewis White Beck. Indianapolis: Bobbs-Merrill, 1959.

Kenneson, Philip D. *Beyond Sectarianism: Re-Imagining Church and World*. Harrisburg, PA: Trinity, 1999.

Kenney, John Peter. *The Mysticism of Augustine: Rereading "The Confessions"*. New York: Routledge, 2005.

Kettle, David J. *Western Culture in Gospel Context: Towards the Conversion of the West: Theological Bearing for Mission and Spirituality*. Eugene, OR: Cascade, 2011.

Kidder, Tracy. *Mountains beyond Mountains: The Quest of Dr. Paul Farmer, a Man Who Would Cure the World*. New York: Random House, 2004.

Koskela, Douglas M. "Healing Practice of Ecclesial Reconciliation." In *Immersed in the Life of God: The Healing Resources of the Christian Faith*, edited by Paul L. Gavrilyuk, Douglas M. Koskela and Jason E. Vickers, 109–22. Grand Rapids: Eerdmans, 2008.

Kurz, Joel R. "The Gifts of Creation and the Consummation of Humanity: Irenaeus of Lyons' Recapitulatory Theology of the Eucharist." *Worship* 83/2 (March 2009) 112–32.

Lash, Nicholas. "Performing the Scriptures." In *Theology on the Way to Emmaus*, 37–46. London: SCM, 1986.

Leithart, Peter. *1 & 2 Kings*. Brazos Theological Commentary on the Bible. Grand Rapids: Brazos, 2006.

Levering, Matthew. *Participatory Biblical Exegesis: A Theology of Biblical Interpretation*. Notre Dame, IN: University of Notre Dame Press, 2008.

Lightman, Alan. "Relativity and the Cosmos." NOVA Online. September 9, 1997. http://www.pbs.org/wgbh/nova/physics/relativity-and-the-cosmos.html.

Lipovetsky, Gilles. *Hypermodern Times*. Malden, MA: Polity, 2005.

Gallagher, Michael Paul. "The Tone of Culture: From Prometheus to Narcissus." Online: http://gospel-culture.org.uk/Gallagher.htm.

Lohfink, Gerhard. *Does God Need the Church?: Toward a Theology of the People of God*. Collegeville, MN: Liturgical, 1999.

Lubac, Henri de. *Corpus Mysticum: The Eucharist and the Church in the Middle Ages: Historical Survey*. Translated by Gemma Simmonds, Richard Price, and Christopher Stephens, edited by Laurence Paul Hemming and Susan Frank Parsons. Notre Dame, IN: University of Notre Dame Press, 2006.

———. *Medieval Exegesis*. Translated by Mark Sebanc. 4 vols. Grand Rapids: Eerdmans, 1998.

———. *Scripture in the Tradition*. Translated by Luke O'Neill. New York: Crossroad, 2000.

Luther, Martin. *On Christian Liberty*. Translated by W. A. Lambert, revised by Harold J. Grimm. Minneapolis: Fortress, 2003.

MacIntyre, Alasdair. "A Culture of Choices and Compartmentalization." Presented at the "Culture of Death" conference, Notre Dame Center for Ethics and Culture. University of Notre Dame, October 13, 2000. Online: http://brandon.multics.org/library/Alasdair%20MacIntyre/macintyre2000choices.xhtml.

Mangina, Joseph L. *Revelation*. Brazos Theological Commentary on the Bible. Grand Rapids: Brazos, 2010.

Mannion, M. Francis. "The Church and the City." *First Things*, February 2000. Online: http://www .firstthings.com/article/2007/01/the-church-and-the-city-6.

———. "Rejoice, Heavenly Powers!: The Renewal of Liturgical Doxology." *ProEcclesia* 12 (2003) 37–60.

Marshall, Katherine. "Creating Peace in War Zones: The Roman Catholic Community of Sant'Egidio." *Huffington Post* blog, October 12, 2010. Online: http://www .huffingtonpost.com/katherine-marshall/praying-for-peace-the-co_b_756818 .html.

Martens, Peter W. "Revisiting the Allegory/Typology Distinction: The Case of Origin." *Journal of Early Christian Studies* 16/3 (2008) 283–317.

McClendon, James W., Jr. *Biography as Theology: How Life Stories Can Remake Today's Theology*. Philadelphia: Trinity, 1990.

———. "Embodying the 'Great Story': An Interview with James McClendon," by Ched Myers. *Witness*, December 2000. Online: http://thewitness.org/archive /dec2000/ mcclendon.html.

———. *Ethics*. Vol. 1 of *Systematic Theology*. Nashville: Abingdon, 1986.

McFadden, John, and David McCarthy. *Preparing for Christian Marriage*. Eugene, OR: Wipf & Stock, 2001.

McGinn, Bernard. *The Doctors of the Church*. New York: Crossroad, 1999.

Miles, Margaret. *Practicing Christianity: Critical Perspectives for an Embodied Spirituality*. New York: Crossroad, 1988.

Moore, Scott H. "Interview." *Academic Alert: IVP Academic's Book Bulletin for Professors* 18/1 (Winter 2009).

———. *The Limits of Liberal Democracy: Politics and Religion at the End of Modernity*. Downers Grove, IL: InterVarsity, 2009.

Morris, Colin. Introduction to *Pilgrimage: The English Experience from Becket to Bunyan*, by Colin Morris and Peter Roberts, 1–11. Cambridge, UK: Cambridge University, 2008.

"Mosaico Di S. Clemente." Booklet. Rome: Collegio S. Clemente, 1988.

Mujica, Barbara. *Sister Teresa: The Woman Who Became Spain's Most Beloved Saint*. New York: Overlook, 2007.

———. *Teresa de Ávila, Lettered Woman*. Nashville: Vanderbilt University Press, 2009.

Myss, Caroline. *Entering the Castle: An Inner Path to God and Your Soul*. New York: Free Press, 2007.

Newman, Elizabeth. *Untamed Hospitality: Welcoming God and Other Strangers*. Grand Rapids: Brazos, 2007.

Newbigin, Lesslie. *The Other Side of 1984: Questions for the Churches*. Geneva: World Council of Churches, 1984.

Origen. *Dialogue of Origen with Heraclides and His Fellow Bishops on the Father, the Son, and the Soul*. In *Treatise on the Passover; and, Dialogue with Heraclides*, translated by Robert J. Daly. Ancient Christian Writers 54. New York: Paulist, 1992.

O'Connor, Flannery. "A Good Man Is Hard to Find." In *The Complete Stories*. New York: Farrar, Straus and Giroux, 1979.

Ong, Walter. *Orality and Literacy: The Technologizing of the Word*. New York: Routledge, 1982.

Parker, Temple Lee. "Interior Castle (Revisited)." Temple's TangleWave Art Gallergy. 2009. Online: http://www.tanglewave.com/interiorcastlerevisited.html.

"Peace and Dialogue between Religions: Ecumenism and Interreligious Dialogue." Community of Sant'Egidio. Online: http://www.santegidio.org/index. php?pageID=671&idLng=1064.

Poteat, William H. *A Philosophical Daybook: Post-Critical Investigations.* Columbia: University of Missouri Press, 1990.

———. *Recovering the Ground: Critical Exercises in Recollection.* New York: SUNY Press, 1994.

Potter, Kyle. "Encountering the Christian Colony: An Evaluation of Hospitality as Proclamation in the Post-Christian West." ThM diss., University of Oxford, 2007.

The Psalter, or, Psalms of David, from the Book of Common Prayer. New York : Church Hymnal Corp., 1997.

"The Question of Michel Certeau." *New York Times Book Review*, May 15, 2008. Online: http://www.nybooks.com/articles/21375.

Radner, Ephraim. *The End of the Church: A Pneumatology of Christian Division in the West.* Grand Rapids: Eerdmans, 1998.

———. *Hope Among the Fragments: The Broken Church and Its Engagement of Scripture.* Grand Rapids: Brazos, 2004.

———. "To Desire Rightly." In *Nicene Christianity: The Future of a New Ecumenism*, edited by Christopher R. Seitz, 213–28. Grand Rapids, Brazos, 2001.

Ratzinger, Joseph. *Salt of the Earth: Christianity and the Catholic Church at the End of the Millennium.* An interview with Peter Seewald. Translated by Adrian Walker. San Francisco: Ignatius, 1997.

Renan, Ernest. "What Is a Nation?" In *Becoming National: A Reader*, edited by Geoff Eley and Ronald G. Suny, 42–53. New York: Oxford University Press, 1996.

Riccardi, Andrea. *Sant'Egidio: Rome and the World.* Translated by Peter Heinegg. London: St. Pauls, 1996.

Riccardi, Andrea, et al. *The Sant'Egidio Book of Prayer.* Notre Dame, IN: Ave Maria, 2009.

Rogers, Eugene F. *After the Spirit: A Constructive Pneumatology from Resources outside the Modern West.* Grand Rapids: Eerdmans, 2005.

Rougemont, Denis de. *Love in the Western World.* Translated by Montgomery Belgion. New York: Pantheon, 1956.

Schindler, David. *Heart of the World, Center of the Church: Communio Eclessiology, Liberalism, and Liberation.* Grand Rapids: Eerdmans, 1996.

———. "'Threads' Interview of David Schindler." The Christocentric Life. September 13, 2010. Online: http://christocentriclife.blogspot.com/2010/09/threads-interviews-david-schindler.html.

Schlumpf, Heidi. "A Mystic for Our Times." Religion Bookline, Publishers Weekly. Online: http://www.publishersweekly.com/article/CA6409698.html?q=mirabai+starr.

Second Vatican Council. "Decree on Ecumenism: *Unitatis Redintegratio.*" Rome, November 21, 1964. Online: http://www.vatican.va/archive/hist_councils/ii_vatican_council/documents/vat-ii_decree_19641121_unitatis-redintegratio_en.html.

Shurden, Walter B. "The Coalition for Baptist Principles," *Baptist Studies Bulletin* 6/6 (June 2007) Online: http://www.centerforbaptiststudies.org/bulletin/2007/june.htm.

Smith, Neil. *Uneven Development: Nature, Capital, and the Production of Space.* Atlanta: University of Georgia Press, 1990.

Steinmetz, David. "The Superiority of Pre-Critical Exegesis." In *The Theological Interpretation of Scripture: Classic and Contemporary Readings*, edited by Stephen E. Fowl, 26–38. Cambridge, MA: Blackwell, 1997.

Steinmetz, David. *Taking the Long View: Christian Theology in Historical Perspective.* New York: Oxford University Press, 2011.

Taylor, Charles. *A Secular Age.* Cambridge, MA: Belkap Press of Harvard University Press, 2007.

———. *Sources of the Self: The Making of the Modern Identity.* Cambridge, MA: Belkap Press of Harvard University Press, 1989.

Teresa of Ávila. *The Book of Her Life.* Translated by Kieran Kavanaugh and Otilio Rodriguez. Indianapolis: Hackett, 2008.

———. *The Collected Works of St. Teresa of Avila.* Translated by Kieran Kavanaugh and Otilio Rodriguez. 3 vols. Washington, DC: Institute of Carmelite Studies, 1976–85.

———. *Interior Castle.* Translated by E. Allison Peers. New York: Image, 1961.

———. *Interior Castle: Study Edition.* Translated by Kieran Kavanaugh and Otilio Rodriguez. Washington, DC: ICS Publications, 2010.

———. *Las Moradas.* New York: toExcel, 1998.

Wainwright, Geoffrey. *Embracing Purpose: Essays on God, the World and the Church.* London: Epworth, 2007.

Wannenwetsch, Bernd. "Inwardness and Commodification: How Romanticist Hermeneutics Prepared the Way for the Culture of Managerialism—a Theological Analysis." *Studies in Christian Ethics* 21/1 (April 2008) 26–44.

Weber, Max. *The Protestant Work Ethic and the Spirit of Capitalism.* Translated by Stephen Kalberg. New York: Oxford University Press, 2011.

Williams, D. H. "Scripture, Tradition, and the Church: Reformation and Post-Reformation." In *The Free Church and the Early Church: Bridging the Historical and Theological Divide*, edited by D. H. Williams, 101–28. Grand Rapids: Eerdmans, 2002.

Williams, Rowan. "The Body's Grace." In *Theology and Sexuality: Classic and Contemporary Readings*, edited by Eugene F. Roger Jr., 309–21. Oxford, UK: Blackwell, 2002.

———. *Teresa of Ávila.* Harrison, PA: Morehouse, 1991.

Wilson, Jonathan R. "The Christian Way of Knowing." In *Where Wisdom Is Found*, edited by Robert B. Kruschwitz. Christian Reflection 30. Waco, TX: Center for Christian Ethics at Baylor University, 2009.

Wittgenstein, Ludwig. *Philosophical Investigations.* Translated by G. E. M. Anscombe. New York: MacMillan, 1953.

Wood, Susan K. "I Acknowledge One Baptism for the Forgiveness of Sins." In *Nicene Christianity: The Future for a New Ecumenism*, edited by Christopher R. Seitz, 189–202. Grand Rapids: Brazos, 2001.

Wren, Brian. "Christ Is Alive." Hymn #318 in *The United Methodist Hymnal.* Nashville: United Methodist Publishing House, 1989.

Yeago, David S. "The Catholic Luther." *First Things*, March 1996. Online: http://www .firstthings .com/article/2007/10/004-the-catholic-luther-43.

Yoder, John Howard. *The Politics of Jesus: Vicit Agnus Noster.* 2nd ed. Grand Rapids: Eerdmans, 2004.

Subject Index

Abbey of Regina Laudis (Bethlehem, Connecticut), 124–25, 125–26n61

Abraham (biblical figure), 106, 115, 154

abundance
common good and, 87
economy of, 70, 92–93, 104
of God's gifts, 86, 86–87n56
grace and, 54n50, 86

Adam (biblical figure), 51, 131n76

agency, divine versus human, 131

Ahab (biblical figure), 155, 158

alumbrados (the "illuminated"), 30, 122

Ambrose, 34, 34n84

Ananias (biblical figure), 150

Anderson, Benedict, 42–45

Angels and Demons (Brown), 11, 11n3

Antony of Egypt (Saint), 22, 164

Apostles' Creed, 4

Aquinas, Thomas, 85

Arianism, 1

Asad, Talal, 109, 120, 174

Athanasius, 1, 128n70

Augustine
biography of, 78n32
on divine mediation, 62
as doctor of the church, 34n84
on Eucharist, 130
on evil, 80
on God within, 22
on God's dwelling, 61
on great Physician, 3

on heart restlessness, 78, 78n31
influence of on Teresa, 21–22, 78
as inventor of modern self, 61
literal and figurative readings of, 8, 8n16
on memory, 60–61, 61n66, 62
on one body with many members, 149
on Platonism, 128
on right ordering of loves, 95n77
surgery analogy of, 149
on understanding of Scripture, 25–26

Avila, Bishop of, 147n24

Balthasar, Hans Urs von, 24, 139–40, 160, 180

baptism, 37, 156n43

Baptist World Alliance, 39

Baptists, 1, 1–2nn2–3, 6–7, 39

Barron, Robert, 178n59

Barth, Karl, 32, 93, 169n32, 176

Bauerschmidt, Frederick, 27n62

Baxter, Michael, 37n2, 64n80, 89

Bayer-Saye, Scott, 113–14

Benedict (Saint), 100, 169n32

Benedictines, 172, 183

Berger, Peter, 66

Bernard of Clairvaux, 100

Bernini, Giovanni Lorenzo, 10, 11n3, 150

Betti, Claudio, 164, 168

bodies, taught, 120, 124

women
    Christ as vine touching, 180
    as doctors of the church, 147n24
    in Teresa's time, 142–43
Wood, Ralph, 6
Wood, Susan K., 37
Word, the. *see* Jesus; Scripture
works, versus faith, 88–92,
    91–92n69
worship, 166–67
worth, human, 91–92

youth ministry, 75n24

zeal, 157–58, 158n61
Zion, 55–56

Scripture Index